THE GREAT PHILOSOPHERS

KARL JASPERS

THE GREAT PHILOSOPHERS

XENOPHANES   DEMOCRITUS   EMPEDOCLES   BRUNO

EPICURUS

BOEHME   SCHELLING

LEIBNIZ

ARISTOTLE   HEGEL

EDITED BY MICHAEL ERMARTH AND LEONARD H. EHRLICH
TRANSLATED BY EDITH EHRLICH AND LEONARD H. EHRLICH
FOREWORD BY MICHAEL ERMARTH

A Helen and Kurt Wolff Book
Harcourt Brace & Company
New York   San Diego   London

Requests for permission to make copies of any part of the work should be mailed to:
Permissions Department, Harcourt Brace & Company, 8th Floor, Orlando, Florida 32887.

Quotations from Hegel's *Phenomenology of Spirit*, translated by A. V. Miller, Oxford, Clarendon
Press, 1975 and C. Bailey, *The Greek Atomists and Epicurus*, Oxford, Clarendon Press, 1928 are
reprinted by permission of Oxford University Press. Quotations from Kathleen Freeman, *Ancilla
to the Pre-Socratic Philosophers: A Complete Translation of the Fragments in Diels, Fragmente der
Vorsokratiker*, Cambridge, MA, Harvard University Press, 1971, are reprinted by permission.

Translation of Die Grossen Philosophen, Nachlas 2

Library of Congress Cataloging-in-Publication Data
Jaspers, Karl, 1883–1969.
The great philosophers.
Vol. 3 has subtitle: Xenophanes, Democritus, Empedocles, Bruno, Epicurus, Boehme,
Schelling, Leibniz, Aristotle, Hegel. Edited by Michael Ermarth and Leonard H. Ehrlich.
Translated by Edith Ehrlich and Leonard H. Ehrlich. Foreword by Michael Ermarth.
Vol. 3 published by: Harcourt Brace and Co.
"A Helen and Kurt Wolff book"—Vol. 3.
Includes bibliographical references and index.
1. Philosophy—History. 2. Philosophers. I. Title.
B82.J313   190   62-9436
ISBN 0-15-136942-9

Printed in the United States of America
First edition
A B C D E

CONTENTS

HEGEL

Foreword

Reading Karl Jaspers requires an active effort of thinking along with him in "loving struggle," as he often termed the basic undertaking of philosophizing itself. This effort is required for all his works, but especially for this and the subsequent volume of *The Great Philosophers*. Not shaped into final form by Jaspers, they were to be part of a project encompassing the "world-history of philosophy" from remote origins to recent developments. Translated from the German edition of unpublished writings left at Jaspers's death in 1969, they complement and extend the two volumes of *The Great Philosophers* published in authorized English translation more than twenty-five years ago, in 1962 and 1966. Conceived within the larger plan, these last two volumes belong naturally with their earlier counterparts; yet they can stand independently on two counts: as searching interpretations of the individual thinkers under consideration, and as a sustained demonstration of Jaspers's unique way of philosophizing in dialogue with others.

"Loving struggle" and "dialogue"—these are vigorous, untechnical words for the more formidable term "dialectic," that dynamic and reciprocal movement of thinking that Jaspers considered to be the impulse driving philosophy throughout its history. His plain but resonant words convey his desire to render philosophical issues in terms familiar to the layman and to conduct his thinking as an interactive effort of communication.

He distilled, but he rarely diluted. He is direct, but he does not offer shortcuts or easy access. The reader should be prepared to enter a conversation that has several levels and voices, and to come to grips with several blocs of meaning: the one constituted by the original thinker and his specific ideas; the accumulated legacy of interpretation about these ideas; and Jaspers's own interpretation. And ultimately—as Jaspers would be sure to point out—the reader must struggle with himself. The Socratic injunction "Know thyself" remains the crux of philosophical effort, but there is no privileged road to this improbable kind of knowledge, which is perhaps the most difficult in the world. We must proceed along indirect and often unfamiliar byways, working our way through others' efforts toward such wisdom. Jaspers's "way of wisdom"—to use the title of one of his most celebrated works—is not solitary inner reflection, freewheeling speculation, or abstract word-watching. It is only through communication with others that we come to ourselves.

Jaspers would take satisfaction from the fact that he has remained a controversial thinker, for such contested status would attest to the unsettling function of philosophy itself, while confirming his role at its vital core. His writings have been translated into more than twenty languages and have gone through many editions all over the world. He is widely and popularly known, perhaps to an extent that does not always enhance his reputation as an academic philosopher. For readers in many countries and cultural traditions, he has assumed a secure place in the company of the great philosophers he wrote about; he is present in many anthologies of modern thought.

Yet he is also sometimes considered a throwback to philosophy's grand but faded past, rather than a decisive force in its present and future. Despite his own strictures against much of metaphysics and the philosophy of history, he is branded by some a nostalgic metaphysician or philosopher of history in disguise. It has been said that he is more a relic-bound historian of philosophy than an original philosopher in the genuine sense.

He would have observed that these critical, even nullifying characterizations say as much about their source, and the orientation of that source in the larger tradition of philosophy, as they do about him. He was given to quoting Kierkegaard's warning about popularity and its price ("When it is fashionable to read my books, then I will be misunderstood"); but he also constantly emphasized that even *mis*understanding can be productive in shedding light on what we strive to understand.

His thinking remains both timely and perennial, both time-bound and time-conscious in a way difficult to convey. The reader will come to feel a tensile relationship between his commitments: between an abiding past and an urgent present; between respect for the metaphysical heritage of philosophy and for modern scientific rigor; between regard for religion, myth, and poetry and concern about current issues in politics, international affairs, and educational reform.

He was *in* his age but not wholly *of* it. He stood "athwart his age, like a rock in a stream," to use the image of his contemporary Golo Mann. Such was the posture Jaspers attributed to the ancient sages,

Christian saints, and modern "awakeners" and enlighteners, all of whom struggled against the ruling opinion and doctrines of their age, but also against their own temptations to self-orthodoxy. His characteristic position stemmed from propounding a philosophy of grounded human freedom in an age of conformity of ideas and of slackening communication.

Jaspers does not readily fit into the common classifications of tendencies and schools of thought. He did not like labels, especially the ubiquitous "existentialism," under which he is often placed with Sartre, Heidegger, and Marcel, among others. For Jaspers, human existence and thinking about it, or through it, remain open and transitive, and therefore cannot be resolved into systems and fixed formulas. To underscore this point he employed the word *Existenzerhellung* ("disclosure of existence"), to avoid the implication of closure attaching to other terms. As his own thinking developed, he came to the even more expansively ecumenical view that existential thinking would find its place within a larger "perennial philosophy" (*philosophia perennis*). But in keeping with the nature of philosophy, this integration would be one not of placid accommodation, but of pitched struggle.

His own existence was a struggle with the more intractable aspects of body and spirit, relieved by a sense of continuing communication with others. He did not mistake his own life in particular for human *Existenz* in general, but the course of his life clearly informed the course of his thinking. He was born in 1883 in Oldenburg, Germany, into a family of securely prosperous North German farmers and merchants. As a youth he was stricken with a debilitating lung disorder that severely limited his physical activities and inclined him all the more to intellectual effort. He rebelled, however, against the philological pedantry of the traditional humanistic *Gymnasium*, finding it anything but humane in a true sense. He began university study in law, but shifted to medicine after his own chronic illness was diagnosed by a brilliant physician.

He received his doctorate in clinical medicine in 1909, but was already moving toward psychology, the humane disciplines, and philosophy. He was intent upon studying the human mind in a new way, at once objective and subjective, both empirical and empathetic. His *General Psychopathology* was published in 1913, before World War I, and *Psychology of World Views* shortly after, in 1919. Both were controversial and pathbreaking in their effort to assume an "inside" or empathetic stance with respect to mental illness and mental life as a whole. During this early period, Jaspers developed a friendship and lifelong respect for the sociologist Max Weber, who became, somewhat surprisingly to some observers, the very incarnation of the philosophical spirit for Jaspers. Philosophy for him did not necessarily reside in its appointed quarters.

After 1920 he held a position in philosophy at the University of Heidelberg, but published little for more than a decade and came to be regarded as something of an amateurish outsider by academic colleagues. He and Martin Heidegger became friends, but their friendship turned stormy and bitter over issues both philosophical and political. At the center of Jaspers's endeavors was the relationship established with his wife, Gertrud Mayer, whom he had married in 1910. Their relationship became his living "cipher" of loving struggle and remained his model of human communication for the rest of his life.

In 1931, in the midst of the political and economic chaos that was to destroy the Weimar Republic and usher in the Nazi regime, Jaspers published *Die geistige Situation der Zeit*, soon translated as *Man in the Modern Age*. In this widely read work, he characterized existentialism as "a philosophy that does not cognize objects" but "elucidates and makes actual the being of the thinker." Such elucidation, he argued, was mankind's most pressing assignment, but it was threatened by ready-made, totalizing ideologies, especially fascism and communism. Moreover, and more subtly, reflective thinking was undermined by the silent dominion of technology, superstitious faith in science, and the conditions of mass existence. This pithy book, widely praised and condemned at the time, remained sufficiently resonant to have five German editions and to call forth vehement responses even fifty years after its first publication.

Jaspers's main systematic treatises, *Philosophie* and *Philosophische Logik*, were written in the darkening conditions of the 1930s, as were other studies in the history of philosophy, including a brilliant interpretation of Nietzsche that was at odds with Heidegger's. Both the systematic and the historical works of this period were oriented toward the question of human existence, and were intended to show the "self-interpretation of mankind through the great thinkers."

In 1933 Jaspers lost the right to participate in official university affairs; in 1937 he lost his teaching position, and then his right to publish. During the war his Jewish wife was constantly threatened with deportation; at the very end of the war both husband and wife were saved from being sent to a concentration camp only by the arrival of American troops in Heidelberg. The "boundary situations" of suffering, guilt, separation, sickness, and death, which Jaspers interpreted as the conditions shocking a person into self-recognition, were concrete realities of the time, not remote theoretical abstractions.

After World War II he became a major public figure in West Ger-

many, summoning his countrymen to moral reflection and civic participation. *The Question of German Guilt* (1946; English translation, 1947)
was a careful but unsparing treatment of German responsibility for the
enormities of the recent past. It was followed by heated controversies
with Georg Lukacs, Rudolf Bultmann, and others, concerning a whole
range of political and cultural issues. Shunning what he called "false
heroizing" and celebrity status as the new "Praeceptor Germaniae" (he
had been considered as a candidate for the presidency of the new Federal
Republic), he moved permanently to Switzerland in 1948, where he held
the chair of philosophy at the University of Basle. His concerns in the
1950s and '60s centered upon the conditions of democracy and civic life
in Germany and in Europe as a whole. He wrote and spoke on nuclear
armaments, NATO, German reunification, and reform of higher education. He continued to be attacked by both the political right and the
left, as well as by academic philosophers.

Until shortly before his death in 1969, Jaspers argued that philosophy
must become concrete and engaged in practical matters without losing
touch with its remote origins. He worked to bring philosophy to wider
audiences, lecturing to large gatherings, making radio and television
broadcasts, and writing books for the general public. He neither bowed
nor condescended to common opinion, but sought to bring it to searching
reflection.

He stood across his age but not aloof from it. He lived and thought
in light of a maxim that runs counter to many ingrained habits of living
and thinking: "Neither to fall victim to the past nor the future; the
important thing is to be wholly in the present."

For Jaspers, philosophy is unavoidable—no matter whether practiced
deliberately or half-consciously, systematically or haphazardly. It is
grounded in human existence itself, in the conditions and limits of our
being human, including the sense we have for being and beings other
than ourselves. Our awareness of the world and ourselves brings a sense
of cleavage between the world and ourselves, as well as cleavage within
ourselves. Unlike discernible objects and logical relations, our own being,
as existence, comes to our conscious attention by way of frustration and
intractability. Philosophy rests as much upon a sense of incompleteness,
of failure and foundering, as upon a sense of being, of reality. "Man is
fundamentally more than he can know about himself," Jaspers said in
The Way to Wisdom.

Jaspers writes that in its encounter with itself "existence is not without
transcendence." He occasionally calls this transcendence "God" or "the

Encompassing" or simply "what encounters existence." Far from any conventional theism, he treats the notion of God as a kind of personified incomprehensibility. When man tries to think beyond his own restricted grounds, categories, or accepted opinions, he encounters transcendence, but only in "ciphers," available to what Jaspers called "philosophical faith," not to certain or empirical knowledge.

Jaspers's sense of *Existenz* harbors an element of resistance, even defiance. It is less the routine of daily life in ordinary conventions than the call to be oneself despite those conditions. This self is, however, anything but a lonely, self-absorbed, alienated ego, for, he insists, human existence becomes available to itself only in communication with others; "the individual by himself cannot be reasonable." Jaspers remains one of the few philosophers to put a high valuation on ordinary language, marriage, family and civic life as genuine ways to wisdom, rather than as sources of mystification and distraction. He sees a common root to reason, respect for the dignity of all mankind, and the institutions of democratic civil society.

With his Kantian heritage, Jaspers remains a firm supporter of science, but not of its elevation to dogmatic scientism. He does not expect science to provide absolute knowledge, ultimate meaning, or grounds for choice among competing values. The basic questions of existence remain neither provable nor disprovable by science. Scientific knowledge is, to use his image, not the pure light of unencumbered truth, but a torch of smoky pitch pine that lights a few steps ahead, but also obscures.

Philosophy is not science, not errant pseudoscience, and not some crowning science of the sciences. It is not knowledge of objectivities, nor is it simply the analysis of logical, linguistic, or factual-empirical relations. It is bounded by, but also transcends, science, language, and culture. It remains rooted in human existence but not confined to strictly human horizons. Philosophy begins in wonder—wonder in the presence of what is and what is taken for granted. It calls into question what is usually taken for granted, whether by science, by custom, or by categories of thinking. Hence there can be no firm lines dividing philosophy from other areas of thought. In its development, philosophy retains but transforms earlier connections to myth, poetry, art, and sociopolitical life. Circularity, contradiction, and the foundering (*Scheitern*) of thought are inevitable in philosophy.

Jaspers felt that, besides dealing with these fundamental ruptures between thinking and being, he was living through a new stage, one of extreme questioning, questioning of philosophy itself—different from previous questioning *through* philosophy. Modern existence was taking more and more for granted, including its forms of understanding, and therefore blocking off many sources of philosophical thinking. Philosophy then becomes doubly undermined, from within and from without, as its radical questioning comes to be deployed against itself, converging with indictments from other modes of thinking. Philosophy thereby comes to be suspected rather than expected in the modern world. Jaspers's path through this quandary was to retrace its stages in a world-history of philosophy—not through the tortured deconstructive etymologies of Heidegger, but in dialogue with the great thinkers of the past.

The history of philosophy remains integral to its essential task and is especially important today precisely because we pride ourselves on self-surpassing novelty. This history shows, not progress, but openness; it serves to keep questions open rather than to resolve them or dissolve them. The axial ideas of the past are still with us, although often unreflectively; the history of philosophy retrieves these ideas without surrendering their activating power. As Jaspers says over and over: "The deeper our foundations in the past, the more outstanding our participation in the present."

His histories remain as controversial as his systematic philosophy (with which they are co-eval), because they engage the reader in a strenuous dialogue, in which textual refinements are subordinated to the issue under discussion. Through his long career as professor of philosophy, Jaspers was impatient with what he called "professors' philosophy," which vested primary questions in cumbersome commentary and qualifications. *The Great Philosophers* treats Socrates, Buddha, Confucius, and Jesus together as "paradigmatic individuals," for example, allowing no neat line between sages and philosophers, between lives and ideas.

Jaspers does not try to find an inner logic in a temporal sequence of before and after; he is more inclined to step outside historical chronology altogether. He takes history and actual historical dialectic seriously, but not to the point of intellectual self-evisceration or denial of the possibility of communication across time. He says of the great philosophers as a whole that "in their suprahistorical character they are like eternal contemporaries."

His world-history of philosophy was intended to revitalize and deprovincialize European and Western thought by setting it in a wider context and approaching it from outside its customary categories and ingrained classifications. With present tendencies toward globalization on many fronts, especially in cultural and intellectual suppositions, Jaspers's efforts take on crucial significance. *The Great Philosophers* includes, for example, studies of Nagarjuna, Lao-Tzu, Buddha, and Confucius, which caused some of his more blinkered interpreters to wonder whether Jaspers knew what philosophy was all about. He often used unconventional grids of time, space, and subject matter to explicate and to link his thinkers. The section headings in this text impel us to rethink positions encrusted in familiar Western terms. Here Jaspers's dictum that philosophical truth consists in "moving on," both with history and beyond it, assumes vital importance.

Of the three great models of truth in Western thought—the first stressing the correspondence of thought and reality, the second stressing the logical coherence of propositions, and the third placing primary emphasis on the communication of meaning—Jaspers clearly inclines toward the last, while striving to bring the other two into conjunction with it. This kind of communicative philosophy becomes even more valuable in a world of accelerating interdependence but continuing cultural difference.

There can be no "Jaspersism" or doctrinal edifice built on his thinking. As with Socrates, Kierkegaard, and Nietzsche, his real message is incompatible with discipleship. With Kant, he contended that the spirit of reason is polemical, or dialectical, rather than dogmatical. This may be the surest proof that he belongs to that company of great philosophers he wrote about, revered, and challenged. For he was critical of all love—including the love of wisdom—that did not struggle with itself.

Jaspers held that "the procedure for understanding texts is a simile for all comprehension of being." In such a view texts must retain fundamental—indeed originary—significance for all thinking, but they should not therefore be allowed to become idols of the mind. This edition, Volumes III and IV of *The Great Philosophers*, aspires to convey, with a minimum of interference, Jaspers's understanding of other thinkers and their texts, especially his way of addressing them through the entire tradition of philosophy. It presents those thinkers with a deep and abiding relation to Jaspers himself. It includes Lessing, Weber, and Einstein, who were not philosophers in the strict sense, and excludes Aquinas and Hobbes, among others, who were of undoubted importance.

The text has been drawn from *Die grossen Philosophen: Nachlass 1, Darstellungen und Fragmente* and *Nachlass 2, Fragmente, Ammerkungen, Inventar*, edited by Hans Saner, published in German in 1981. The selections were translated by Edith Ehrlich and Leonard Ehrlich, who have drawn upon a collaborative lifetime of close study of Karl Jaspers, their former teacher. In format and style, the selections are in keeping with the earlier two volumes in English. Illuminating sections from the large volume of Jaspers's supplemental notes ("Zusätze") have been incorporated in the text without special note. A short bibliography has been supplied for each volume.

—MICHAEL ERMARTH

Translators' Acknowledgments

The preparation of this volume was made possible in part by a grant from the Division of Research Programs of the National Endowment for the Humanities, an independent federal agency. It allowed Leonard H. Ehrlich to take one semester's leave from the University of Massachusetts at Amherst. The grant was one of the last processed by Susan Mango prior to her retirement as Texts Program Officer of the NEH Division of Research Programs. We are certain that we are speaking for hundreds of former grantees when we say that the courtesy and care she took in guiding NEH support toward worthwhile projects is remembered with deep appreciation.

The translators gratefully acknowledge the care with which Helen Wolff has brought her rich experience and professionalism to bear on the fruition of the project. Also indispensable for its successful completion was the close interest that two associates have taken in the project, Hans Saner (Basel), Jaspers's literary executor, and Richard Wisser (Mainz).

—EDITH EHRLICH
LEONARD H. EHRLICH

The Projective Metaphysicians

INTRODUCTION

The "Metaphysicians" constitute the largest group in Jaspers's typology of the great philosophers. He distinguishes several main types of metaphysicians. Volume II of *The Great Philosophers* consists of Jaspers's interpretation of the first type, "The Original Thinkers." In what follows, Jaspers treats other types of metaphysicians under the common heading "The Projective Metaphysicians." In the Introduction below, the Projective Metaphysicians are contraposed to the Original Thinkers; the latter are meant when Jaspers speaks of "speculative metaphysics."

For speculative metaphysics thought and actuality are one. Whatever there is, speculative thought allows to become present in such a way that Being is not seen as subject confronting object, even though thought inevitably takes place in the dichotomy of subject and object.

Projective metaphysics proceeds in a fundamentally different manner. It displays configurations of the world or visions of suprasensory happenings that transform the world, processes visible in the world, or conceptual developments of what manifests itself in the world as appearance.

Projective metaphysicians consider their cognition as absolutely valid. They are utterly convinced that they are in possession of the truth. Since, however, the vehicle of this truth is formulated knowledge, they open themselves to criticism. They present thoughts in analogy to natural science, which proceeds by hypotheses, but without applying the methods of scientific inquiry. They can be accused of shallowness since they fall short of philosophical depth. The entirety of Being is projected by them as the entirety of the world, in analogy to scientific hypotheses derived from objective knowledge. But, unlike their positions, scientific hy-

3

potheses are modified through the constant progress of research. This is the crucial difference, of which they remain unaware.

Among the projective metaphysicians I differentiate the following subgroups, highlighting the philosophers discussed in this volume:

Piety toward the World: **Xenophanes, Empedocles, Democritus,** Poseidonios, **Bruno.**

Tranquillity without transcendence: **Epicurus,** Lucretius.

Gnostic Dreamers: Origen, **Boehme, Schelling.**

Constructive Minds: Hobbes, **Leibniz,** Fichte.

These ways of thinking can be found in all ages and have continued to this day, even if in weaker and unoriginal ways.

Piety toward the World

XENOPHANES

DEMOCRITUS

EMPEDOCLES

BRUNO

Under the heading "Piety toward the World," I present a group of philosophers who have most likely determined—if not dominated—the consciousness of the Western world to this very day. Here, as with all the other groups, we are not dealing with a universal for which the philosophers under scrutiny would serve as examples or case histories. Rather, each of these philosophers stands, irreplaceable, by himself; each a unique individual. Although the group character eludes definition by a generic term, it may be delineated as follows.

1. These philosophers live in the world, which is also our world, no matter how differently they might perceive it. They do not draw the dividing line that differentiates the world as it exists from its origin, and the self in its freedom from the transcendence through which it is—not, anyway, in a manner that makes this separation the fundamental problem of certainty and the gap between us and the transcendental the cause for the disquiet of our Existenz. They do not articulate the cipher of the supramundane, extramundane God who created the world out of nothing. The world is eternal, whether in its duration or in the eternal recurrence of its revolutions.

For them the world is the ultimate, the abode of gods and men. Within it we are secure. To be sure, it shows us its horrible countenance, terrifying at the limit like that of the Gorgon. But beyond all this it is still magnificent and beautiful, exhilarating and calming. It allots us our tasks, which have to be worked out in the world itself. Ethos is grounded in the world. The attitude toward life of these philosophers is piety toward the world. Transcendence is unknown to them.

2. Their thinking takes the form of graphic visions of the world and is absorbed by the plenitude of appearances and by man as a natural being that is part of this world. It proceeds in accordance with the intellect and can be grasped with ease. Authentic speculation is unknown to them.

But the something that, according to this characterization, seems to be missing makes itself felt all the same, since it belongs to man qua man and to Being qua Being. Their world of actuality, so intellectually

7

lucid and vivid, seems illuminated by a light that emanates from else-where. Their thinking then touches upon transcendence, upon specu-lation, upon existential freedom. There is no classification that locks philosophers or even human beings into compartments. Our conscious-ness is primarily struck by what is typical, but that does not exhaust the human being's potential. According to his potentiality, each human being encompasses everything. In actuality no one is everything.

3. I am speaking here of something to be found in all ages. The individual persons in the garb of the eras in which they live and think demonstrate enduring problems of philosophy. We are interested in them because they may concern us at any time.

XENOPHANES

The fragments of Xenophanes come from lost poetic works, from elegies, satires, and epic poems.[1] Even though the Milesians and Heraclitus considered prose to be the more suitable form of imparting philosophy, Xenophanes chose metrical language. Up to Hesiod and the cosmogonic writers, poetry had been the vessel of myth possessing philosophic content. Xenophanes made it the vessel of philosophy itself. He was followed in this by Parmenides, Empedocles, and, later, Lucretius.

I. LIFE

Xenophanes (between 570 and 465 B.C.) is the first from the early Greek period whose person and life we can envision, even if only in a few of its features.

In his youth he left his home polis of Colophon because he was not prepared to live under the hegemony of the Persians, who after 546 B.C. had subjugated all Greek cities on the coast of Asia Minor. He went to Sicily and Greater Greece (Southern Italy). Throughout his life he migrated from polis to polis. At the age of ninety-two, he wrote: "By now, seven-and-sixty years have been tossing my care-filled heart over the land of Hellas" (F8). He glorified his native country in a lost epic about the founding of Colophon. But he also leveled critical accusations: "(*The men of Colophon*), having learnt useless forms of luxury from the Lydians as long as they were free from hateful tyranny, used to go to the place of assembly wearing all-purple robes, not less than a thousand of them in all: haughty, adorned with well-dressed hair, steeped in the scent of skillfully-prepared unguents" (F3). The catastrophe brought about by the Persians (Medes) was the great event of his life. "Talking by the fire in winter," he relates, the questions are: "Who are you among men and

---

[1] Wherever this volume uses Kathleen Freeman's translation of Diels's *Die Fragmente*, the fragment number is preceded by an F. Numbers alone in parentheses refer to B fragments in Diels; A fragment references are preceded by an A.

where from? How old are you, my friend? What age were you when the Mede came?" (F22).

Having become homeless, Xenophanes journeyed alone through the world, receptive to his fellowmen, rich in information about cities and countries. His plight awakened his inner independence. Neither an aristocrat nor a citizen of a polis, he was dependent on patrons or on earning his livelihood; was nowhere at home, yet he found the point whence he proclaimed his wisdom (*sophia*).

Xenophanes has been denigrated as a rhapsodist who in public recited the Homeric poems as a means of livelihood while in private he recited his own poetry, which rejected Homer. An anecdote reported by Plutarch (*Reg. apophth.*, 175e) was quoted: Xenophanes, they said, pointed out to his patron, the tyrant Hieron of Syracuse, that his income was too small; he could keep but two slaves; Hieron is said to have answered: And yet you make derisive remarks about Homer, who even after his death feeds a great number of people—that is, rhapsodists such as Xenophanes.

II. POSITION AND MEANING OF THIS PHILOSOPHY; *THE SYMPOSIUM*

Xenophanes represented only himself—without mystery, without claiming authority as *vates* and poet, without charisma, and also without an organized school. The poetic works in which he imparted his *sophia* he recited at symposiums. These were neither empty social occasions nor unmotivated entertainments, but a concerted educational act that disciplined and elevated the individual. He himself gives us a picture of their solemnity and piety.

Room, people, and objects are properly prepared. "The floor is clean, and so too the hands of all, and the cups. One (*attendant*) places woven garlands round our heads." The symposium begins as a cultic act. "The altar in the centre is decked with flowers . . . incense sends up sacred fragrance. . . . Praises are sung to the God with devout stories and pure words," and the prayer is recited "to give us strength to do what is just, for this comes before everything." After this it is "no desecration to drink just so much that everyone who is not infirm with age can find his way home by himself. . . . The mixing flagon stands there filled with joy (*euphrosyne*), and ready in the pitchers is still other wine, which promises never to cease flowing, a mild flower-scented one. . . . Breads are prepared . . . the table bends under the load of cheese and thick honey . . . song surrounds the house and the joyous feast." "But the man whom one must praise is he who after drinking expresses thoughts that are noble, as well as his memory [*mnemosyne*] (*and his endeavour*) [*arete*] concerning virtue allows . . . always to have respect for the gods, *that* is Good" (F11).

In this early period something is peculiar to Xenophanes that becomes prevalent only much later, and is then turned into its opposite. Within the solemn form in which he speaks to us there appears the enlightened view that whatever happens in the world is natural (as against magic and prophecies), that there is one God (as against the invention of myths opposed to God), that there is a moral, natural way of life appropriate to man (as against the high value set on victory at the Olympic Games and on the fighting spirit generally), that there is an awareness of the limitations of human cognition (as against the false claims of human knowledge and ability).

III. THE NATURAL CONCEPTION OF THE WORLD

Starting with Thales, the Milesians introduced the natural explanation of things. Its principle is to comprehend things, events, the world as models, in analogy to the immediate observation of the mechanical connections in space and time rather than on the basis of personal and impersonal powers having mythical character. Xenophanes took over this way of comprehending in the form of numerous images, which are by no means without inconsistencies. For example:

The sun is composed of fiery particles that collect from moist emanations, from clouds that have begun to glow. They go out during the day and begin to glow again every night like coals. The moon is a compressed mass of clouds and has its own light. It goes out every month and renews itself. Comets and meteors and the rainbow (which "people call Iris" [32]), the St. Elmo fire on ships: all these are glowing clouds in motion. Lightning is caused by the clouds being lit up owing to their motion.

The stars move in a straight line in the heavens, as do the clouds. Circular motion is an optical illusion. There is infinity on all sides: on the surface and down into the earth, which is rooted in infinity. Xenophanes did not understand the clear and revolutionary cosmological notions of Anaximander.

The ocean is the origin of all winds and clouds and waters. The moisture is drawn up from the ocean by the sun. Its salt-free components are separated out and condensed into fog and clouds, which come down as rain and produce the winds. "The mighty ocean is the womb of clouds, winds and rivers" (30).

"All things that come into being and grow are earth and water" (F29). "For everything comes from earth and everything goes back to earth at last" (F27). "We all have our origin from earth and water" (F33).

From time to time ocean and earth have intermingled. The proof for this is "that inland and on the mountains seashells have been found; in Syracuse, in the rock quarries, impressions of fish and seals; in Malta, impressions of all kinds of ocean creatures." Xenophanes concludes that at one time everything had turned to mud and that the impressions in the mud had then hardened. This event can be expected to recur. "All people would perish if the earth slid into the ocean and then became mud. But afterwards the earth would start again to come into being, and all worlds would be subject to this alternation" (A33).

In spite of the individual instances of sound observation, Xenophanes represents neither the Milesian mode of thinking in systematic constructs nor the methods of inquiry in the natural sciences. It is all a matter of ad hoc inspiration or accidental observation or borrowings from the Milesians or the monotonous repetition of explanations based on "clouds." Xenophanes did not, as was ascribed to him in analogy to other pre-Socratics, write a book "On Nature."

Something else was decisive for him: the mode of comprehension as such, the rejection of mythical explanations that could not be verified. Perhaps it did not matter to him whether this or that natural explanation was correct or wrong. He rejected divination but admired Thales because he predicted a solar eclipse in a natural way. According to Cicero, he was the only one of the philosophers who, although he believed in the presence of gods, radically rejected the belief in prophecy (*On divination*, I, 3, 5). God, however, was of primary importance for him.

IV. GOD

Xenophanes is the first of the Greek philosophers to have taught there is one God. It is "a single God, among gods and men the greatest" (23).

Deeply affected by God's majesty and his otherness compared to all finite things, Xenophanes attacks the erroneous representations that debase God:

Mortals believe the gods have clothing and voice and body like they do. But God is "similar to mortals neither in body nor in thoughts" (23). Hence Xenophanes ridicules the adoration of the gods in the shape given to them by Greek sculptors: "If oxen and horses and lions had hands and could paint and sculpt with them like the humans, then the horses would paint horselike, the oxen oxlike figures of the gods and would form such bodies as each species itself inhabited" (15). "The Ethiopians maintain that their gods have snub noses and are black; the Thracians that their gods are blue-eyed and red-haired" (16).

Mortals believe that gods are born. But God did not become and is eternal.

It seems that Xenophanes thought the fundamental thoughts of Western monotheism: oneness as opposed to the multiplicity of gods, incorporeality as opposed to the representations of human and other figures, eternity as opposed to the coming-to-be and birth of gods; God as thought, as presence, as all-powerful efficacy; unborn, eternal, infinite, but in ways that are beyond human imagination. What do these early simple notions of God mean?

They are, first of all, the thoughts of the much later so-called negative theology. By saying what God is not, he rises to his exalted height. Man attains a level of self-consciousness by reference to this wholly incomprehensible, yet actual, deity.

But Xenophanes does not stop at this negative theology. The incorporeal deity achieves a rudiment of form through graphic ciphers. God is "all eye, all spirit, all ear" (24); he needs no organs in order to see and to know everything, but he sees and knows everything. He governs irresistibly, without physical force. "With only the spirit's power of thought, He effects effortlessly the revolution of the universe" (25). He is perfect majestic serenity. "He always remains in the same place, not moving at all, and it is not fitting for him to go back and forth, now here and now there" (26); that means he is everywhere.

The following seems to contradict the notion of one God: Xenophanes speaks not only about God but also about gods. "One God is the greatest among gods and men" (23). He speaks about gods when he describes the solemn symposium introduced by ritual. Solemnity and ritual are tied to the gods. For him, the one God has no cult; all cults of the gods are directed toward him without drawing nearer to him. The symposium as described by Xenophanes cannot be interpreted as the founding of something like a new cult of the one God. There is no trace of a religious founder in Xenophanes. His goal is purification, not foundation. His piety lies in polytheistic concreteness joined to all-pervading awe before the encompassing One. His radicality turns against the destructive representations of gods, not against the many gods. The one God, however, who eschews all shape, appears in the shapes of the gods.

This whole problem of the one God and the many gods is not explicitly thought through but for Xenophanes is a natural presupposition. The great battle of the one God of the Bible against heathen polytheism is not as yet a possibility. Hence the passion is lacking which, in the cipher of the one exclusive Biblical God, this personal God, turns against all false gods and all of polytheism (though not without restoring it in another form).

One analogy remains. In the Bible: For the sake of the one God, the world is stripped of its magic, which now becomes the object of rational comprehension. God's actions take place in the world, in history, which God commands and guides through the actions of man. In Xenophanes: For the sake of the one omnipresent God, the whole world is opened up to rational comprehension.

The crucial difference: Xenophanes' thinking does not include God's otherworldliness, or the gulf (*tmema*, Plato) between God and the world. He has no knowledge as yet of what will make its appearance with Plato's *agathon* and then with the Biblical God. Without saying so expressly, he regards the deity as congruent with the universe. The later One and All (*hen kai pan*) is the thought of piety toward the world, with its certainty of the one God.

Even in antiquity there was confusion in understanding Xenophanes, confusion that has been corrected only in our times.[2] Xenophanes cannot be regarded as the teacher of Parmenides. Parmenides' greatness could not have been stimulated by Xenophanes' mode of philosophizing. On the other hand, the idea that the aging Xenophanes derived his conception of God from the younger Parmenides is traceable only to the work of an anonymous author of the Hellenistic period who wrote about Xenophanes, Melissus, and Gorgias, and was falsely regarded as a reliable source.[3] In this work the thinking of Parmenides and Xenophanes has been combined in a patently absurd manner. Parmenides directs his thought toward Being and carries out speculative thoughts, but nowhere does he call Being God. Xenophanes, by contrast, directs his thought toward God in his majesty and does not carry out any speculative thoughts; by God he means neither Being nor a concept. Parmenides

---

[2] See Karl Reinhardt, *Parmenides und die Geschichte der griechischen Philosophie*. Bonn, 1916, 126ff., 152ff.

[3] Jaeger, 51–52.

carries out philosophical thinking in its depth. Xenophanes exhibits the depth of a pious consciousness of God, which excludes from his representation of God all that is unworthy. Parmenides' thoughts could later be used by speculative theology because he developed concepts. This is not the case with Xenophanes because his thinking remains on the level of mere intellect.

It is doubtful whether Xenophanes, as was said at a later time, became a citizen of Elea. He wrote a poem about the founding of Elea, just as he did about the founding of Colophon. What is said about him as an Eleatic probably arose through the erroneous combination of the philosophy of Xenophanes and of Parmenides.

V. THE ETHOS

Xenophanes is incensed by Homer: "From the very beginning all have learnt in accordance with Homer" (F10). That is morally ruinous. For "Homer and Hesiod have attributed to the gods all things that are shameful and a reproach among mankind: theft, adultery, and mutual deception" (F11). Hence one should not sing at the symposia of the "battles of the Titans or of the Giants or even of the Centaurs—inventions of ancient times" (1). Nor should one sing of violent civic strife. Martial spirit and brute force are repugnant to Xenophanes.

Xenophanes is opposed to the important basic value judgments of the Greeks. He despises the honors bestowed upon the victors at the Olympic Games. The Greeks bestow the greatest honors on the winners in footraces, wrestling, boxing, in the pancratium, and in horse races. Xenophanes dares to contest the worth of such victors by saying: "And yet he does not have as much value as I. For my *sophia* is better than the strength of men or of horses" (2). The demand of thought, of philosophy and the sciences, often to be repeated by great philosophers in spite of their lack of resonance, is made here for the first time: If men search for knowledge, truth will dissipate the fog of lies and deception.

If Xenophanes criticizes things as they are—the mores, the cults of the gods, the agnostic frame of mind, the festival plays, the kinds of poetic productions—it is for ethical reasons. Philosophy demands of him a revaluation for the salvation of man. Whereas Pindar in his poems glorified the victors and their cities, Xenophanes pilloried what in Pindar speaks to us in timeless beauty and in the grandeur of pious thoughts.

It must not be overlooked that Xenophanes repeatedly uses the con-

cept of "utility" in his reasoning. Reciting mythological fictions and
accounts of civil wars at symposia is not useful. The victors at Olympia
and the honors bestowed on them are not useful. They will not "bring
a better order to the *polis*. . . . These things do not enrich the treasure
chambers of the state" (2).

VI. THE LIMIT OF MAN

Xenophanes' sense of his own worth in comparison with his fellowmen
is combined with his modesty as a human being. He knows nothing of
the philosophical tyranny of absolute knowledge, nothing of the Hegelian
"courage of truth" to which everything must open and nothing can
remain hidden.

Human cognition is unable to reach what it aspires to. "Perfect
knowledge (or the absolutely certain, *to saphes*) has never been glimpsed
by man, nor will there ever be anyone to have done so with regard to
the gods and all the things I maintain in this work. Even if someone
above all others were to be successful in expressing what is actually
present, he still would not draw his knowledge from his own experience.
Rather, there is conjecture in all things."

We must constantly remain on the way: "Truly, the gods did not
disclose everything to mortals from the beginning; instead, seeking, they
gradually find what is better."

VII. HISTORICAL PLACE AND INFLUENCE

Xenophanes belongs to the early stages of Greek philosophy; contemporaneous with and shortly after the Milesians (Thales, Anaximander)
and Pythagoras, he is a unique phenomenon. He is not, like the former,
a theoretical thinker and scholar nor, like the latter, a religious-political
founder. He is the herald of an ethical attitude toward life based on
unlimited enlightenment. He desires the purification of the soul, not
through mysteries and atonements and magical acts but through clarity
of thinking as one leads one's life with the one God, who is present in
the infinite universe.

Xenophanes precedes the beginnings of the speculative philosophy
of Heraclitus and Parmenides—a philosophy that, by means of a new
way of thinking, penetrates to the ground of things. He, unlike them,

however, is devoid of the pride of superhuman wisdom that lifts man above the folly of the crowd and alienates him from it. Instead, he is self-assured in his enlightened natural way of thinking that links him to fellow human beings. For him, this mode of thought is the best man can attain and share with others.

He remains the naïve enlightener, unaware of potential criticism, to which his way of thinking is vulnerable, criticism leading to confusion. He has no notion of the perversion brought about by means of this artifice for the calculated manipulation of minds, which the later Sophists understood. They first brought about the change in the life of the mind that opened the way to Plato and Socrates.

Heraclitus says contemptuously of Xenophanes, whom he mentions alongside Pythagoras, Hesiod, Hekataios: "A smattering of many things does not teach one to have reason (*nous*)" (40).

The doctrine of one deity, pure and noble, conceived without the falsification of anthropomorphic representations appears first in Xenophanes, to become the common property of the philosophers and tragedians. Immediately after him, Empedocles formulated: "He is not equipped with a human head on his body . . . he is spirit, holy and ineffable, and only spirit, which darts through the entire universe with its swift thoughts" (134). Plato, Aristotle, the Stoics, and all sublime philosophy, stand within the continuity of this thought.

The tragedians adopted it, Jaeger calls attention to Aeschylus: "Zeus is the ether, Zeus the earth, Zeus the sky; Zeus is the All, and what is higher yet than this."[4]

And in the *Heracles* of Euripides, we read:

> But I do not believe the gods commit
> adultery, or bind each other in chains.
> I never did believe it; I never shall;
> nor that one god is tyrant of the rest.
> If god is truly god, he is perfect,
> lacking nothing. These are poets' wretched lies.[5]

[4] Jaeger, 70.
[5] Tr. W. Arrowsmith. Lines 1341–46.

VIII. CHARACTERIZATION

Xenophanes is not the creator of new ciphers or the inventor of configurations of thought, or the deep thinker whose statements are pondered
for millennia, or the founder of a religious movement. He had no school,
because he had no doctrine. There were Pythagoreans, Milesians, and
later Eleatics and Heracliteans. But there was no school of Xenophanes.
No luster surrounds this philosopher.

Xenophanes represents a clear morality and good sense that protect
him from being led astray. His trust in this good sense, his innate
humanity, his joy in the beauty of existence, his sobriety—all draw their
strength and substance from the one, unimaginable, unthinkable God
superior to everything.

In his approach, however, this philosopher from the earliest period
of Greek philosophy clearly exhibits the limits that from his day to ours
are linked to this mode of thinking. Such piety toward the world is
blind to the awesome forces that not only destroy man but lead him to
surpass himself. He knows nothing of the courage of sacrifice, or the
meaning of great decisions, or the fighting spirit not content with a
critical stance but ready to risk life itself. Alien to him is the man whom
reason alone will not satisfy. He does not see the greatness of such a
being or sense the powers speaking through the gods.

A further limitation lies in the fact that this good sense finds its
expression primarily in criticism and polemics. Though not grounded
in negation per se, this view has a natural basis that, in its abstractness,
may seem flat and dull. Hence as a great philosophical personality Xenophanes is not symbolic of great thinkers who seem to know more
than they are able to express.

Yet, Xenophanes, for the first time in philosophical thinking, exhibits
the good sense that looks around in the world with an unprejudiced
eye, the theoretical earnestness of a sublime conception of God, and the
awareness of the limits of human knowledge.

I do not agree with the generally negative or even scornful evaluation
of Xenophanes, for he occupies a position that, though narrow, is indispensable. His thinking originates in his rejection of a perverted admiration for a frame of mind that tyrannizes the spirit, though it may
be linked to a creativity that is indeed admirable (palpably so in Parmenides and Heraclitus). He refuses to submit, even to one whom he
acknowledges to be great. He does not follow the widespread tendency
of idolizing human beings. He repudiates the inhumanity that searches
for the superman or supposedly recognizes him in an individual, or even

claims such suprahuman status for himself. For him, there is no supremacy of one human being over another. Each person remains a human being, in spite of the tremendous differences in rank.

Xenophanes addresses himself to an audience, namely, to everyman. He did not isolate himself to pursue lonely truth in a small circle. He participated in human affairs, eager to enlighten and morally to purify himself and his fellowmen.

DEMOCRITUS

BACKGROUND; DEMOCRITUS AND ATHENS

Democritus (c. 460–370 B.C.) was born and lived in Abdera, on the coast of Thrace, where he was a member of a school of philosophy. He undertook journeys of long duration to Greece, Egypt, and the Near East. The thought of Leukippus—the originator of atomism—was known to Democritus through his work *Megas Diakosmos* (The Great World-Order). Democritus had some contact with the Sophist Protagoras, who was his senior by twenty years, possibly also with the physician Hippocrates. He was held in high regard by his countrymen.

Democritus had no connection to Athenian philosophy. He ridiculed Anaxagoras, who was older than he by four decades, because of his cosmic order (*diakosmesis*) and his doctrine of the mind (*nous*) (5). Unlike his older compatriot Protagoras, Democritus ignored Sophist thought, the grandiose, disintegrative mentality without which neither Socrates nor Plato would have been possible. He knew as little about these contemporaries as they about him. He is reported to have said, "I came to Athens and no one knew me" (116). Plato never mentions him, but must have known about his atomic theory when, in his old age, he wrote his *Timaeus*. Only Aristotle mentions him, often and with great respect. The contemplative life of discovery in the natural sciences and the ethos that went with it could not interest Socrates or Plato. One root of their thinking lay in practice, in the responsibility and frustration of politics, in activism; it went beyond observation of nature, far into the suprasensory realm, which, in turn, would have seemed sheer nonsense to Democritus. Aristotle says: "In Socrates' times inquiry into nature was abandoned and philosophers turned to the examination of practical virtue and of politics" (*De animalium partibus*, I/1). But nature as well as the sciences dealing with it were Democritus' concern, as later on they would be that of Aristotle, who gives as the reason for his high esteem: "Democritus seems to have speculated about everything" (A35). These were two philosophical worlds, which did not touch and which—if they know each other at all—remain barely intelligible to each other even today. Only Aristotle, with his universally organizing objectivity, was able to bring them together.

We see Democritus—in contrast to Athenian philosophy—as an entirely different type of philosophical possibility, complete in itself. Hence we can understand that Christian thought, basing itself on Platonic philosophy, to which it was linked by elective affinity, would allow his writings to disappear. (They were still extant at the time of the Roman emperors.) This is why we are no longer able to view this other great type of philosophy in a complete, structured opus. We can call Democritus to mind only through fragments and reports. If we had a *corpus Democriteum*, as we have a *corpus Platonicum*, the resulting picture would demonstrate his greatness through its richness.

Democritus does not belong to the pre-Socratics. He is a contemporary of Plato and is his counterpart.

I. DEMOCRITUS' ATOMISM

With his atomism, Democritus did not create a philosophical system that would explain everything that exists. His areas of scientific inquiry and realms of thought bear little relationship to atomism. What makes it all cohesive is not atomism, but a mode of thinking that in the model of atomism bears witness to, among other things, the totality of natural events.

1. The theory in outline

Leucippus found atomism to be one of the great designs of Being of the pre-Socratic age. Democritus made it into a link within a more comprehensive philosophy. A schematic presentation of atomism would look like this:

a) There is Being and Nothingness, that is, fullness and the void, atoms and space. The void exists without being something. Democritus expresses it with an artificial neologism: "Being is just as much as Nothingness '*den*' is just as much as '*meden*' " (A37, A49; 156). The old proposition states: "Nothing can arise out of nothing; what is cannot be reduced to nothing." But we must also ask what this Being is. Parmenides answers this question in a speculative manner. The answer of the atomistic theory is: Only the atoms are eternal and immutable.

b) Atoms are the smallest invisible objects filling space. They are indivisible because of their smallness, or their hardness, or because there is neither void nor interstice in them; they are incompressible. They are altogether full (*pleon*), solid and impenetrable.

c) Atoms lack any differentiating qualities; they differ only quantitatively. They are infinite in number. They are infinitely varied, coming in all possible geometric shapes: spheric and angular, provided with hooks, bent into themselves, smooth and jagged. They have no interior condition whatsoever.

d) The atoms move in the infinite void, in which there is no above or below, no center and no outer limit. In eternal motion from the beginning of time, they affect each other through pressure and thrust, through bonding and clustering.

The actual world comes to be with the first collision taking place within the vortex. Like attaches itself to like. The finer particles escape into the outer void.

Thus things come to be in the visible world through the arrangement of the different atoms, of their number, shape, and size.

Motion is necessary; the accidental arises only through the manner in which motions encounter each other. Only through motion do vortices and the formation of the universe come to be. Necessity is the motion of counterthrust, of locomotion, of the impact of matter.

e) The cosmos is infinite. Innumerable worlds are formed; they are simultaneous or successive within the infinite. The world happens by chance, as does motion. There is no point in inquiring after its cause, for the cause has always existed. Time, like motion, has no beginning.

f) Only atoms and the void are imperishable. Worlds and all the things in these worlds come to be and pass away, for they are nothing other than the combination and separation of atoms. What is imperishable does not change. What does change are the particular stratifications and agglomerations of the atoms, each of which has its beginning and its end—each thing and every one of the worlds.[1]

2. *The solution of the difficulties*

There are certain difficulties connected with the theory of the atoms if it is to explain everything there is, difficulties that can be overcome only by adding further presuppositions.

a) *Whence comes the suitability of living things to their purpose?* In the universe of atomic motion there is no purpose and no meaning and no

[1] Wilhelm Capelle, *Die Vorsokratiker, Fragmente und Quellenberichte*. Leipzig, Kröner, 1935, 396ff.

order, but solely motion and mutual chance encounter. Order and, particularly, the formation of living things come to be because only that which is purposive achieves permanence. What has come to be by chance vanishes quickly if it does not assume a configuration that, through special, unplanned accident, is capable of permanence. There are only efficient causes, no final causes.

Democritus calls such events *logos* and *ananke* (necessity). All that occurs does so for a cogent reason—namely, the motion of the atoms —and is accidental only when measured against purpose and meaning.

As letters come together to form words and sentences, so atoms come together to become things. Just as all works of poetry and of thought consist of just the letters of the alphabet, so all efficacious actualities in the world, the living beings, consist of innumerable atoms.

Something else has to be added so that we may understand purpose and meaning in accordance with their origin.

b) *What is the soul?* The soul consists of round atoms, the smoothest and finest, the most mobile, like the floating atoms of fire. Aristotle tells us that a writer of comedies maintains that Daedalus had made it possible for the wooden Aphrodite to move by pouring mercury into her. Similarly, Democritus maintains, according to Aristotle, that the spherical atoms activate the whole body through their motion, since, as is their nature, they are never at rest (A104).

Even thinking is a bodily state and occurs when the atoms are properly mixed. It changes when the mixture becomes too cold (A135).

In perception and in dreams, images (*eidola*) penetrate into the soul as projections of themselves from all kinds of things. This is how household utensils, clothes, plants, living things are seen in a dream (A77).

Something more, however, is needed for us to comprehend the inwardness of psychic experience according to its origin. The outwardness of atoms, no matter how fine, mobile, or fiery they may be, is not sufficient.

c) *What is cognition?* If atoms and empty space alone are constitutive of Being, then what we perceive are appearances. Our senses do not show us reality itself. We do not know through perception, but through thought. This, in fact, is what Democritus says. But now he has to explain what perception and cognition are.

What we know is never actuality itself, for only atoms and the void are reality-in-itself and permanent. The combinations of atoms change. All that is, is such a compound of the infinitely various atoms: things, living beings, stars, souls, and gods. Information about all of these is received by way of perception. Perception is due to images (*eidola*) pro-

jected from objects making contact with the senses. Hence the senses
show us only these appearances and not the actuality of the atoms and
the compounds of atoms themselves. Sense perception never shows us
atoms; only, according to customary opinion (*nomos*), black or yellow or
red, bitter or sweet, cold or warm, and hence never that which corresponds to the nature of things.

This essence of things—atoms and the void—manifests itself only
to thinking. Hence thinking has preeminence when it comes to truth.
There are two sorts of knowledge. To the obscure one belong sight,
hearing, smell, taste, and touch. Genuine cognition arises when obscure
cognition can do no more. When it can "neither see more minutely, nor
hear, nor smell, nor taste, nor perceive by touch—and a finer investigation is needed, then the genuine comes in . . ." (F11), that is, thought.

According to Democritus, there are three criteria of truth. First: In
order to grasp the invisible things one has to consider the visible ones.
Second: Investigating the road is thinking. Third: For choosing and
avoiding, one listens to the emotions (*pathe*). "For we are to choose that
toward which we are well disposed and avoid that which is alien to us"
(A111). (We shall not deal with this third criterion here; it applies to
ethics.)

Democritus lets the senses speak: " 'Miserable Mind, you get your
evidence from us, and do you try to overthrow us? The overthrow will
be your downfall' " (F125). But this is by no means his last word. The
senses are the point of departure at every step of cognition, even though
thought surmounts the nature of appearance proper to the entire sensible
world. But the progression does not, as in Plato, move from becoming
to the eternal ideas as the primal images and to the power of the idea
of the Good which effects all and illuminates all; rather, it moves from
the sensory qualities to the everlasting forms of the atoms (also called
"ideas" by Democritus, since idea equals form).

For Democritus there are two limits of cognition. First: "We know
nothing in reality; for truth lies in the depth" (117). Our interpretation:
To be sure, thinking advances as far as actuality itself, to the atoms; yet
thinking is not able to bring about sensations; for fundamental cognition
permits only the fundamental deduction of a world of appearances and
not its complete explanation encompassing the concreteness of realities
open to experience.

Second: "Our knowledge of actuality is never safe from deception
but changeable according to the constitution of our bodies and of those
things that flow toward and impinge upon it." No matter how far we

progress, we remain tied not only to our senses but also to our natural proclivities.[2]

d) *Are there gods and what are they?* In distinction from all other pre-Socratic schemes of Being, the atoms of Leucippus could not be termed divine because the crude image of a spatiality replete with incompressible little lumps made this impossible. Thus Democritus too never used the term divine as an attribute of the atoms; that designation was given by Anaximander, Heraclitus, and Empedocles to the ground of Being as they conceived it. It was also possible with the Being of Parmenides and the *nous* of Anaxagoras. What Democritus called divine was the nature granted to Homer, the endowments of the soul (37) in distinction to those of the body (21). "It is the mark of the divine intellect to be always calculating something noble" (F112). The poets "think divine thoughts with their mind" (F129). Democritus did not deny the gods.

In the first place, he sought to explain certain phenomena within the framework of his theory of atoms: Demons are *eidola*, and these—as is the case with sense perceptions—are thin clusters of atoms detaching themselves from objects and pouring into the soul, in both the waking and the dreaming state. They can be either beneficent or harmful. Democritus wished to meet auspicious images (166). These, he said, are of supernatural size, do not pass away easily, but are not imperishable. They make known to man the future in advance. Just as there are premonitions, there are also tangible signs of things to come. For this reason Democritus believed in the wisdom of inspecting the entrails of sacrificial animals, in order to recognize the signs of health, epidemics, bountiful harvests, or crop failure (A138).

For Democritus these belong to the realm of natural realities that properly do not concern God or the great gods; they are explicable within the framework of nature as it is conceived in accordance with the theory of atoms.

In the second place, Democritus sought to derive the fact that men believe in gods from the nature of man. If the gods are put in doubt, and if, as with nature generally, the nature of man is the subject of thought and investigation, then the question arises how the belief in gods originated. For this belief in itself constitutes a reality even if gods did not exist.

When prehistoric men saw what happened in the space above, such as thunder and lightning, the conjunction of stars, and the eclipse of sun

[2] Capelle, 428ff.

and moon, they were struck by fear, since they believed that divine beings were the originators of these phenomena. Hence Democritus began to explain the ideas about gods as being based on natural phenomena: Ambrosia, the food of the gods, is the vapor that nourishes the sun (25).

Other sources are the sense of guilt and the fear of punishment, which, added to the belief in an afterlife (a belief that Democritus repudiates), turn into fear of the gods.

In the third place, however, Democritus has an entirely different conception of God, which is neither confirmed by the *eidolon* theory nor in any way relates to the theory postulating a psychological origin of belief in gods. Rather, it has its origin in his philosophizing, in which the theory of atoms and encyclopedic scientific inquiry are only partial areas.

Democritus speaks of the early sages (the *logoi*, thinking men) as though they were still valid prototypes for the philosopher of his day—his own prototypes. They did what was essential: "Of reasoning men, a few raised their hands toward the place which we Greeks now call 'air' and said: Zeus considers all things, he knows all and gives and takes away all and is king over everything altogether" (30). These early sages prophesied as individuals to the nations. It is an image that makes us think of the actuality of Moses but simultaneously reveals the dim distance from this historic reality. Yet this precisely is philosophy: the trust in insight in view of the all-embracing divinity, the will to become authentically human on this path, and the expectation that all men can enter upon it. Democritus clothed divine efficacy in the language of popular religion:

"But the gods are the givers of all good things, both in the past and now. They are not, however, the givers of things which are bad, harmful or non-beneficial, either in the past or now, but men themselves fall into these through blindness of mind and lack of sense" (*agnomosyne*) (F175).

At this point, at the very inception, it becomes quite evident—though not as a conscious element in Democritus' thought—that the theory of atoms as such does not necessarily lead to materialism and godlessness. This can happen only when the atoms usurp the place of divinity. But at the same time the unresolved contradictoriness in Democritus' overall conception of world and man is made evident. This is resolved only when the theory of atoms, in a particular science, is taken to be merely a thought-pattern for inquiry into matter, a pattern that does not determine faith or philosophy in any decisive way.

II. THE SCIENCES IN RELATION TO THE
THEORY OF ATOMS

Some physical facts can be explained by means of atoms:

The larger atoms are heavier than the smaller ones, and the substances that contain less emptiness and more atoms are heavier than those with more empty space and fewer atoms. By sinking to the bottom the heavier ones propel the lighter ones upward.

The mixture of substances consists in the positioning of the atoms. Hence the intermingling is in fact an illusion. In the smallest parts— the atoms themselves—there is no mixing.

Magnetism is explained as follows: The magnet (which consists of the same atoms as iron) is composed of fine atoms, is less compact, and contains more interstices.

What one sees here at the inception is similar to the atomism of Epicurus and Lucretius: Explanations are not based on scientific investigation but on plausibilities of trivial and unproven character. Something more becomes evident: The clarity and simplicity of the schema of atomism collapses when it is used to explain more than inanimate matter.

But even with regard to inanimate matter, the fruitfulness of atomism did not manifest itself until the seventeenth century, when metaphysical atomism was presented again by Gassendi and when Boyle and the chemists made use of the model of atomism in their research, calling it the theory of corpuscles. Ever since then, atomism has played a role in the process of modern scientific progress, though in constantly changing form. With the aid of mathematics, which first made possible quantitative precision and control, atomism became a means of cognition within a particular perspective of the world.

Up to then, atomism remained one metaphysical world-vision alongside others and, as such, based its evidence on grounds utterly different from those of scientific cognition. It functioned as a cipher and was used as such by Epicureanism and so-called materialism in a variety of ways, including totally opposite attitudes toward life.

Most areas of cognition that engaged Democritus are wholly independent of atomism.

III. ETHOS AND ETHICS

What is preserved of Democritus' writings is a large number of maxims (*gnomai*) and several longer fragments—disorderly debris. The struc-

turing of this presentation is intended to characterize the meaning of
this thinking in its coherence, and is directed, equally, toward nature
and ethos.

1. Overview

Democritus' focus is the human being. His ethos has man as its origin
and goal.

What is man? Democritus repeats the dictum of the ancients: Man
is a small universe (*mikros kosmos*) (34).

He does not offer an interpretation of this universe. He asks what
is best for man, wherein lies his salvation. Salvation is not found in
something outward for which man exists, but in himself.

To find the solution, man must be seen according to his nature, hence
the need for psychological and physiological observation. He is body and
soul, subject to the necessities imposed on him by nature in his drives,
conditions, and situations. But man cannot be exhaustively investigated
by exclusively objective means. What he makes of what he is, is his own
responsibility. He himself is answerable for many ills, for his actions,
for his entire inner constitution. In short: As the object of inquiry, man
is a natural being; through the nature peculiar to him, he is his own
task.

2. What becomes of man is of his own choosing

What man will become is of his own choosing; it depends on his natural
endowment, which varies among individuals; he himself determines his
own goal in his substance, his dignity, his salvation.

Observation teaches us that inclination and aversion are man's mo-
tivating forces. "Pleasure [*terpsis*] and absence of pleasure [*aterpia*] are
the criteria of what is profitable and what is not" (F4). Our feelings
(*pathe*) move us "to choose that which we like and to turn from that
which is alien to us" (A111).

But critical examination shows that it is not a matter of inclination
as such, but of the object of inclination.

3. The goal

Judgment and choice can be measured against the question: What is
man's ultimate goal? The Greeks called it *eudaimonia*, meaning to have
a good *daimon* as guide and with his aid to achieve the integration of

life. The *daimon* does not dwell in gold and possessions but in the soul only. "The soul is the dwelling place of the daimon" (171). This *daimon* may be a good or evil genius. Democritus, in his ethical advice, postulates the potential efficacy of a good *daimon*.

For him, the goal is an ordering of life, a state of the soul. He does not use the term *eudaimonia* but designates it by a variety of terms: joyousness (*euthymia*), well-being (*euesto*), imperturbability (*ataraxia*), steadfastness (*athambia*), a state free of apprehension (*athaumastia*), serenity (*galene*), harmony (*symmetria*) of the soul.

There are two ways to reach the goal (*telos*).

One might see the desired state of the soul as a consequence of inclination away from perishable things toward things exalted and eternal, in the purity of motives, in the fulfillment of obligations. This advice to seek after noble things might easily be interpreted as not posited for its own sake but because of its influence on the state of the soul (hence as a means to an end).

The other way points to psychological motivation and seems to calculate what would further a tranquil state of the soul.

Our own question to Democritus might be whether the state of the soul as such should be given this ultimate value. Does this calculated purpose not throw a shadow over whatever great and beautiful aims men set themselves? Is it not self-limiting in scope, regressive?

An ethical mode of thought such as this is shot through with ambiguity. It allows psychological motivation derived from natural attributes to intermingle with ethical motivation based on substantial meaning. The nobility of the true is damaged by psychological advice (such as comparing oneself with those who are worse off); in such borderline cases this amounts to advice to adopt a base attitude as advantageous to our well-being.

Thus there evolves a mode of thinking restricted to the aim of achieving purely human tranquillity. The goal here is the condition of the individual, his cheerfulness, not an elevation of spirit whether in fear or in bravery, or in facing one's destiny with the powers of love and reason. The tragic element of life disappears from our range of vision. Destiny is eliminated. The contentment of contemplation is sufficient unto itself. The trials and dangers inherent in life are to be expunged, risk is to be avoided. The meaning of life finds its fulfillment in the private sphere, or, rather, in that of the single individual, in his peace of mind. We shall see how this ambiguity manifests itself in further developments as they are particularized: the excellent insights and the disconcerting absolutization of the banality of existence.

4. The origin: reason

Rarely does Democritus mention a god by name. But the title of one of his works is *Athene* (*Tritogeneia*, thrice-born) (2). He calls this goddess "prudence" (*phronesis*). "However, out of this prudence arises this triad: thinking well (*kalos*), speaking appropriately, and doing one's duty."

Thinking, intellect, reason (*logis, logismos, nous, phronesis*) is the wellspring of the good, the means for shaping one's life, the goal reached by way of disinterested cognition. This is philosophy (still called *sophia*), and philosophy produces joyousness.

5. Independence, freedom from the fear of death, dignity

The goal of the ethos is *euthymia*, the tranquil state of the soul, which is well-being, pure happiness in contemplation of the beautiful, independence and freedom.

This happiness is in harmony with nature. It is characteristic of how Democritus views the ages of man and death.

He compares the ages of man without regrets, without yearning for the past, and without impatience for the future. To each age he apportions what is proper to it, and refrains from comparing them.

For Democritus, death is not an object of dread, but a fact of life. There is no life after death. This is a mere fable invented out of fear about what follows death. It is foolish to avoid thinking about death because of fear, and to want to quicken the pleasures before death comes upon us unawares (1a).

Yet whoever studies Democritus has to become aware of the shadow that darkens these insights, as the soul's state of *euthymia* becomes the ultimate goal.

Democritus nowhere asks whether this very state he postulates for each human being does not require something beyond it, whether it can be attained in this world without fulfillment through something else. This something, it is true, leads to peace of soul, but again and again breaks through tranquillity in a movement that allows us to rise above ourselves by the force of restlessness. According to Democritus, neither pleasure nor tranquillity as a state of mind is the ultimate goal. Instead, the question is always not only pleasure in what, but also tranquillity through what.

In his concrete value judgments it is evident that Democritus does not address this question in its substance: vide his fundamentally apolitical attitude, his comments on women and children. Even friendship, as he sees it, is not solidarity when faced with the misfortune of men subject to alien forces, not the endlessly renewed struggle of loving communication, but the peaceful contentment of men joined in the civilized enjoyment of the beautiful, men who are decent, no doubt, though possibly agitated by unconscious drives and moods. The degree to which this tranquil friendship moves into the center of life, indeed becomes its real culmination, undermines the validity of this ethos.

IV. CHARACTERIZATION

Three aspects of this philosophy seem to stand out as separate components, each of them taking its direction from its origin. The *theory of atoms*—the schema of Being in itself—is developed independently. *Universal scientific inquiry* grows out of a limitless thirst for knowledge and is self-delighting. He "would rather discover one causal explanation than gain royal dominion over the Persians," Democritus said (118). The *ethos* desired tranquillity and achieved this goal by directing light upon all human activity.

These three blocks of thought seem to stand, unintegrated, side by side. Democritus did not develop a system of the whole. The systematic theory of atoms stands within this whole but does not encompass it or give it a foundation. We must ask ourselves how all this is held together. If there is no system of the whole, then perhaps there is a way of thinking the whole. Since Democritus does not supply the answer, it may be arrived at by trying to highlight what is specifically characteristic of him.

A recurrent feature is his striving for vividness, comprehensibility, naturalness. He seeks the concrete, that which manifests itself. He shirks the imaginary; the theory of atoms itself seems to him in accordance with nature, using as his guide what is most easily grasped, the body in its compactness and resistance in space. He rejects the unnatural and suprasensory, denies immortality and a realm of the beyond. He knows no transcendence, renounces speculation into the ground of Being, since atoms have taken the place of transcendence. The function of the theory of atoms seems to be, at least to some extent, the expunging of speculative philosophy. This seemingly superior disillusionment amounts to a somewhat misleading reasonableness.

The basic stance of this philosopher is characterized by a cool temper, lack of a sense of destiny, and, finally, lack of transcendence. Democritus, by the very existence of his great thought, demonstrates that it is possible to live, without God, in tranquillity, serene and active, without fear and without a trace of despair.

Alongside all this we discover a plenitude of posited problems with regard to questions of knowledge, but an absence of problems in the existential realm. Such reasonableness does not correspond to the great matter-of-factness of reason, but reveals an obliviousness of man's concern in the face of his limits. This thinking contains a tendency to banality even as we view the pinnacles fleetingly attained by him along his way.

Though deeply moved by a notion of the dignity of man, Democritus touches on it only marginally, that is, without making it an integral part of the totality of his thinking. Here too, as with everything else, he brings openness to his contemplation; similar in this, perhaps, to the early sages who looked up to divinity and proclaimed it. When he touches on delight in the beautiful and the great, on duty recognized and fulfilled, on self-examination and the notion of inner purity, he does not inquire into their origin. Their ground lies solely in themselves. As an autonomous being, the person sufficient unto himself sees the beautiful, recognizes the ought, and has commerce solely with himself. He does not need transcendence and does not inquire after it. Thinking so blatantly and exclusively rooted in nature leaves beyond the horizon the mystery of perplexities, the possibility of higher orders through which those natural orders are fulfilled, their insufficiency revealed, and in the end penetrated and transcended.

We see here the fundamental mind-set of piety toward nature. All that is human is nature and conceived as nature. Tranquillity lies in contemplating the fullness of a world without end.

This interpretation of nature is based on the following principle: As the world is conceived as arising from the atoms, so the sublime from the lowly: rationality grows from necessity, culture from necessity and need, religion from fear. Everything in the world comes to be through the motion of the smallest parts (the atoms); everything among men, out of the attributes and actions of individuals. All becoming is development: all that has come into being and to completion, everything large is derived from the smallest that did not come to be, from the simple, the incomplete, the insignificant. This kind of thinking denies meaning and purpose to what occurs. Everything is accessible to natural causal explanation.

The relationship of the three origins (theory of atoms, encyclopedic knowledge, ethos) seems to be the following: Perfect tranquillity resides in knowledge; it brings about man's absorption in the unchanging, in the things that are "not mortal."

This knowledge finds its perfection in the theory of atoms, which is the cognition of what authentically is and of all there is. The fundamental mind-set of the person who philosophizes in this manner finds sufficient satisfaction in the theory of atoms.

This is a rich world-philosophy, a highly disciplined individualistic ethos. But this self-satisfied thinking breaks down again and again, astonishingly, pitifully obtrusive—symbolized by the theory of atoms as the authentic knowledge of Being.

EMPEDOCLES

LIFE; THE SICILIAN WORLD; LEGENDS; WRITINGS

The span of Empedocles' life is usually given as sixty years, the date of his birth supposed to be around 490 B.C. (cf. Diog. Laertius, VIII, 52, 74). His native city was Akragas (today Girgenti), at that time one of the wealthiest and most splendid cities of Sicily. He was of noble birth and a member of the democratic faction. It is said that he was exiled in his old age and that he died in the Peloponnese following an accident (a fall from a carriage).

Sicily was then at its historical apex. Following the victory over the Carthaginians at Himera in 481 B.C. (contemporaneous with the Greeks' victory over the Persians at Salamis), rapid colonial development in the sixth century led to its highest flowering. The catastrophe began in 409 B.C. with the destruction of Selinus and Himera by the Carthaginians, the saving of Syracuse by Dionysius, a series of wars. The risky nature of life lived in great insecurity and among rapid changes engendered a tendency toward excess. Temples of enormous size, only partially completed, were in keeping with the pride of the citizens and the merciless exploitation of the vanquished, like the captive Athenians who perished in 413 B.C. from working in the stone quarries of Syracuse. It was believed that protection of the gods could be gained through the splendor of religious worship. The style of Sicilian life presented itself to the Greek world in its grandiose participation in the Olympic Games, in splendid festivities, in the development of a sophisticated culinary art, ostentatious dress, and every kind of gratification.

The true greatness of this Sicily, however, was owed to the spirit of its poetry, its rhetoric, its thought. A high-mindedness towering above the ordinary found expression there. As an example: a *heroon* (monument) erected by his Sicilian enemies honored a youth killed in battle, celebrating his beauty, according to Herodotus. But among all the wonders that Sicily produced, says Lucretius, the most splendid is Empedocles (*De rerum natura*, I, 716ff.).

In his hometown, Empedocles took part in the battle against tyranny; as an itinerant physician and prophet, an Iatromantis (a wonder-working physician), he roamed surrounded by disciples, to one of whom, Pausanias, he dedicated his book *On Nature*. Not content with appropriating what the Milesians, Pythagoras, Parmenides, and the schools of physicians had created, he used them as foundation for his own work, filled with new ideas, thoughts, and poetic-philosophic visions. This intellectual labor was put entirely at the service of practical life. He was there to help people; in the free atmosphere of this Sicilian-Greek century, he was able to act in complete independence.

Soon legends grew up around his life. He was said to have refused the throne proffered him by the citizens; to have successfully protected Akragas against violent winds by spreading the skins of asses as a screen; that, by diverting streams, he freed Selinus of marshland and malaria. But the legends surrounding his death were the most striking.

After a banquet in his honor, his friends found that by morning he had disappeared. A slave told of hearing a powerful voice at midnight calling for Empedocles. He got up and saw a blaze of light but nothing further. Empedocles had gone to join the gods.

Skeptical jealousy cast a different light on this disappearance: After rising, Empedocles, it was told, had journeyed toward Mount Etna. Having arrived at its fiery maw, he leaped into it and disappeared, in the hope that this would further the belief that he had become a god. But the truth prevailed when one of his brazen sandals was cast forth by the crater.

Legends possess an inherent power. They achieve symbolic truth. What Greek malice invented about his suicide on Mount Etna, Hölderlin—who, like Nietzsche later, felt almost magically attracted to him—understood as the tragic truth of Empedocles' greatness.[1]

There have come down to us about 450 lines from two of his poetic works, *On Nature* (*Peri physeos*) and *Purifications* (*Katharmoi*). In addition, there are a number of reports. The beauty of the poetry, the terse diction, the images and situations grip us even today.

The contents of the two works from which these fragments derive seem to be mutually incompatible. They have been assigned to different periods in the philosopher's life. But this is countered by other voices (Bignone, Jaeger), who claim that Empedocles' entire work should be understood as an integrated whole expressed in different psychic states.

[1] Cf. Walther Kranz, *Empedokles*.

I agree with this claim, which, based on the nature of Empedocles' contribution, has proved to be justified.

THE BASIC EXPERIENCE

Grounded in Orphic-Pythagorean tradition, Empedocles expressed his view of the world: It is "a joyless place where murder and rancor and swarms of other spirits of calamity, debilitating illnesses, and corruptions and consequences of floods (*Sepsis* and *Rheuma*) roam hither and yon in the gloom of the meadow of misfortune" (121). We live in a "roofed cavern" (120). Therefore: "Alas, poor mankind, woe unto you who are pitifully wretched: out of such quarrels and sighs were you born!" (124).

Yet this world is ambiguous. There is always an opposite: "Here were the Earth-Mother . . . and the far-seeing Sunshine-Nymph . . . bloody Discord, and Harmony with her serious mien, Beauty and Ugliness, the Speed-Nymph and the Nymph of Delay, and lovely Infallibility and dark-eyed Uncertainty" (F122).

Because we experience this ambiguous state, we sense the possibility of an unequivocal one. Thus, even at birth: "I wept and wailed when I saw the unfamiliar land" (F118). "Cast forth from which level, from what fullness of bliss do I dwell here?" (119). The basic experience of our finding ourselves in the world, with no explanation, but immediately given, leads to the questions and answers Empedocles develops.

How is the origin of this human condition to be understood? His answer is the world-vision of a cyclical, eternal recurrence. Our awesome, beautiful world is a phase in this cycle. So far the theory.

To this, practice must be added. What is up to us and what ought we to do? The answer: What we are here we are through prior guilt. If we understand our origin in guilt, we know what we ought to do: become pure for our return.

I. THE THEORY

1. The world-vision as a whole

a) *Love and strife; the four roots of all things*. The state of the world varies. There are periods in which things are better or worse than today.

Two fundamental forces are the cause of motion: love and strife (*philia* and *neikos*). They contend with each other. If love achieves preeminence, the perfect state of harmony, of the sphere ("*sphairos*") prevails.

Strife is kept at bay. If strife dominates unchecked, there is total disorder (*akosmia*); love is extinct. Both of these outermost limits are turning points: strife soon penetrates *sphairos, akosmia* invades love. Events in the actual world fall between perfection (*sphairos*) and disorder (*akosmia*), between defection from *sphairos* and reconstitution out of *akosmia*. The world is in constant motion. There is rest only in the two transitional moments when the world is not yet or no longer. The end of the world is reached in the motionless perfection of love as well as in the fullness of disorder. The world comes to be through motion, which enters either the *sphairos* by way of strife or the *akosmia* by way of love.

The *sphairos* is not set in motion by universal unification. It is a single whole under the domination of love. There is no differentiation of the "swift limbs of the sun," nor of the "shaggy power of Earth," nor of the sea. "Thus the globe-shaped *sphairos* lies bound in the fast keep of harmony, enjoying the quiet all around" (27). This globe-shaped *sphairos* is not limited but "on all sides equal and everywhere infinite (*apeiron*)" (29).

The substance of world-motion consists of the four roots of all things, *rhizomata panton* (6): earth, water, fire, air. In a state of complete harmony their combination is such that they no longer exist as separate elements. In *akosmia* they have segregated themselves from each other so that they exist only as separates.

b) *Mixing and unmixing*. Aristotle can therefore say that, in Empedocles, love is sometimes the divisive principle, strife the unifying one. For love separates the like elements from each other in order to combine them in the configuration of the world. Strife, on the other hand, unifies the elements into homogeneous aggregations of fire, earth, water, and air. This is the destructive process of unmixing: "Fire increases fire, earth increases its own substance, air increases air" (37). In *akosmia* the elements are completely separate; in *sphairos*, totally combined. Within the actual world they are at once divided and combined.

In the world, it is true, the aggregations of the four elements are segregated into sun, earth, sky, and sea, but in these aggregations they are all mutually "bound together in harmony" (22).

Among the innumerable substances, those that are similar to each other are joined in love, but those that differ most greatly are mutually repulsive. "Water is more able to combine with wine but unwilling to mix with oil" (91).

c) *The wealth of configurations*. The wealth of configurations in the actual world is infinite. Empedocles contemplates them with both wonder and comprehension—configurations which "came pouring out" of the mix, "an infinite host of mortal creatures, in a thousand forms, a marvel to behold" (35).

Just as painters harmoniously bring multicolored substances to harmony by taking more of some and less of others, and just as figures come into being out of these combinations, so also the substance of things on earth, as many as we have come to know in their infinite plenitude, are to be sought in the four roots (23).

Empedocles contemplates the marvel of this inexhaustible wealth that has grown out of simple substances through their mixture: "Look at the sun . . . and the immortal heavenly bodies and at the water which, dark and cool, manifests itself in everything, and how the durable and solid substances come forth from the earth. . . . Everything grows out of them, everything that was and is and will be. Trees grew up and men and women, wild animals and birds and the fish in the waters, and the long-lived gods." For only the four roots "exist, and as they circulate among each other they assume the most divergent shapes. So great is their transformation due to their mixing" (21).

Right away, however, the configurations of living things are again "disunited by the evil spirits of strife. Alone, each by itself, they wander along the shores of life. And the same struggle occurs among the trees, the fish in the water, the animals in the forest, and the seagulls gently moving with their wings" (20).

d) *Are we in ascending or descending motion?* If we pose the question whether, according to Empedocles, we find ourselves in an ascending or a descending world-process, on the road toward *akosmia* or toward *sphairos*, no explicit answer can be found.

Because of the notion of the ascending and descending world-process, Empedocles' cosmological view appears twofold: The world comes to be through the incursion of strife into the *sphairos*; the world is actualized through love.

Strife brings about world-motion through explosive unmixing. The air is separated from and surrounds the sphere as its shell. The outermost layer becomes a crystal vault. Fire separates from the remaining mass and breaks through the air layer. It dislodges the air from the upper hemisphere. In this way, two hemispheres come to be, one light and fiery: day; and one consisting of dark air: night. This does not prevent Empedocles from stating in another context: "The Earth is the cause of night by setting itself against the rays of the sun (passing below it)" (48). Out of the earth, which is compressed from all sides, the water bubbles forth. Finally, all four elements are segregated.

Simultaneously with the catastrophe of the origin of the world, emerging from the *sphairos* through a primal explosion, as it were, re-action sets in. When strife reigns within the vortex, love arises. In love everything unites to form a single unit; this does not happen all at once but by a spontaneous drawing together from all directions. Out of this mixing an immense host of mortal creatures arises. Whatever is still held back by strife remains unmixed. By as much as strife retreated, "the gently disposed immortal impulse of flawless love" moved forward (35). The world exists through the enduring effect of love.

Then, in this world, organic beings—plants, animals, humans— grow through the uniting power of love. Love prepares the ground for the reestablishment of *sphairos*. After the primal catastrophe, we find ourselves in ascending motion.

The other aspect is descending motion. The central state in the cycle is, as such, the same, but reverses into its opposite, in accordance with the path that proceeds either upward or downward. Aristotle says: "Em-pedocles maintains that the world, under the sway of strife, is now in the same state as earlier under that of love" (A42).

The doctrine of the Golden Age as portrayed by Empedocles accords well with this: Once upon a time the gods were not Ares (god of war), nor Zeus, Poseidon, Kronos, but only Kypris (Aphrodite). No blood was shed at the sacrifices. To deprive other beings of life was considered the greatest pollution among men (128). In those days, the trees were always in leaf and were resplendent throughout the year in the superabundance of their fruit. All the animals were tame and trusting. There was then living a man of surpassing knowledge, a master of many skills of wisdom. When he exerted all his mental powers, his view encompassed with ease each one of existing things, in his ten and even twenty lifetimes (129). This golden age is not the *sphairos*. For the world and its many config-urations already exist, though they are still drawn together and unified by love.

This vision of the world does not imply that Empedocles considers himself to be at a turning point in the world. There are only two turning points, the *sphairos* and the *akosmia*. He perceives the cyclic nature but does not see himself as prophet at a turning point in the historical process. Nothing in him aspires to the level expressed in such a variety of modes by Virgil, the Gnostics and Apocalyptics, by Buddha and the Christians.

e) *Being and becoming.* The world-vision of Empedocles shows ex-ternal being and external becoming at the same time.

1) The cycle of world-periods is the being that is immutable. Time is annulled by closing on itself in a circle. It remains infinite time because the cycle is infinite. Time is revolution, not progression into infinity.

Thus, what is endures. Thus, what endures are the four roots of things (elements) and the two forces, love and strife: "in so far as they never cease their continuous exchange, in this sense they remain always un-moved (unaltered) as they follow the cyclic process" (F17); but in so far as things arise out of them, these things have no constant time (*empedos aion*). Never shall love and strife cease to be; they were before and also will be and never will for ineffably long time (*aspetos aion*) be free of them. The whole of the time that returns in the *kyklos* is Being that is no longer enclosed. If, as it were, time in the *sphairos* stops for a moment, then strife "has reached the outermost limits of the *kyklos*" (35), but it is and remains there. At the turning point at which it could be completed, the *kyklos* begins anew.

2) The other fundamental idea underlying Empedocles' world-vision is the following: Being as a whole does not remain constantly the same. Instead, within the chronological sequence, the opposites that bring about this sequence themselves become different phenomena.

Heraclitus, says Plato (*Sophist*, 242d), sees the opposites coming to-gether and separating. Compared with this stricter understanding, the gentler one of Empedocles (the "Sicilian Muse") has weakened the state-ment that it is such for all eternity by the assertion that, in turn, the universe is either united in love under the influence of Aphrodite, or, in a state of enmity against itself, it becomes a multiple. The strict view holds to the combined action of the opposites; the gentle view envisions a successive process implying distress and restoration. In Empedocles unity resides only in *sphairos* or in the world-process as a whole, whereas in Heraclitus it resides in every present moment. In Empedocles unity is lost to the extent that harmony does not embrace its opposite but is brought about by elimination of the opposing calamitous divine power of the *neikos*. Hence Heraclitus is able to call strife the father and king of all things; but Empedocles calls it calamity.

Being can be understood in the phenomena of the world only through the power of the One, of love. Yet it contains a counterforce as the ground of the multiple and as that which does not allow the work of love, the *sphairos*, to endure; but, instead, destroys it.

2. *Specific natural phenomena*

Empedocles is noted for his observation and interpretation of specific natural phenomena, for his graphic explanations and conjectures, which, as an anticipation of natural science, strike us as modern. He exhibits a wealth of ideas, of figurative and conceptual schemata that have dominated the understanding of nature in later times. We sense his passion for exploring the actual world, to see what is there, and to make known what he has seen through interpretation. Following are a few examples only. (They are merely of historical interest; in substance they are irrelevant for us today.)

a) *The origin of living beings.* Empedocles is familiar with the notion of development. Living beings did not start to exist in their present form. They have come to be and, in the course of time, to unfold their various forms.

First to emerge were raw clumps of earth. "They did not yet exhibit a lovely body with limbs, nor voice, nor genitals" (62). Next, fragmentary parts came to be as if the earth were gravid with individual limbs. "There grew out of the earth many heads without necks, arms wandered unattached to shoulders, and eyes strayed about lacking brows" (57). These members united: "Many creatures were created with double faces and double chests, with the body of cattle and the face of man, and, conversely, human bodies with the heads of cattle, hybrid beings that in part had the shape of men and in part that of women" (61). Only at the end did such whole bodies come to be which kept themselves alive by taking nourishment from outside and were "enticed into wedlock by the beautiful forms of women" (64); (Nutrition and Procreation). Whatever was not viable perished quickly. Whatever had conjoined out of mismatched limbs could not survive.

The power of love has effect without intention and in chance events of mixtures. Thus, in the formation of the eye "the mild flame happened to receive only a slight admixture of Earth" (85). Hence the media of the eye are transparent. And: "All beings possess consciousness by the will of chance" (103).

Nature looks like a large testing ground but lacks purposive intention. Love lets things come together as it chances, and those that cannot survive as a particular form through nutrition and propagation disappear.

b) *The comparative morphological view.* Empedocles sees the same basic material in hair, birds' feathers, and scales on strong limbs (82). He sees "earth deposited as the skin of the heavily armored denizens of the sea, especially that of the sea snails and the stony-skinned turtles" (76).

c) *Astronomical ideas.* The solar eclipse comes about through the moon: The moon "cuts off his (*the sun's*) rays whenever she goes below him, and she throws a shadow on as much of the Earth as is the breadth of the bright-eyed moon" (F42).

d) *The speed of light.* Aristotle reports that Empedocles had assumed without justification a certain velocity of light when he said that light arrives earlier from the sun in the intermediate region than on Earth or within our view. The movement of light remains hidden from us because of its great speed (*Metaphysics*, 985a, 21ff.).

e) *The respiration of the skin. Klepshydra* was the name of a tube, open at both ends, which is immersed in water while its upper end is held closed. Only when it is opened does the water stream into the tube from below, something that could not happen before because of the "weight of the air." This is Empedocles' way to explain breathing, which he applies universally to all things: "everything breathes in and out" (100).

f) *The theory of pores.* How do the things that are separated in the world come together? The pores make it possible. They explain magnetism, nutrition, respiration, the growth of organisms, and sense perception. The pores of magnets are symmetrical to the effluences of iron, hence the attraction. Respiration comes about through pores in the blood vessels that take in air. Perception originates through the pores of each individual sense organ. Only effluences that fit a particular organ combine with each other; the smaller ones flow through, the larger ones do not even get in.

The pores are not simply empty spaces that are filled (for there is no void anywhere). They are adapted to receive the effluences of other bodies as their complement, the way a keyhole fits the key. Where this fitting does not occur, no combination is possible. Things that in part repel each other and in part can be combined encounter each other in nature.

Reciprocal rejection occurs when no forms capable of receiving the effluences are found. Reciprocal combining is due to the fact that all things emit effluences, animals and plants, earth and sea, stone, copper, and iron. This is the constantly moving, never completed process of nature. *Sphairos* is of an utterly different character. Where love is sovereign no such combining—for example, no sense perception—is possible or necessary. When all matter is combined, there are no effluences. In perfect union there is also perfect rest.

3. The significance of this conception of nature

Empedocles' views cannot be brought together in a cohesive theory of natural science. His big schemes of the four roots and the two forces of love and strife are a means of portraying cosmic events as well as the actions of men. Nor does any investigation in a critical sense take place here. Particular plausibilities do not constitute cognition. It is a thinking in pictures which, for this reason, cannot be regarded as initiating natural science.

Rudiments of scientific thinking are actually present among the Ionians in the area of biology and in the medical schools in the collecting of observations. Plato turned his attention to the grand beginnings in mathematical physics and astronomy. Empedocles had no part in any of this.

Yet he exhibits two ways of thought substantially at variance with each other. Not only does he see images expressing actuality in the way of myth, but he also presents mechanical models (such as pores) meant to explain what happens in nature. Mythic actualities and physically conceived models, however, are merged. For him there is no distinction here in the quality of cognition.

To elucidate once more the mythic side of this thinking by way of examples: When, in his metaphor of the painter, he makes the marvelous configurations of nature arise out of a fitting-together, he does not mean just the mixture of four elements. He imagines them as the product of the craftsmanship of love (Aphrodite). She built the eyes (86); the animals are joined together by Kypris's hands (75), which fit the bones together by cementing them (96). The mutual attraction of likes—"Thus sweet seized on sweet, bitter rushed towards bitter, sour moved towards sour, and hot settled upon hot" (F90)—is obvious from the many pictorial accounts. Love and strife lack the physical precision of the later concepts of "attraction" and "repulsion" and are, here, comprehensive divine forces. The four roots of all things are not what would later be understood as elements—something like the minutest parts of a variety of components. Empedocles gave no thought to the structure of his four roots.

Is this thinking obsolete and hence meaningless for us? It has meaning in a negative sense: as we do with most of the early philosophers, we ask, to clarify for ourselves, why natural science is absent. In a positive sense, however, this thinking takes its importance from its illuminating actualities, which are missed by the natural sciences. The natural sciences by no means exhaust what is experienced in the actuality of nature. They gain their knowledge always and precisely by disregarding certain actualities in order methodically to cognize their particular limited actuality within their own sphere. Art and poetry do not alone bear witness to these other actualities. Prior to Schelling, a "philosophy of nature" has been formed throughout the ages which is neither another natural science nor objective knowledge. Instead, it expresses and makes us aware of what can be experienced in the actuality of phenomena but eludes investigation. In this realm, Empedocles speaks to us even today.

II. THE PRACTICE OF SALVATION

Cosmic vision presents an object for contemplation. But Empedocles wants to serve the salvation of man. The soul desires to escape the calamity in which it finds itself: It does not know what it is and what it should do.

The soul which originates in the world and passes away like all things is not the soul which is concerned with itself for the sake of eternity. It senses that it comes from somewhere, has been dropped, as it were, and that it is headed somewhere—toward its salvation or its calamity. The word "soul" does not occur in the fragments, only in the narratives. Empedocles speaks of the *daimon*. This *daimon* does not merge into the *kyklos* of the world. It has experienced a fall and has a fate.

This process cannot be comprehended via the concept of the cosmic *kyklos*. Something entirely different enters here: the migration of the soul, which is oriented by the desire for salvation. It is guilt that determines the path taken in this pilgrimage. The *daimon* of each human being was present in previous births and will return in later lives in order to atone for its guilt.

1. The migration of the soul

The doctrine of the migration of the soul states that the soul assumes one body after another, entering into many forms of life. "I have been born as boy, girl, plant, bird, and mute sea fish" (117).

2. Guilt

Guilt is not inescapable participation in "strife" (*neikos*) which rules the world as its one pole; it is the free guilt of the individual *daimon*.

What is the *daimon*? Is he, like the gods, one of the forms emerging from the mingling in the world-process? Nowhere is he mentioned in this context. He seems to differ from these forms by undergoing constantly new incarnations in the migration of souls. But whence does he come, where lies his origin? Empedocles does not answer this question. In his world-vision, man, as natural being, stands with other such beings as part of the whole of nature, he occupies no special position. But the *daimon* does have a special position. He has no allotted place but roams through the forms, of which only one is the natural form of man.

Out of the torment of this life—Empedocles' fundamental experience—begins the ascent to higher forms. "Among the animals they become lions . . . but among the trees [they become] laurel" (127). "But ultimately they become seers and bards and healers and princes among men on earth, from which they grow upward as gods, those richest in honor" (146). Finally they are again "companions of the hearth of the other immortals, fellow partakers at table, exempt from human suffering, indestructible" (147), the image of the community of the blessed.

Quite different is the fate of the guilt-ridden *daimones*. "It is the decree of necessity, a decision of the gods, ancient, arch-eternal, sealed with broad oaths: if one . . . sullied himself with the blood of murder . . . committed perjury," then he must "roam for thrice ten thousand *horae* far from the company of the blessed, being born, in the course of time, in all possible shapes of mortal creatures that tread the laborious paths of life. For the powerful air chases him to the sea, the sea spews him onto the earth, the earth to the rays of the blazing sun, and the sun throws him into the whirlwind. One takes him over from the other but all hate him. Now I am one of those, too, a man banished by god and erring, since I put my trust in raging strife" (115).

3. What should you do?

What should you do in order to put your *daimon* back on the right path? "To sober up from evil" (144). For if you are "torn this way and that by vile evildoing you will never free your heart from wretched torment" (145).

The main commandment: Do not kill animals, eat no meat, and make no bloody sacrifice. Because these beings lacking reason are related to us, we stand in communion with them as we do with the gods. "Will you never cease from this clashing slaughter? Do you not see how you tear each other to pieces in the thoughtlessness of your minds?" (136).

Empedocles also prescribes certain rites peculiar to the Orphics and Pythagoreans: Keep away from beans; do not touch the leaves of the laurel tree, which belongs to Apollo (140, 141).

4. Immortality

For Empedocles, man, as a natural being, is mortal, as are all things put together by mixing and later dissolved (15). Immortality is the attribute of whatever neither comes to be nor passes away as phenomena change, but endures as foundation. Immortal in this sense are the four elements and love and strife. For being to become nothing is unthinkable (12). There is only mixing and exchange of what has been mixed (8). Birth and death are merely names for these processes. As things circulate through each other, they become different things at different times, and thus it goes in all eternity (17).

There is an entirely different immortality, the immortality of the *daimones* which we are. We have fallen out of the bliss of their company and strive to return there, being, in this world, merely "clad in the alien cloak of the flesh" (126).

III. COGNITION AT ITS LIMITS

Empedocles' theory of the world and his message of salvation did not fully satisfy him. In his questioning, he goes further: By what means do I know? What is cognition and what is its effect? Which cognition is true? It is only through reflecting on cognition that Empedocles achieves self-awareness.

1. The senses

Empedocles is aware that cognition begins with the senses, which he trusts. "Observe with each of the senses by which way all that is individual becomes manifest (*delon*)" (3); with *each* of the sense organs, for neither the eye, nor the ear, nor the tongue, nor the remaining sense organs are entitled to preferential trust. Each yields one path to cognition. Hence: ". . . use whatever way of perception makes each thing clear" (F3). Being open to the world with all of one's senses: that is the foundation of knowledge.

Immediately he stresses the limitation of the senses: "Narrowly limited are the tools of the senses (graspers)." Of all of life, they observe only a small part, "convinced by this [part] alone, which each individual [sense] happened to encounter in its various wanderings; and yet each boasts that it has found the whole" (2). It is not through passivity that we gain sensory truth; rather, truth manifests itself to the senses only where they are permeated by thinking. Hence the demand: "Observe with the mind, and do not sit there with wondering eyes" (17).

But then the content of what the senses encounter becomes problematical: "Much that is paltry (*deila*) assails them, which blunts the thoughts" (2). Hence the demand for purity and clarity in our devotion to things.

Devotion to inferior things makes us inferior too. In thinking that has not been dulled, things would not be inferior either. Only where we cognize in purity with our whole being do we become one with things as we cognize. The relation of the knower to the known is a relationship between equals grounded in world-being.

2. *Likes are known only to likes*

"If the eye were not sun-like, it could never see the sun." In Goethe's dictum we find again a theme that, originating with Empedocles and continuing with Plotinus, runs through the ages.

In man there is everything. Hence the statements: "We see Earth by means of Earth, Water by means of Water, divine Air by means of Air, and destructive Fire by means of Fire; Love by means of Love; Strife by means of baneful Strife" (109).

This corresponds to the view that there is an unrestricted relationship between man and everything else. Empedocles maintains that we have something in common not only with fellowmen and the gods but also with the nonrational animals.

Things in the world are held together through the love (*philia*) that unites all. She is "believed to be implanted in mortal limbs also; through her they think friendly thoughts and perform harmonious actions, calling her Joy [*gethosyne*] and Aphrodite" (F17).

Even though men are related to all things animate and inanimate (even plants know longing and sorrow and joy); even though everything in the world shares "in breathing and smell" (102), "in consciousness (*phronesis*) and in thought (*noema*)" (110), Empedocles speaks of cognition only in reference to human beings.

3. *Possibilities and limits inherent in cognition*

Since man resembles the object of his cognition and bears resemblance to all, the elements as well as the gods, his cognition appears to be unlimited. But since, being human, he is limited, his cognition is subject to the condition imposed by his finiteness. From this arise his great opportunities as well as his great errors. Empedocles shows us both.

a) *The whole.* Truth is the whole; untruth is the result of division and narrowness and of exaggerating the particular to be everything. Hence Empedocles, ". . . Touching on summit after summit, does not want to follow a single path of discourse to the end" (F24).

But the whole "cannot be grasped by eye or ear, nor can it be encompassed by man's mind" (2). This extraordinary feat was possible only to men of the early ages who, using all their mental powers, saw with ease each particular of all that is (129).

b) *Like strengthens like.* I am, or become, what I cognize because like is awakened when it encounters like. Hence Empedocles warns us of that which dulls: the paltry, lowly, and false. Cognition possesses "truth" in a sense other than mere accuracy: through its object and through the appropriateness of the thought to this object. Hence: "Greatly blessed is he who earned a treasure of divine thoughts for himself, but wretched he in whom dwells a dark delusion about the gods" (132).

c) *The power of cognition.* True cognition confers power. "If you," Empedocles says to Pausanias, "take these teachings deep into your firm mind and view them, well-disposed, with your pure effort," only then does thinking become power. Otherwise it would be no more than a diverting intellectual occupation. What we cognize is not only at our disposal for a lifetime, but man himself is changed: this cognition grows into the ethos of man "according to each man's nature" (110).

The power of cognition and of what is cognized is not there for the taking. It must be earned: "Friends, I know that Truth is present in the story that I shall tell; but it is actually very difficult for men, and the impact of conviction on their minds is unwelcome" (F114).

d) *The limits of man.* Empedocles recognizes the limits of human cognition with modesty and awe. When he promises Pausanias that he will discover the truth, he adds immediately, "not more than mortal intellect can attain" (F2). He calls out to the muse: "I beseech thee also, much-wooed white-armed maiden Muse, convey (to me) such knowledge as divine law allows us [ephemeral] creatures to hear, driving the well-harnessed car [of song] from (the realm of) Piety!" And, as a warning, he adds: "Nor shall the flowers of honour paid to fame by mortals force you at least to accept them on condition that you rashly say more than is holy—and are thereupon enthroned on the heights of wisdom!" (F3).

e) *The promises.* In his book *On Nature*, Empedocles promises Pausanias powers arising from his cognition that seem to contradict his earlier teachings: "You shall learn all the drugs that exist as a defence against illness and old age; for you alone will I accomplish all this. You shall check the force of the unwearying winds. . . . And again, if you wish, you shall conduct the breezes back again. You shall create a seasonable dryness after the dark rain for mankind, and again you shall create after summer drought the streams that nourish the trees. . . . And you shall bring out of Hades a dead man restored to strength" (F111).

What does this mean? Obviously magic, that is, power through knowledge of nature by means of cognition, without causational mediation. These verses were thought to be a parody. But more likely they need a different interpretation.

Contemplation of that which is has an effect on the contemplator. The experience that, through knowledge, I myself become effective testifies to the power of thinking. Another, highly dubious experience is added to this obvious one. My experience of being linked to and at one with all nature turns into the belief that I participate in effecting what nature has brought about—moreover, in a manner heightened by my consciousness of such knowledge. This grandiose error of man's union with the processes of nature, experienced in thinking, runs through all the ages.

Within his view of the whole, Empedocles arrived at his methods of healing. Magical-cognitive consciousness is linked to specific medical operations as the theory of the world-vision is linked to the understanding of specific natural phenomena. This world-vision together with the magical knowledge grounded in it becomes the means of medical practice.

The world-vision itself arose in a way quite distinct from that of theoretical knowledge. The universal linkage of all beings is supposed to create a knowledge that, in the end, amounts to an illusion. This illusion indulges itself in unfounded metaphysical assertions. It had been radically rejected already by the contemporary empirical physicians of the school of Hippocrates, whose methods were built by piling observation upon observation.

4. Not a system

It would not be in keeping with Empedocles' thought for him to design a system, since the whole eludes cognition. It cannot be known to thinking human beings because of their present condition. Hence the multiplicity of aspects does not converge in a coherent whole. In his thinking, Empedocles beholds his visions, and in writing them down gives them their particular order. They revolve around a center that is not fixed with finality at any specific point, neither in the *sphairos* nor in the group of six realities, the four roots and the two forces of love and strife.

Does Empedocles hint at something that is ultimately necessary and reaches beyond all else? Why the progression of world-periods in this sequence and these appearances? Why the guilt, which brings about calamitous incarnations?

Empedocles does not respond to these questions, for he constructs neither a system of Being nor a self-completing history of the fall and salvation of the soul. But he touches upon its boundaries:

1) In the *sphairos* of love the mighty battle begins anew. Why? Because "the time was fulfilled that is laid down for each of them in turn in a tightly bound sworn covenant" (30).

2) Four elements and two forces constitute the aspects of the world. But then, where is the ground of the whole, the one that orders and rules them? Empedocles' answer: They "are all equally strong and equally ancient in their origin but each of them has a different function, each its specific manner, and each in its turn gains ascendancy in the revolution of time" (17). Expressed in political analogy: The world is not a despotism of the One, but is engaged in a mutual, eternally ordained battle of the powers that brings about an alternating predominance.

3) Why guilt? There is something universally valid that has no further grounding, the contravening of which brings about guilt. "The law valid for all stretches far throughout the widely dominant ether and through the boundless light" (135).

These thoughts at the limit mean: All events in the world are guided by an all-embracing law, which itself is not formulated but determines when "time is fulfilled." All fundamental forces are integrated into a whole that assigns to each in turn its "office" in its time and does not permit preeminence or domination by one of these forces. All action on the part of the *daimones* is subject to judgment based on the all-permeating, all-present law.

Is guilt itself a necessary component in the totality of subordinate necessities? True, we are told why it is to be judged as guilt, but not why it has occurred. Is guilt built inescapably into necessity itself? Empedocles is silent.

5. Digression about asking questions

It seems that there is no end to the asking of questions. They have to be asked, regardless of whether they are meaningful.

Nowadays it has become fashionable to ask and then not to give an answer. This gives the appearance of thoroughness and depth, but actually it is superficial and cheap: perhaps the expression of merely rational empty schemata. It can be carried into indifferent infinity. One ought not to set a limit to questioning, but the questioning itself can become meaningless.

Whoever asks should also answer. This guideline would only be inapplicable if the question is such that it excludes an answer, which would apply to the ultimate question. With this question I touch the limit where the question as such is an insight in view of the open horizon.

Is there such a question?

Does questioning cease here by means of a question?

In that case, the question would have to express the ultimate ground, and thus cease to be a question, becoming the form of cognition itself.

Such an "ultimate question" would be possible only if everything that is were to become present by it.

That would be the One through which everything exists. If the being of the One is beyond question, then the question is "how is this One possible?" and all that is further contained in this question. But then the answer too becomes impossible.

What is the ultimate ground in the face of which all questioning ceases or changes its meaning?

IV. THE DEITY, THE GODS, THE DIVINE

Nothing in Empedocles is untouched by divinity. In antiquity, his explanations of nature were called Nature hymns. The following forms of divinity can be differentiated in his thinking:

The one all-pervading deity is like that of Xenophanes: "One cannot bring the deity close enough to reach with our eyes or grasp it with our hands" (133). "The deity does not possess a head and limbs similar to those of humans. . . . A spirit (*phren hiere*), a holy and inexpressible one, moves there alone, one that rushes through the whole world edifice with swift thoughts" (134).

Sphairos is discussed in a similar way. "The back does not sprout two branches, nor feet, nor agile knees, nor members full of creative energy; it was a sphere, rather, like to itself on all sides" (29).

The *sphairos* is not the spirit that rushes with its thoughts through the world edifice, but the round complete Being of quietude in contrast to the constant motion in the world.

The four roots and the two polar forces are also called gods. Empedocles names fire, air, earth, and water: Zeus, the shining one, and Hera, the giver of life, as well as "Hades and Nestis, who, through her tears, makes the fountains flow on earth" (6). *Philia* and *Neikos* are gods. *Philia* is called Aphrodite; *Neikos*, Eris.

Sanctity surrounds the perduring powers: "The dictum of Necessity (*ananke*) is called divine decree" (115). *Charis* hates "hard-to-endure necessity" (116).

The souls that have fallen into this world because of their guilt are called *daimones*.

The universal sanctity of things, in all its gradations, in the free movement of representations and thoughts about them, without any conclusive rational order, corresponds to a basic trait of his Greek piety. Everywhere, in all landscapes and all human configurations, it senses this Something More. It objectifies the latter in mythic representations and cult localizations. It is expressed in Thales's statement: "All is full of gods" (A22) and in that of Heraclitus, spoken from his cave: "Even here there are gods" (A9).

V. EMPEDOCLES' SELF-CONSCIOUSNESS

The early philosophers experienced thinking as it had never been experienced before. To them it revealed the actual world. Overcome by that experience, many confined their philosophic reflection in this sphere. Others—Heraclitus and Parmenides—attained as individual thinkers an overwhelming alienating self-consciousness. Empedocles' self-consciousness is of a different order. In worshiping the divine, he practices moderation. Praying to the muse, he desires only such knowledge as is granted to ephemeral man (whereas Parmenides wrests absolute truth from the goddess). But Empedocles has his own way of self-consciousness: "I go about among you as an immortal god, no longer a mortal, held in honour by all [as is proper], crowned with fillets and flowing garlands. When I come to them in their flourishing towns, to men and women, I am honoured; and they follow me in thousands . . . some desiring oracles, while others ask to hear a word of healing for their manifold diseases . . ." (F112).

Thus Empedocles roams through the cities in the guise of prophet, savior, physician. People take him to be what he purports to be. Does he really consider himself an immortal god?

His way of thinking is: Like is known by like, the outside god is recognized by the god in us, the *daimon*. He who achieves the highest cognition becomes what he knows.

The bliss of philosophic cognition allowed him to sense that realm out of which, guilt-laden, our *daimon* has fallen.

He was conscious of the great gap between his insight and that of other men. He stands in the radiance of his inventive powers, demonstrated in his ideas on nature, the grandeur of his cosmic vision, the abundance of his poetic talents. His words—". . . as if I were achieving something great in that I surpass mortal men who are liable to many forms of destruction" (F113)—testify once more to and at the same time temper a self-consciousness which is the echo of his powerful personal influence.

Aside from the philosophical charlatans of late antiquity, such self-apotheosis is unique in the history of Greek philosophy. But antiquity virtually never questioned Empedocles' self-glorification. To thinkers of those times it did not seem as monstrous as it does to us.

What appears to be mutually exclusive shows itself as equally real: on the one hand, his modesty in addressing the muse; on the other, his promise of the domination of nature through magic. Added to this was the consciousness of the guilt-ridden, fallen *daimon* who knows that in this respect he is not different from all other mortals, and the claim to be more than man, to be a god. Empedocles has to be understood within this tension.

VI. CRITICAL CHARACTERIZATION
AND HISTORICAL POSITION

Empedocles takes philosophy into the streets. He does not close himself off from the multitudes in order to be with a few like-minded people. "Democratically," he addresses everybody. Crowds of enthusiasts follow him. Let us consider his roles as political activist, as religious savior, as helpful physician.

Politically, Empedocles did not become active as a statesman. He did not participate in the founding of a *polis*. He did not establish a political party, as was done by the Pythagoreans, who strove for government of the *polis*, off and on with success, until a political catastrophe swept away their regime.

Nor did Empedocles found an apolitical mystery religion. Though his claim to be a savior is evident, he is also the lone individualist unwilling to take upon himself the obligations of a founder. He proclaims *sophia* as the road to salvation. This savior is himself a man steeped in guilt and suffering like his fellowmen.

Being a physician, he wanted to help, but he did not join the scientific and research-oriented medical community of the Hippocratics.

Empedocles was familiar with the great philosophical thought of his predecessors: the Milesians, Pythagoras, Xenophanes, Parmenides, and Heraclitus, as well as the religious movements. His thinking was influenced by an already developed philosophy. He was the first to summarize a great inheritance through new fundamental ideas. These enabled him to reconcile opposites, to accept nothing as absolute, but to assign each view its proper place, as it were. The specific stringency peculiar to what he appropriated was lost. The plasticity of a thinking open in all directions was *de facto* repudiated, although Empedocles did not realize this. Parmenides' thoughts about Being were lost in the four ineradicable roots and the *sphairos*, as was Xenophanes' unconditional idea of God. The religious movements ended in the individualization of a specific man. Milesian-Ionian inquiry into nature disappeared in sketches which were plausible but distractive. Empedocles is the poetizing philosopher who cultivates many fields of expression and different impulses of faith.

Empedocles did not arrive on the scene as the late fruit of the priests of purification and the soothsayers of the sixth century. In him operated that mythic force which endures in the metaphysical attempts of philosophy. As itinerant savior, he performed miracles but absorbed them into the continuity of philosophical self-consciousness. Renan said of Empedocles that he was "Newton and Cagliostro" in one. But in his mode of thinking he was in no way a precursor of Newton and not at all a deceiver. Eduard Meyer called him "thinker and charlatan." "Thinker"—a well-chosen term if one knows what is to be understood by it. But "charlatan"? The use of this word is incomprehensible in light of Empedocles' deep seriousness. It is comprehensible only as an outgrowth of the modern scholar's arrogance and lack of respect.

In Empedocles there operates the mythical mode of thinking that absorbs the rational as its instrument. He carries out magical procedures, which, in an undifferentiated way, make use of technical means. He has visions that lack rational grounding, but also acknowledges ingenuous discoveries and observations in nature, as well as rational mechanistic explanations. In him is found an ever-recurring seduction: rationalized mythical and magical thinking combined uncritically with cognition and technique.

Aristotle speaks of Empedocles' "clumsy manner of expression," since it lacks the clarity of logical deduction and does not correspond to Aristotelian categories (*Metaphysics*, 985a, 5ff.). Conversely, this lack can be interpreted favorably. In Empedocles, phenomena still emerge as the language of eternal Being without being robbed of their mythic power by logical-systematic thought. Wherever this happens they become empty but gain, simultaneously, a false form of truth that fits them for doctrinal and scholastic use. To the extent that later metaphysics has substance— that is, considers, in its ideas, phenomena out of the ground of things —it is closer, in its transformations, to self-interpreting and reinterpreting myth than to our science, which, from the standpoint of Aristotelian philosophy, is pseudoscience.

The influence of Empedocles on his successors is considerable. The magic of his poetry and his person inspired Lucretius, who counts him among the wonders of Sicily: "It has surely held nothing more glorious than this man, nothing holier, nothing more wonderful, nothing more precious. Indeed, the songs that took shape in his divine breast proclaim in ringing tones such glorious discoveries that he scarcely seems a scion of mortal stock" (I, 729ff.).

Empedocles was frequently quoted in antiquity and by the Church Fathers. Many found their own views, modes of thought, pictorial sketches prefigured in him. His name continued to be mentioned up to the Middle Ages.

Out of the various traditions, Hölderlin fashioned the tragic figure of a man who founders upon himself and then upon others. It is no longer primal guilt that destroys him; rather, it is the entirely different guilt of having elevated himself to divine stature and the guilt of having used his—initially correct—cognition in order, sacrilegiously, to make the forces of nature submit to his bidding. As a result of this guilt, the priest and the head of state originally subservient to him gain material ascendancy over the philosopher. The multitudes turn away from him and toward other authorities. And he, who may despise them, atones for his wretched emptiness far from God by his voluntary death in Mount Etna.

Nietzsche oriented his youthful visions in the sphere of Empedocles and later crystallized them under the name Zarathustra. Still later in his career he wrote: "My ancestors Heraclitus, Empedocles, Spinoza, Goethe."

The four elements, the notion "like known to like," the medical terms *sepsis, rheuma*, all survived—anonymously—the passage of time.

His significance for us: He presents the image of the suprahuman role to which philosophy could at one time lay claim through the person of a philosopher. This role for philosophy has no place for a successor.

Empedocles could achieve such greatness only in an intellectual climate still unenlightened by science and not yet arrived at encompassing reason. At that time, savior figures could still hold their own without radical falsehood or foolishness. Today such attitudes would be considered mischief caused by esoteric circles or a minor matter on the part of blindly enthusiastic crowds, both owing to people who are not equal to what the intellectual situation of our age demands. We cannot turn back the clock, either on our modern, scientific, methodically clear, universal inquiry, or on the Kantian critique of reason.

The error of Empedocles' claim to be a savior was an error in the grand style, as was that of the dictatorship of thought in Heraclitus and Parmenides, or the all-inclusive political planning of Plato. Their substance of truth (if we subtract their errors), expressed with unrestrained self-confidence, makes them imperishable. The Greek path from *sophia* to philosophy, first pointed out and taken by Plato, ought never to be forgotten.

What appears to us acceptable or even glorious in a historically perceived existence becomes also, from the perspective that scans three millennia at once, a reverse image that we cannot follow. Empedocles can seduce us if, impressed by his greatness, we desire the garment still possible in this day and age, or even wish to don it. But remember: Empedocles infringed the limit. He forgot the boundaries set for man. Only once could philosophy go astray in such a grandiose manner.

BRUNO

Editors' Note

Giordano Bruno (1548–1600) was born into a noble family in Nola, near Naples, and was educated by Augustinian monks. Ordained a Dominican priest in 1575, he was soon charged with heresy and left the order in 1576. During the following fifteen years, he witnessed the spreading effects of the Reformation as he taught and studied at Oxford, in England, and at Marburg, Wittenberg, and Frankfurt in the Germanies. His defiant views and flamboyant conduct often caused him trouble with local authorities; he was censured and driven out of both Catholic and Protestant precincts. On returning to Italy in 1591, he was arrested in Rome and imprisoned for seven years by the Inquisition. He was burned at the stake in 1600, on charges of pantheism.

I. ORIENTATION IN INTELLECTUAL HISTORY: MYTHICAL PHILOSOPHY OF NATURE

In the fifteenth and sixteenth centuries, man looked at nature with renewed and lively interest, perceiving it as an independent actuality, no longer as merely God's revelation. Secular interest in the variety and richness of natural phenomena came into play, and also the will to harness them and thereby enhance the quality of human life.

But as yet there was no clear system of the various ways of comprehending nature, hence no clear picture of the world. Mythical philosophy of nature, ancient and eternally present, undergoes a far-reaching development; experience grows in the workshops of artists and technicians and has its greatest representative in Leonardo. Exact science is, at most, intimated for a moment in its earliest stages but not yet comprehended (its germ is theoretical abstraction, subsequently tested experientially and applied); only later will it find its clear and final actualization in Kepler and Galileo.

The natural philosophy of the age is essentially mythical, but it considers itself rightly to be experiential science. Its representatives keep their eyes open, observe and collect ad infinitum, without, however, a guiding principle: everything marvelous and curious, all inner experiences which we understand only psychologically and subjectively, such as apparitions, are taken to be objective substance and treated as experience. Whatever any persons active in a practical field report about their sphere is quickly appropriated. Thus there evolves, to be sure, a great difference in relation to a merely deductive mythic construction, an abstract natural philosophy; but the mass of experience remains in chaos and experience has not yet become critical in any way. It is not yet able to separate actuality from appearance. It falls prey to any deception. It does not know any methods of proof. Hence it combines with the endless supply of individual items of actual and supposed knowledge a deductive picture of the whole, or, rather, a vision developed a priori in concepts and then filled in everywhere with that mass of material. This natural philosophy gives an impression of richness and fullness through concrete intuitions of personal experience as well as through the incorporation of all myths and fairy tales. A mysterious life is shown to us in which poetic abundance alternates with sterile discussions of concepts which are supposed to signify cognition. It is something which endures through the millennia, does not progress, always seems new but is actually ancient.

The modes of observing nature are still intermingled here, which is detrimental to the progress of cogent insight. Fantasy and opinion still smother actual cognition, which as yet cannot be differentiated from it. This separation will occur later. But there persists the idea of a synthesis without intermingling; the question remains whether mythic natural philosophy is totally meaningless or what its meaning is. For this reason it has reawakened time and again up to the present, most effectively in Schelling and his school. To this day no such synthesis has been found. Instead, so far only two alternatives proved to be possible: As a distinct feature of the great and successful achievement of disciplined, truly scientific cognition mythic natural philosophy has been completely set aside by modern science. Or it has been reconstituted as a mere opposition to modern science, fantastic and uncritical, romantic and ineffectual. When we consider the natural philosophy of the Renaissance, we come to know a world which poses problems that may concern us even today. It is a world of thoughts and intuitions, coherent in itself, which as a creation of the human spirit deserves to be brought to our knowledge.

II. A PHILOSOPHER IN THE GRAND MANNER

With Bruno we return to a philosopher in the grand manner.

His life was a struggle for purity and nobility, a battle that he finally won in an unexpected manner.

He hated neither mankind nor the world. All he did was to develop, in grandiose solitude, the positive nature of his worldview, a love for the universe as the infinitely beautiful configuration of the divinity, and his philosophical enthusiasm.

Seven years of incarceration and constant moral coercion could not force him to recant his philosophy.

Almost all his ideas derive from Plato, Plotinus, and mysticism. What is new is the momentum which impels these ideas in Bruno: his genuine struggle in failure, his humanity in the most exalted demands as well as in the recognition of what is unachieved, his turn to the sensuously concrete and toward the world while soaring toward transcendence.

I confess that in my student days his *Eroici Furori*, next to Dante's *Vita Nuova*, awakened essential impulses in me, though the truth to be found there is not present in a pure and identically repeatable form. But something unforgettable speaks here to us in a historical garment, that arises out of the depth.

III. PHILOSOPHY BECOME RELIGION

The pervasive impetus is not a logical proposition, but philosophy become religion.

Bruno was filled with an enthusiastic new philosophical spirit that ran counter to the scholasticism that dominated the universities of his day, counter to the ecclesiastical institutions, whether Catholic, Calvinist, or Lutheran. Gazing in wonder at the Copernican picture of the world and what it implies, Bruno proclaimed the infinity of the world and the countlessness of the solar systems.

At his trial, he recklessly endeavored to save himself by way of an ambiguity: applying the doctrine of the twofold truth, he offered to submit to all doctrines of the Church, return repentantly to its bosom; but abjure his philosophy—that he would not do.

Enthusiastically, he drew the consequences: For him, the act of redemption by the Son of God, His crucifixion and resurrection were no longer the unique pivotal point of universal history, but a fleeting guest performance in insignificant places, repeated on one star after another.

This blasphemy reveals the religiously questionable nature of a doctrine that ejects the earth from its central position in the world.

Bruno's "pantheism" is not unequivocal. In contrast to completely consistent pantheists, he upholds God's transcendence, at least at certain points, and allows a theology of revelation to subsist alongside philosophy.

His thinking is metaphysical; he takes nature, and especially the cosmos as a universe of stars, as his guide. Decisive for him are: the divinity; man's ascension through love (eros and cosmos in their ancient conjunction, but now with a new, human imprint); the truth of his religion, into which his philosophy increasingly turns, up until his death as a martyr.

With him, and for the first time, the relationship of philosophy to Church and theology became for a philosopher a question of life and death. But this, with all its consequences, did not become wholly and fundamentally clear to Bruno until the very last.

IV. THE NEW ATTITUDE TOWARD CHURCH AND THEOLOGY

Giordano Bruno is the first modern philosopher, in the sense that, at the end, he took his stand consciously, wholly, and exclusively on philosophy; philosophy, for him, is not merely an intellectual exercise but something that animates him completely with fiery enthusiasm.

From now on, theology and the Church are no longer the obligatory background that, more or less effectively, more or less undecidedly, remains sanctuary or guidance; rather, an alternative had been put forward, proved itself and was sealed by martyrdom.

For Bruno, philosophy had become his religion; it was sufficient unto itself. Not only did he dispense with the Church, but also he affirmed the truth of philosophy in sacrificial death, and in rejection of Christ's divinity at the stake in the face of death, and in prophetic awareness.

What do we mean by this?

1) It was not Bruno who raised the question; it was the Church. Only under the pressure, the blackmail and demands of the Inquisition, were things clarified in Bruno's mind.

Bruno did not abandon his earlier position, that is, God's inaccessibility to reason, the meaning of a theology based on a possible revelation. In practice, it had not meant much to him before, and was important only for setting limits. Now it no longer mattered at all. He did not need it; he was certain of the truth out of the philosophical origin into which the profound philosophic contents of the Bible—the concept of God—had entered as a matter of course and no longer required specific revelation.

Bruno did not want to fight against Church or theology as a matter of principle; even later, the meaning of his philosophy did not demand this fundamental denial. But it did demand that he maintain the independent origin of the consciousness of and relationship to God.

Only one thing was determined: When Church and theology act intolerantly, demand exclusivity of truth and—as they will do whenever they have the power—want to obtain this exclusivity by force, there is a point of resistance in man. With God as his ally, he resists such human presumption, stands up against brute force and for freedom of thought and speech.

2) To this day the true significance of the Church's actions—seven years of torture of this noble man, culminating in his murder clothed in the mantle of justice—is still debated: Is it a mistake by the Church (attributable to the nature of the times, fateful to be sure, but not crucial overall), an error with grave consequences but none that were ruinous for the Church, an error that the Church itself regrets? Or are these acts revelatory of what must ensue when a human organization able to exert power and force raises the claim of exclusivity?

This matter—an extraordinary and complex problem—need not be discussed here; we have only to see in the historical context that Bruno's death was to become a symbol of the first order, the first summit of a movement that drew ever-widening circles in the seventeenth century and became evident to the priests in the frightening, unconcealable fact that so many morally pure men and women no longer felt the need, at the hour of their death, of the consolations of the Church; indeed, refused them.

3) This report of Bruno's teachings and philosophy must rest on those of his writings which predate his great decision. The rejection of theology was not integral to his philosophy; most likely it was forced on him as a consequence of the situation.

V. THE SINGING FIGHTER

Bruno's writings are voluble, repetitive, full of contradictions. They do not form a coherent system, and lack an aura of clear intelligibility. No clear logical method, no principle, no systematic form prevails. They are rhetorical. He was the typical singing fighter and not an accomplisher.

His writings reveal an awareness of his shortcomings, alongside the exuberance of the knower.

They exhibit an overpowering stimulation by the momentary thought, an overflowing of words and phrases, a joy in metaphor and in the collection of metaphors and recollections from his readings in philosophy. He does not cognize; he unburdens himself.

This thinking is a remembering and awakening, an illuminating and urging onward, but it is not a knowing. It renders possible the recognizing of what is known, but not a new learning of what is unknown.

Bruno operates throughout with inherited concepts, which he brings together, interprets in an original manner, and unites in a great stream, by limiting himself to Existenz. "Subjectivity" and "individual person" are inappropriate terms here, since both terms are overcome within the movement he encounters. But he neglects the objectivity of the concepts, which in the end he needs for his interpretation. He is different in nature from Plato and Augustine. Seen superficially, he is essentially psychological in his manner of expression and goal orientation.

A comprehensive philosophy, all-pervasive truth, hence the unity of all philosophies—this is Bruno's basic position, though held instinctively, naïvely, neither methodically nor consciously.

VI. THE VISION OF THE INFINITE UNIVERSE

In Bruno there is a pervasive affinity with the thoughts of Cusanus. Although in the latter everything remains symbol—for example, the infiniteness of the world is a symbol for the true infiniteness of God—in Bruno there is secularization of this thought.

There is no new thought, but, rather, appropriations, in the flow of thought, without precise methodological differentiation. It is the vision of being swept away into the All, expressed in the ancient supreme speculation of all ages. In this vision, God and the world, Being and symbol are taken as one, only to be separated again in thought.

What is decisive is the thought of infinity; not as mathematical problem, but as actuality of the universe. Logical and cosmological problems still coincide undifferentiated. In Cusanus, symbol of the true infinity of God; in Bruno, the infinity of the universe is itself God.

The world is the necessary explication of the deity. (Herein lies the antithesis to Cusanus.) What is the relation between world and God? There is neither emanation nor creation; no unitary, final formula. Relation of the One to multiplicity, of transcendence to immanence, of the eternal to the temporal remains varied and vague; Bruno constantly wrestles with it. And yet, there is always the idea that the relation of God to world is that of necessity. Potentiality and actuality converge in God. There is nothing in God that, unfolded, does not exist in the world as effect.

God and nature—the world and the worlds—flow into one. It is as though the animate universe replaced God. The categories in which God was thought speculatively serve to think the entirety of the world.

Not specific cognition, but the worldview satisfactory to him— infinity, the whole, movement of an earth become tiny, and the grandiose picture of the infinite universe.

Tremendous upheaval of the whole worldview and consciousness of Existenz [through Copernicus]: In proceeding from the rejection of immediate appearance, the ground was lost, the heavens, the secureness. From this upheaval arose the freedom of reason, ethical self-awareness, enthusiasm. In this groundlessness, Bruno cultivated pantheism.

This is a philosophy of nature and a turn of mind; it is not an insight, nor is it related to exact scientific investigation that leads from Copernicus to Kepler and Galilei.

VII. HEROIC LOVE

There is a doctrine corresponding to the contemplative vision of the universe, the doctrine of active behavior, of a sequence of stages of surrender to the universe, a widening of the self to participation in the infinite universe. This is the true religion of the few heroic natures. The transposition of man from the anthropocentric standpoint of the way things seem to the senses into the cosmocentric one is merely one side of the revolution; the other one is a revolution in the religious-ethical realm. By relating to the divine universe, the false demands on the divine order are made to disappear, demands that stem from the longings of the individual who wants to become eternal in his duration. "The philosopher, the artist and the heroic man are one for him and one in him."[1]

The infinite upward movement is the ultimate that man can attain in this world divided by opposites. In the case of heroic love, what matters is not possession but this movement, disposition and passion.

[1] Wilhelm Dilthey, *Weltanschauung und Analyse des Menschen seit Renaissance und Reformation, Gesammelte Schriften*. Leipzig, Berlin, B. Teubner, 1921, II, 340–41.

Somehow the lover reaches the goal at each moment, yet remains in motion. He always lives in vital concrete configurations, but is always urged beyond them, onward on the ladder into the infinite.

The infinite end of taking hold of the object with love is the mystical union. Bruno reminds us explicitly of the teachings of Plotinus and the mystics.

The mark of heroic love is self-sacrifice, being consumed, and not merely putting oneself at risk.

Thus the One in the lover and the One in the beloved give structure and hierarchy to beings. The enthusiastic attitude contains a "sense of the One" that goes beyond all rational assumptions of a monistic kind. It is the root, the "Nothing" of the striving for unity—so empty in its rational formulation—which is no longer a "monistic prejudice" but the power of enthusiasm and love. This unity recurs in all realms of love; in sexual love it receives its most concrete and paradoxical configuration.

What matters is the intention, determination, and decision that turn the soul toward the One and toward the ultimate goal.

For enthusiasm itself contains unity. It is creative in the genius.

VIII. CRITICAL APPRECIATION

Bruno's originality may be schematized under these captions:

1) Vision of the world, nature, and God: here he is the source of all modern pantheism.

2) The experience and doctrine of heroic madness, of enthusiastic love.

3) Abstract thoughts about the minimum, about the *monas*, strongly influenced by Cusanus, but not the vehicle for further development of dialectic.

The mark of Bruno's greatness: an early feeling for the "exception," sense and experience of the pathological, helpless stumbling in the rush of exaltation, love of reason and tranquillity, inner strife, excessiveness; all this while living in historic, existential groundlessness, wandering, exposing, and sacrificing himself.

However, there are also these reservations:

1) His blindness for the "theologia crucis."

2) His prescientific condition—in accordance with the age, as yet no scientific cast of mind.

3) His lack of precision, his verbosity, a baroque exuberance.

Tranquillity without Transcendence

EPICURUS

EPICURUS

INTRODUCTION

Epicurus and Epicureanism occupy a unique position in the history of philosophy. A special distinction was bestowed on Epicurus: almost all philosophical schools, although battling fiercely among themselves, were unanimous in their opposition to him, the wrong-headed man. For the Skeptics, he was a dogmatic fool. Christianity, taking its cue from the Greek philosophies, excluded him. The usual opinion, current since antiquity though refuted over and over again, is that Epicurus is the godless teacher of a life of unbridled pleasure-seeking, for whom sensual pleasure is the greatest bliss and who knows nothing beyond material things. Hence Horace, himself strongly influenced by Epicurus (that is, by what Epicurus genuinely stood for), could call himself, ironically, "a pig of Epicurus' herd" (*Epistolae*, I, 4).

It is also noteworthy that Epicurus and his disciples evinced something in their lives and attitudes that is analogous to religion. Whereas the other philosophic schools underwent changes in the course of the centuries, examined their traditional doctrines, and brought forth new independent thinkers, Epicurean doctrine always remained faithful to itself. No new, original Epicurean thinker came forward. The ancient Epicurean circles of friends held together like religious sects. Epicurus was the inviolable personal ideal to be revered and followed.

LIFE AND WORKS

Epicurus (342–270 B.C.), the son of an Athenian, was born on the island of Samos. When, after completing his military service in Athens, he wanted to return home, the Athenians had been driven off Samos. His father had fled to Colophon, and he followed him there.

He declared himself to be a self-taught philosopher. He did not belong to any philosophical school but was well-versed in the writings of Democritus. The only Athenian among all the heads of academies active in Athens at the time, he remained aloof from the sphere of influence of great Athenian philosophy. He had no understanding whatsoever of either Plato or Aristotle.

Circa 310, he founded his academy in Mytilene, then moved it to Lampsakos (all of his influential students come from these two cities) and in 306 to Athens. There he bought a piece of land, his "garden," where he would teach. In accordance with his testament, this garden remained the site of his school for generations.

The academy consisted of a circle of friends who, in a communal spirit, centered their lives on the course set by Epicurus' teaching. Slaves, women, and hetaerae were allowed to participate. It was a self-selecting community, not aiming at mass influence, an aristocracy of the spirit and not of birth.

The school was founded, for all time, on the sole and unique personality of the Master. He was said to have been sickly from childhood. His mode of life was austere, his food simple. His concern for his friends and their children is evident from his extant testament.

It is said that he retained his capacity for happiness, attained by means of his philosophy, right up to his death. His last letter, to a friend, states: "On this truly happy day of my life which is also my last, I write these lines to you. Strangury and dysentery have afflicted me, with pain that transcends all imaginable bounds. But against all this is the joy in my heart as I remember my conversation with you. Do, as I expect it from you, provide for the children of Metrodorus, in accordance with the affectionate regard you have shown for me and for philosophy from boyhood on" (Diog. Laert., X, 22). A disciple said about him: "Epicurus's life, when compared to that of other men, might in regard to generosity and self-sufficiency be thought a legend" (Fragments, B36).[1]

Epicurus wrote approximately three hundred scrolls, one of the most voluminous corpora by philosophers of antiquity. Only the titles and a few remains of this output have come down to us, among them letters, collections of maxims, and fragments of larger writings. These remains were collected and interpreted by philologists and give us a relatively complete picture of his thought. The writings deal with nature, cognition, ethics. The letters he addressed to his friends are also counted among his works. Didactic letters were one of the main forms of his philosophical intercourse.

---

[1] The Fragments of Epicurus are cited in accordance with Cyril Bailey's numbering. Where his translations are used, the numbers or titles are preceded by a B.

SURVEY

1. *The point of departure of his philosophy*. The fundamental question for Epicurus is: What is happiness (*eudaimonia*) for individual man? His answer: Pleasure (*hedone*). He finds the proof for pleasure's being the highest good in the fact that we enjoy it from birth, whereas by nature we revolt against suffering (N198).[2]

All of late antique and Christian philosophy wrestles with the question of what matters most to man. What constitutes the greatest good (*summum bonum*), after the blissful life (*vita beata*)? Question and answer meet widely differing interpretations and solutions out of a deeper source. Peculiar to Epicurus is the radical realization of his answer: Happiness (*eudaemonia*) lies in pleasure (*hedone*).

But the fact that the fundamental question comprises the meaning of all of philosophy, that it is a matter of attaining to bliss, makes philosophy man's most urgent, constant concern: "Whoever says that the age for philosophy has not yet come or is already past is like the man who says that the age for happiness is not yet come to him or has passed away" (B, Letter to Menoikeus).

2. *Why the query about happiness?* Because man stands squarely within misfortune. He lives in disquiet, anxiety, and fear and often in bodily pain. Misfortune has three causes: first, the belief in gods whose intentions and acts interfere in the world and in our life and who are unpredictable in the way they care for us; second, false ideas about death and what will come after; third, the needs and the suffering of our bodily existence. Fear of the gods, fear of death, and bodily pain constitute the misfortune that must be overcome.

Philosophy intends to demonstrate that the fear of the gods is groundless, that the fear of death is based on wrong ideas, that pain can have no effect on the happiness of the soul. In this way philosophy demonstrates the remedy for the threefold misfortune; in the first place, "one does not have to be afraid before god or the gods"; second, "death means absence of sensation and hence is nothing to us"; third, "the good can be obtained easily, the bad can be borne with ease" (N220). If this third point is counted as two separate ones, we have the so-called *tetrapharmakon* (the fourfold remedy) of Epicurean philosophy.

3. *Comparison of philosophy with medicine*. It was traditional in ancient Greece to compare philosophy, the remedy for the soul, with medicine.

---

[2] References preceded by N are to Wilhelm Nestle.

Democritus drew this comparison, as did Socrates and Plato. It played the greatest role in Stoicism. Medicine cures the ills of the body; philosophy liberates the soul from the passions. Hence Epicurus says: The philosopher "whose words do not heal any human passions is an empty windbag. For just as medicine is useless if it does not rid the body of disease, philosophy is useless, too, if it does not liberate the soul from passion" (N210–11).

4. *Survey.* First we have to show what is meant by saying that happiness is pleasure. Then we must ask what has to be done in order to achieve genuine pleasure. What must I know, in order to be happy, about the world, the soul, the gods, the nature of death? How can I act properly toward my body and its drives?

Further, we have to demonstrate the nature and meaning of cognition and the cognitive life and what constitutes freedom.

And finally, we have to show how the philosophic actualization of life is put into practice and to sketch out the ideal of the sage.

1. WHAT IS PLEASURE?

a) We call happiness (*eudaimonia*) the life of a man that has turned out well, is in harmony with itself, is present in every moment and as a whole. Epicurus' fundamental question is: How does this happiness come about? His answer: Through pleasure (*hedone*).

In order to comprehend the way of salvation and to understand the thesis that happiness lies in pleasure, we must know what Epicurus means by "pleasure."

b) Pleasure is baseless. It is the pure consciousness of existence as such. Pleasure, as such, is always present but under cover and interfered with. Hence it cannot be brought about, but can only be liberated and restored.

For this reason pleasure is determined by negatives: freedom from displeasure, absence of pain (*alypia*). "We feel a need for pleasure only when, due to its absence, we experience pain. But if we do not feel pain, pleasure is not needed any longer, either" (Letter to Menoikeus). Thus the greatest pleasure does not lie, for example, in the strong, overpowering pleasure of intoxication, which is never pure, but carries displeasure with it or has it as a consequence. Pleasure is to be increased only to the point where pain is dissolved. It cannot rise to a higher degree.

c) As soon as pleasure has reached the point where displeasure ceases, it assumes various forms by manifesting itself not only in repose but also in motion. "Serenity of the soul and the absence of pain are quiet pleasure experiences. For joy, on the other hand, and for gaiety motion is the distinguishing characteristic" (Diog. Laert., X, 136). Serenity of the soul is motionless stillness; bodily pleasure is pleasure in motion. Serenity of soul flourishes and is grounded in the appropriate manner in which these motions take place. Bodily pleasure is precious as such; it is essential for the pleasure of the painless serenity of soul. Epicurus expresses this quite boldly: "I know not how I can conceive the good if I withdraw the pleasures of taste and withdraw the pleasures of love and those of hearing and withdraw the pleasurable emotions caused to sight by beautiful form" (B123).

"The beginning and the root of all good is the pleasure of the stomach; even wisdom and culture must be referred to it" (B135). "The stable condition of well-being in the body and the sure hope of its continuance holds the fullest and surest joy for those who can rightly calculate it" (B123).

d) However, bodily pleasure too is a state of the soul, and its purity is serenity. Bodily pleasure also becomes serenity in borderline cases: "Nothing so gladdens the soul naturally and nothing puts it into a state of tranquillity akin to an ocean becalmed as does bodily pleasure either present or anticipated" (N206).

Pure serenity of the soul is much more than mere bodily pleasure. The state of the soul in this serenity is called imperturbability (*ataraxia*), effortlessness (*aponia*), self-sufficiency (*autarkeia*). "Just as one understands, when one speaks of the stillness of the ocean, that not even the faintest breeze ripples the waters, so does the state of the soul appear serene and still when all disturbance ceases that might excite it." Once this state has been achieved it is master over the body and also a match for physical pain. The high value ascribed to the pleasure and pain of the body seems to be changed into its neutralization: "The sage is happy even when he is being tortured and he moans and laments" (N211).

e) He still retains the pleasure of remembering. "We are all ungrateful toward the past insofar as we do not recall all the good that we have received, whereas, after all, no pleasure is more certain than one that cannot be taken from us any more" (N206).

But all life is lived in the present. The future is uncertain. What matters is the present moment and hence the enduring philosophic stance that always takes hold of what is present as the actual and certain. Horace, the poet attuned to Epicureanism, expressed this in two words: *carpe diem!* Every day, at every moment pluck the fruit that life holds out to you (*Odes*, I, 11, 8).

f) Pleasure is the absolute: Since it is not grounded in something else, it cannot be questioned further. Since it is always present, it is timeless. Therefore, it is a matter of indifference how long it lasts, whether for one moment, a short or a long lifetime.

Because pleasure is the absolute, it is the state of the gods. Hence mortals who achieve the freedom of their pleasure are akin to gods. Gods and men differ in that gods possess the perfect purity of painless pleasure and possess it for a long stretch of time.

Philosophy "transports us into a godlike mood and lets us discover that, in spite of our mortality, we need not fall short of the immortal and blissful nature of the gods. For as long as we are alive we are happy just like the gods" (Diogenes of Oinoanda; N294). "The flesh cries out to be saved from hunger, thirst, and cold. For if a man possess this safety or hopes to possess it, he might rival even Zeus in his happiness" (Fragments, B33).

2. WHAT MUST WE DO TO ACHIEVE PURE PLEASURE?

If pleasure is recognized as "the first innate good" (Letter to Menoikeus) and regaining it to be our goal, then all of man's thinking and striving will direct itself to that which is already there, ever ready, present at every moment, if only it is liberated. The road toward salvation runs through philosophy, that is, first, through the proper knowledge of the universe, the actual worlds, of men and gods (liberation from fear of the gods); second, through apprehending the nature of death (liberation from fear of death); third, through a sensible attitude toward the body and its needs (liberation from the constraints of corporeal existence).

Three paths:

A. Proper cognition of the universe, Being and the worlds, of the soul, of the gods

1) *The universe (Being and the worlds).* Democritus' theory of atoms supplied Epicurus with his all-governing view. There are atoms and the void. They alone are constant, eternal, did not become, are indestructible. In a large opus used as a basic text in his academy (the thirty-seven

books on nature), Epicurus worked out in great detail the theory of atoms. The universe, to him, appears like this:

There are atoms and the void. Nothing can come from nothing. What is cannot become nothing. If it could dissolve into nothing, all things would have perished already. But the universe exists, whereas everything in it comes to be and passes away, is formed out of the atoms, and dissolves again into the atoms, which alone are immortal.

The universe has always been the way it is now and always will be that way. The atoms are constantly in motion. There is no beginning and no end.

The universe is boundless. Nothing beside it exists. It cannot be viewed in comparison with another universe. In this universe there are countless worlds. The infinite number of atoms has not been used up on one world, or on a limited number of worlds.

Individual worlds come and go. One of these worlds is our world. It is a section cut out of infinity, an internally cohesive part embracing the stars, the earth, and everything that is visible to us. In the dying worlds and in the interstices between the worlds, new ones come into being out of the whirling motion of the atoms, by chance.

Perhaps the boundary of our world is something that is in the process of change, or perhaps it is standing still; perhaps its outline is round, or triangular, or has some other shape. All this is possible, since none of the phenomena in this world allow us to recognize its boundaries. "That such worlds are infinite in number we can be sure, and also that such a world may come into being both inside another world and in an interworld, by which we mean a space between worlds; it will be in a place with much void . . ." (B, Letter to Pythokles).

The other worlds are in part similar to ours, in part dissimilar. We have to assume that there are living beings as well as plants in all worlds.

2) *The soul.* The soul is corporeal, but in a special way. Embedded in the aggregation of atoms that forms the organism are the most delicate atoms of all, comparable to suffusion by a warm breeze. A part of these atoms is still more delicate; it is manifest in feelings and in the excitation by thoughts. When we lose that part of ourselves, we die.

That the soul is corporeal is proven by the fact that it is able to act or be acted on and can suffer only by means of motion, for only bodies possess motion.

The soul has perception. Something from the external world enters into us which the soul comes to meet and thus brings about perception. ". . . the soul possesses the chief cause of perception: yet it could not have acquired perception unless it were in some way enclosed by the rest of the structure" (B39, Letter to Herodotus). Perception is possible only with the whole of the structure, with the organs of the body. The soul-atoms by themselves would lack the ability to perceive.

What enters into us from the exterior world are "contours of solid bodies whose delicacy, however, surpasses by far that of the visible objects" (N169). These contours (or impressions) are called pictures (*eidola*). They are continuously flowing from the surface of the bodies. This emission is a motion as rapid as thought. The continuity of this emission constitutes the depth, density, and corporeality of perception.

Pictures, however, do not reach us merely by way of our sense organs. Space is full of infinitely multitudinous images, which reach us individually, but lack density and corporeality and become visible to us in our dreams. These pictures, floating freely in space, are fragmented or combine fragments into strange configurations that do not correspond to any visible object. All this is a natural process in dreams. Dreams lack a divine nature or prophetic meaning. There is no reason to be frightened by them.

The pictures do not make us perceive what is in itself, that is, the atoms, but merely the aggregations of atoms. These do not possess the attributes of visible objects except for size, shape, and weight. Here the difference lies only in the small size of the atoms, which, for this reason, can never be perceived, but stand in the same relation to each other, because of size and shape, as do visible objects. The essential difference between atoms and visible objects consists in the fact that the former are unchangeable, whereas the latter are subject to constant change.

Thus sensory perception remains the guide to the representation, in thought, of the atoms. Certain modes of this perception, that is, optical ones in regard to size and shape, and haptic ones as regards resistance, have priority.

3) *The gods.* If the universe of the worlds is nothing other than the eternal play of atoms, then, it would seem, there are no gods. But Epicurus by no means denies their existence. He knows what they are. They do not live in any of the worlds, but between the worlds (in the *metakosmia, intermundia*). There they originated out of the most sublime atoms.

Their images (*eidola*) move, like other *eidola*, through space with the speed of thought. They have assumed human form. They appear to the people of all nations in their dreams. "The first human beings thus had an idea of imperishable natural beings" (N185).

Although Epicurus conforms to the testimony of all peoples as regards the existence of the gods, he differs in regard to their nature. Most people harbor a false picture of the gods. "For gods there are. . . . But they are not such as the many believe them to be." When accused of godlessness, Epicurus replies: "And the impious man is not he who denies the gods of the many, but he who attaches to the gods the beliefs of the many" (B83, Letter to Menoikeus).

For the philosopher, the following perceptions of the gods are of decisive import:

First: The gods are immortal and blissful beings. They do not concern themselves with human beings. They become known to men through their *eidola* and man's thinking about them. If the gods were to concern themselves with the world and men, this would be inconsistent with their life of sublime bliss and draw them into pain and care. Their perfect blissful tranquillity would be disturbed.

Therefore all fear of the gods is groundless. "One must not let man continue to believe that God is the cause of either his injury or his advantage" (N185).

Second: The world was not created by gods, for it is full of wickedness and in this state would be unworthy of a god. Nor is it altogether bad; rather, it is full of instances of beauty, and was not by any means brought forth by a devil. It has come about through chance and necessity, and happened through the motion of atoms; thus it is comprehensible in principle in its very detail.

A god cannot have created the world. Why should he have done so? Why should there be something novel? Was he bored? Or for the sake of man? But man had not yet appeared on the scene, and the world today displays so much calamity and menace for man and indifference toward him that it cannot have been created for his sake.

If God were involved with the world, we would have to ask, in view of all the badness and evil in it: Does God want to liberate the world of its ills (the bad, the evil), but is unable to do so, or is he able but not willing, or neither of the two? If he wants to and is unable, he is weak, which is not in his nature. If he is able and unwilling, then he is envious (malevolent), which is alien to God. If he neither wants to nor is able to, then he is both malevolent and envious, hence again not God. If he is willing and able, which is proper only to God, then why do these ills exist? Why does he not do away with them? Answer: Because the world does not exist through God, nor does he rule over it. It exists out of itself and is left to its own devices. By its very state, the actual world proves that God or gods have nothing to do with it.

Third: The gods live effortlessly, without work, without passions.

Exertions necessary to man, be it labor or statesmanship, are alien to them. They are the image of eternal bliss; the sage attains happiness by keeping this image before his mind's eye. He sees in it the state he himself desires to reach and is able to reach. He venerates the gods not because he seeks their aid or is fearful of them, but because contemplation of their glory is fitting for him and furthers him.

Fourth: The world is free of God. The stars, the tranquillity and regularity of their orbit in the heavens—this cosmos is neither god nor divine. We must not believe "that what is merely the coalescence of fire possesses bliss and assumes these motions according to its own will." Rather, we have to "assume that at the time when these vortices originally were spun off, when the world came to be, this necessity and these regular orbits too were perfected at the same time" (Letter to Herodotus).

The "world free of God" is one of the great fundamental conceptions that can exert their rule over man.

B. Proper insight into death

"We are born once and cannot be born twice and life must come to an end" (N215; Fragments, 14). The inevitability of death causes fear. But whoever cannot find peace as he contemplates death cannot find peace at all. Insight into the nature of death can be helpful.

1) *What is death?* In death the soul-atoms also are dispersed. Then the soul, a combination of the finer soul-atoms with the organism, ceases to be stimulated and to convey sensations. It is unthinkable that soul-atoms are capable of feeling without organs, and organs to feel without being part of the whole living organism. Only because the soul is enclosed by the organism can it feel and operate, can it remember and have consciousness.

To achieve Epicurean tranquillity, a crucial insight is necessary: With the death of the body, the soul too passes out of existence; there is no "after death" for the soul. This insight, once accepted, does away with the questioning anxiety over whether nothingness is truly nothing.

The Epicurean Philodemos writes: A corpse has no feeling. The corpse left behind after death does not contain my soul. To mistreat it means "to mistreat mute earth" (N245). There is no difference whether we lack sensation above or below the earth, whether we are devoured by fishes, eaten by worms or maggots, or destroyed by fire; in each instance we are equally insensate.

2) *The consequence of this insight*: Death "is nothing to us" because what does not feel does not concern us. And it is nothing to us since

"so long as we exist, death is not with us; but when death comes, then we do not exist. It does not then concern either the living or the dead" (B85, Letter to Menoikeus). There is nothing dreadful inherent in not being alive.

It is only this understanding "that makes the mortality of life enjoyable" (B85, Letter to Menoikeus). The wonderful thing is that I am alive. I no longer yearn for immortality.

3) *The lives of fools are wrong* because they do not achieve clarity regarding death. They neglect what there is in the present because they are thinking about the tomorrow over which they have as yet no control. They are consumed by vacillation and "die" in the midst of their active lives. Now they flee death as the greatest of evils, now they seek it in their flight from the evils of life. "It is ridiculous to throw oneself into the arms of death because one is tired of living" (N208). "Yet much worse still is the man who says it is good not to be born" (B87 and Letter to Menoikeus).

4) *How different the life of the sage!* He neither scorns life nor fears its cessation. He loves life.

"And just as with food he does not seek simply the larger share, but instead the most pleasant, so he seeks to enjoy not the longest period of time, but the most pleasant." When he thinks of the future he is mindful "that it is neither ours nor yet wholly not ours, so that we may not altogether expect it as sure to come nor abandon hope of it if it will certainly not come" (B85, 87, Letter to Menoikeus).

Metrodorus, a personal disciple of Epicurus, expresses the triumph of the philosopher over death: "I have anticipated you, chance . . . we shall not submit to being your prisoner nor that of any kind of circumstance. But when it is time for us to leave we shall scorn life and those who cleave to it in vain. We shall make our exit with a beautiful hymn of praise, proclaiming how well we have lived our lives" (Fragments, B47; Metrodorus, No. 222). The Epicurean Philodemus (first century B.C.) gives this description of the sage's attitude toward death: It is impossible for death to pounce upon the wise man suddenly, like an enemy. He knows that man is a creature that lives for a day, for whom not only the tomorrow but even the next moment is shrouded in darkness. He will not consider the timing of his death unreasonable or unexpected, but will deem it miraculous should he live to an old age. He who has become inwardly independent "counts each individual day as if he had gained an eternity." He accepts "every accretion of time like an unexpected stroke of luck and is accordingly grateful for the course of things" (N251). He breathes his last, when death comes, "in the knowledge that he has enjoyed everything and will now enter a state of complete absence of feeling" (N252).

C. *Discerning attitude toward the body and its drives*

The Epicurean description of true pleasure was astonishing and open to misunderstanding, especially in its affirmation of all bodily pleasure and its playing down of even the most violent physical pain.

It contradicts and challenges all devaluation of bodily pleasure, all demonizing of the sensual, all tendencies toward asceticism. Physical pain, the absence of which is considered to be so urgently necessary to the tranquillity of the soul, is declared to be wholly surmountable through the philosophic attitude. We must look more closely at this ambivalence of the high and low values assigned to the corporeal.

1) All our *appetites urge us toward pleasure*. This is all they desire. We cannot blame them. No pleasure is evil in itself.

But appetites blindly obeying their urges produce increasing displeasure by the evils that may ensue. Seduced by the appearance of pleasure we are drawn into unanticipated displeasure. In this respect pleasure can be an evil.

Hence the appetites can be recognized by their effects, and on the basis of this understanding have to be guided by calculating the maximum of pleasure, its duration and certainty.

To be sure, pleasure is always our standard "for all our choosing and avoiding" (Letter to Menoikeus). It is our touchstone. But the difference consists in whether this choosing and avoiding is done blindly or guided by understanding. "Pure pleasure" is possible only by way of such guidance.

"Pure" here does not mean "morally pure," but cleansed of displeasure and pain. Appetites and moral imperatives are on an equal level. They are not valid as absolutes, but as controllable means for the purpose of achieving pure pleasure. "Nobility, the virtues, and such are to be valued if they bring pleasure; if they do not, avoid them" (N199).

It is the task of philosophy to recognize the reasons for choosing and avoiding and to cancel out mere opinions that lead into the labyrinth of urges and of morals.

2) *The appetites are either natural or unfounded*. The natural appetites are either necessary or unnecessary. The necessary ones are either necessary for happiness or for the satisfaction of the body or for maintaining life itself. This yields the following axioms: "We must not violate nature, but obey her; and we shall obey her if we satisfy necessary desires and

also the physical, if they bring no harm to us, but sternly reject the harmful" (Fragments, B21).

3) Reasonable calculation—"weighing the beautiful against the harmful" (Letter to Menoikeus)—considers *which pleasure is to be chosen and which avoided*, and even what pain to choose in order to arrive, by paying this price, at the greatest pleasure. For it is sensible to forgo pleasure in order to avoid greater pain, to take pain upon oneself to achieve greater pleasure. Even though "every pleasure because of its natural kinship to us is good," we do not choose every pleasure. Even though "every pain also is an evil, yet not all are always of a nature to be avoided." We forgo much that gives pleasure if its result would be "a greater discomfort . . . and similarly we think many pains better than pleasures, if a greater pleasure comes to us when we have endured pain for a long time" (Fragments, B21).

4) The life that grows out of such considerations is not an unbridled life of pleasure. Rather, Epicurus, without disapproving of any pleasure as such, leads us actually to an *ascetic though nonviolent life.*

"We consider being content with little a great good." "Simple food gives the same pleasure as a fancy meal." "Bread and water give us the greatest pleasure if we ingest them out of a need for food." "Becoming accustomed to a simple and inexpensive way of life takes away apprehension of fate and heightens our spirits if for once, as an exception, we enjoy luxurious pleasures." For he who least needs luxury knows how to enjoy it with the greatest pleasure. In addition, "all that is natural is easily obtained and only the superfluous is hard to procure" (Fragments, B21).

Hence pleasure is not at all "the pleasures of the gourmandizer nor that which is based on sensual gratification." Not carousing, not opulent meals, "not the enjoyment of youths and women" are, though pleasures, the highest good. "All pleasure is subject to being judged by the yardstick of pure pleasure" (Fragments, B21).

Thus the sage contents himself with what he possesses. Only the fool "always whines about what he does not have." Only "poorly endowed souls always feel deprived" (N207).

5) *Erotic joys* are considered the height of pleasure. Time and again it has been assumed that these are central to Epicurus, who is thus changed from a philosopher of pleasure to one of lust. Not at all. Epicurus permits them as long as they do not lead to exhaustion, do not consume what is necessary to maintain life, and do not infringe upon laws and morals. All that would cause more displeasure than the pleasure given by the joys of love. Epicurus does not wholly trust them. "For the

pleasures of love never profited a man; he is lucky if they have not harmed him" (Fragments, B51).

6) The calculation of bodily pleasure in order to achieve the maximum or the purity of pleasure seems to have a limit. *Life* as such, the ailing body, *entails pain* that is frequently quite violent and that we cannot prevent even with careful calculation. Not all pain can be avoided through moderation, simplicity, and frugality. Epicurus is no more able to make pain disappear than is the physician. However, opines the philosopher, the afflictions arising from the necessities of existence can be made less acute. It is not pain itself that we are able to avoid; Epicurus does not deny that horrible physical pain is inescapable. But it is up to us whether and to what extent we suffer under it, and Epicurus teaches us how to master it so that it does not disturb the tranquillity of the soul.

The fear of future pain is to be eliminated through the realization that "all bodily suffering is negligible: for that which causes acute pain has short duration, and that which endures long . . . causes but mild pain" (Fragments, B4). Pain is limited by its very violence and reaches a point where it turns into unconsciousness.

But when there is pain, then the pleasure in existence must be preserved through one's attitude toward pain. Though its actuality cannot be denied, it can, owing to our freedom, be kept at bay, as it were. Tranquillity of soul, Epicurus maintains, is possible, as is pure pleasure in the remembrance of beauty experienced earlier. Under all circumstances, life is better than suicide. For life as such, if properly lived, always contains pleasure.

The grandiose paradox remains. Physical pain, the absence of which is, after all, a prime requisite for the tranquillity of soul, is thus declared to be surmountable by way of our philosophic attitude. Adjudging to the corporal both value and insignificance is mutually compatible in this philosophy.

Epicurus explains his intention thus: "We do not want to charge the flesh with being the cause of greater ills, nor do we wish to blame conditions for what is unbearable." We ourselves are responsible. "We would rather seek the cause in the soul . . . and belong wholly to ourselves alone" (N206–07).

3. ABOUT COGNITION AS SUCH

A. *The philosophic significance of science*

For Epicurus the purpose of understanding nature lies in the tranquillity of soul brought about by science. We would not need the natural sciences if we had no anxieties based on false notions and expectations. "A man cannot dispel his fear about the most important matters if he does not know what is the nature of the universe" (B92).

Hence, what Democritus, Epicurus, and Lucretius have in common, namely, the atomistic theory of the universe, was essential for Democritus but not, in itself, for Epicurus and his successors. For Epicurus it is an instrument of cognition or a way of understanding that believes itself to be equal to all realities through anticipatory knowledge. It proves itself in the cognition of all things. This is nothing but the particular excogitated aggregation and segregation of atoms. As ultimate knowledge it serves the Epicurean attitude toward life.

Epicurus, therefore, rejects the true natural scientists. He considers them busy braggarts and babblers who use natural science as a means to dazzle the many, so eagerly receptive to their insights. By contrast, the kind of natural science that alone matters to him is meant to strengthen man's decisiveness, independence, and sense of self-worth. The technical application of science never enters his mind and would surely have been despised by him.

Understood in its essence, the cosmos is the natural course of events devoid of purpose. No gods or demons, no evil or helpful spirits interfere. If I know what is real, basically and as a whole, then the false ideas, threatening omens and the fears occasioned by dreams cease to be. The frightening phenomena have become transparent. Knowledge of the cosmos brings about tranquillity of soul.

B. *Epicurus' basic conception of the whole in its relation to science*

Everything happens "naturally," that is, it can be thought of in analogy to immediately perceived processes. The atoms and the void are the ultimate, sole, ungrounded, and irreducible reality out of which everything proceeds through motion.

The observable configurations of nature and the natural processes furnish the mental images that, as models for the motion of atoms, the configurations of atoms, the clustering of atoms that constitute Being, are thought in forms which themselves remain forever invisible to us.

It is an intellectual abstraction of great boldness in its disregard for color, sound, smell, leaving as residue only volume, shape, movement, space. At the same time, however, it is the grossest abstraction, in which gravity, pressure, and impulse of the tiniest indivisible parts of bodies are Being itself.

The objections against the theory of atoms as doctrine of Being are ancient and simple:

A gap exists between the animate and the inanimate, between corporeality and consciousness, between a physiological process affecting the nerves and the experience of color sensation. One cannot be derived from the other by means of any evident representation.

There is a difference in origin between a causal connection and a connection based on meaning. For the atom theoretician, purpose in organic existence consists in the survival of accidental combinations of atoms. Just as all poetry is the result of the combination of the letters of the alphabet, all things having purpose or meaning result from the combination of the much larger number of atomic configurations. From the small number of basic forms follows an illimitable number of combinations—of linguistic productions on the one hand, of natural configurations on the other. Thus, the Homeric epics, for instance, might have taken shape purely by accident, as a purposeless and accidental aggregation of letters.

In such explanations Epicurus searches for what is evident to intuition and can exist only within the realm of approximation. He operates with "transitions" which elude factual representation, with developments the possibility of which is posited by the assumption of boundless time, infinite space, and an infinite amount of prime matter.

Characteristic of Epicurus' thought is its reliance on possibility rather than on scientific investigation or methodical observation. With him, persuasive power lies in thought, not in experience.

His second characteristic: The basic ideas of the theory of atoms are regarded not as possible but as indubitably certain. Yet all specific explanations are merely possibilities which lend themselves to many formulations. Epicurus wants to differentiate that which operates and occurs in an exclusively unequivocal way from that which comes about in a variety of ways. He posits certainty and exactitude only for the fundamental ideas; that this is the way it is can be grasped only in thought. It is not valid to believe that "things might be different," that this is "possible in various ways" (Diog. Laert., X, 78). The mere determination of facts (as, for example, the rising and setting, directional change, or eclipse of the stars) has scant importance for him. Here various explanatory approaches are possible, not to mention the uncertainty concerning the potential behavior of things. In place of a scientific approach Epicurus contents himself with the view that things, in their appearance, can be thought of as possible in a variety of ways. This, however, implies that he failed to grasp the meaning and possibilities of scientific inquiry, the rudiments of which were present among the Greeks long before his time:

First: Where he claims absolute certainty, that certainty cannot be achieved by scientific means. So far no philosopher or researcher who thinks dogmatically has been able to comprehend this. Fundamental ideas such as these have, as a whole, never been proven scientifically and have, therefore, always lent themselves to attack. Second: Science itself, insofar as it becomes pure science, leads us to the limits at which it preserves its own—always particular—insights from being made absolute in a knowledge of the whole. Third: In its specificity, science achieves results that endure; but there is progressive change in its fundamental concepts.

In all particulars Epicurus contents himself with plausible possibilities. He does not investigate, but interprets everything from his presupposition, his knowledge of the whole. True science takes the opposite course; the projection of possibilities is its point of departure. Research examines them by means of criteria of observation—either sought out or brought about by judicious planning based on experience. It aims at the highest possible accuracy in these observations within the limits of mathematics and measurement.

However, Epicurus properly defined the difference between conceptions of the whole of Being (which alone are important to him) and particular conceptions in their multiple possibilities; he understood correctly that these particular conceptions, being subject to change, are incapable of giving support to life or, in and by themselves, of "providing tranquillity."

Epicurus' misunderstanding of true science is closely connected with the purpose that his "science" is meant to serve. As a result, he despises that which he misunderstands, though for a reason that is itself correct: These sciences, like the many possible plausible explanations of details, are not conducive to tranquillity of soul. If, up to the present day, such peace of mind is achieved by searchers through science, it is not based in science itself but on notions outside the sciences; they falsely presuppose an absolute inherent in the sciences and believe they can find it there. In this regard, scientists of such a mind-set are receptive to what they find in Epicurus and Lucretius. Cognition of details is not enough.

According to Epicurus (Diog. Laert., X, 79), those who are conversant with individual facts, but have no knowledge of their nature and superior reasons for being, are disquieted by emotions of fear, no different from those who are without this detailed information. They may even be exposed to greater anxieties through the investigation of events that, while arousing their astonishment, offer no solution of their mystery. We should, therefore, consider only in passing the various possible ways in which things come about. Only total cognition is absolutely certain and calming; all other cognition is dependent on perspective and hence of no concern for us.

It has been advanced that in Epicurus may be detected the scientific mind-set (which, in modern times, has indeed received stimulation from the Epicurean understanding of nature as discovered by Democritus, especially in the form given to it by Lucretius), namely, the sense of the immutability of causality and of the laws of nature ("nothing is created out of nothing"), as also the notion of the preservation of matter and of energy, and the methods of observing nature.

C. The Canonics

Possessing knowledge is not sufficient. We must be aware of the origin of its certainty in order to test the sureness of the road to it. We want the criteria of truth. Epicurus calls this area of his thinking canonics (in others, it might be called logic, dialectic, methodology).

1) *Clarity about words:* We must see what underlies the words. "For in the case of each word, the first mental image associated with it should be regarded and there should be no further need of explanation." Only then do we have "a fixed point of reference for what we have thought, doubted, or merely supposed." If this is disregarded, we are "dealing with empty words" or "get lost in infinity with our explanations" (Letter to Herodotus).

2) *Points of departure:* What is the mind's referent at the origin of knowledge? It is what is really present, and this is given in immediate insight, in what is evident (*enargeia*, evidence). For this there are three sources: sensory perception (*aisthesis*), feeling (*pathos*), and concept (*prolepsis*). Later on, Epicureans added a fourth: imaginary representations of thought (*phantastikai epibolai tes dianoias*).

Sensory perceptions: "Sensory perceptions have to be firmly and accurately grasped, and equally the attendant stimulations of the capacity for thinking" (Letter to Herodotus). Should sensory perceptions be disregarded, then all of the ground is lost. In denying them, we lose the reasons for our assertions.

Feelings: The feelings (*pathe*) attendant on sensory perceptions are the criteria of pleasure. In sensory perception and pleasure we find the pure presentness of Being. Here is the point of absolute trust. If it were to totter, cognition and tranquillity would be lost at the same time.

Concepts: By a concept Epicurus understands "an internally preserved representation of a general cognition, i.e., the memory of something that has often made its appearance externally, as, for example, 'something like a human being.' As soon as I say 'human being,' its type is represented to me conceptually, guided by my preceding sensory perceptions" (N184).

We "would be entirely unable to examine what we do examine if we were not already familiar with it, e.g., 'Is the animal standing over there at a distance a horse or a cow?'" This question can be answered only if the shape of the horse and the cow is already known conceptually. "Neither could we ever give a name to anything unless we had already made conceptual acquaintance with its type" (N184).

The concept anticipates (that is why it is called *prolepsis*) what is fulfilled in sensory perception, yet has its origin in sensory perceptions. "All thoughts arise on the basis of sensory perception through accidental cause, analogy, similarity, combination, to which, of course, thinking also contributes something" (N183).

3. *From phenomena* (phainomena) *to the nonevident* (adela): Sensory perceptions, feelings, concepts are what is evident. They make present and evident all that exists. In this immediate evidence everything is phenomenon, appearance. There is no visible sign of atoms anywhere. "Hence one must draw conclusions from the visible to the invisible" (N183). The road leads from the appearances (*phainomena*) to the non-evident, unknown things (*adela*).

Epicurus' attitude toward the world is two-sided. Everything is presence; there is nothing beyond it, no purpose, no goal. Yet, beyond everything tangible lies that which is uniquely nonevident: the atoms, that is, something utterly indestructible, imperishably enduring; also their motion in the void, and the infinity of their numbers and of the extension of space.

4) *Truth and falsehood: all sensory perceptions are true:* "All perception is devoid of reason. . . . Furthermore, there is nothing that perception could refute. . . . Neither can one perception refute another" (N182). "Even the imaginings of demented persons and images in dreams are true; for they act as stimulants; if they did not exist, they could not bring about such stimulation" (N183).

It is the condition of all cognition that all perception—whether subsequently referred to as perception, imagination, or dream—is originally true as actuality and cannot be false. "Only if the sensory perceptions are all true will one be able to cognize or grasp anything" (N183).

The location of true and false: Whereas perceptions and representations, in their immediacy, are always true, opinions can be true or false.

"There could be no errors if we did not find in ourselves yet another kind of mental activity. To be sure, this activity is connected with the imaginative activity, yet has its own ways of apprehension. Only through it—if it is not immediately confirmed or refuted—can deception come about; if, on the other hand, it is confirmed or not refuted, truth comes into being" (Letter to Herodotus).

"Hence, deception and error always lie solely in what is thought additionally which still has to await its confirmation or at least nonrefutation" (Letter to Herodotus). "Confirmation and nonrefutation are the sign that something is true: nonconfirmation and refutation, however, are the sign that it is false. Evidence (*enargeia*), however, is the keystone and foundation of all" (N183).

"An opinion is also called an assumption. It can be true or false" (N184). "For this reason the concept of waiting-and-seeing was introduced: e.g., one postpones one's judgment until one comes close to the tower and sees what it looks like up close" (N185). It is only this immediacy that brings evidence with it.

5) *Appraisal of Epicurus' canon:* It is deficient in that Epicurus fails to clarify, either logically or through the theory of knowledge, the method of drawing conclusions from the appearances to that which is not manifest (in Epicurus, to Being as the eternal motion of the atoms, which he sees as true Being as such). He does not submit the process itself to any examination.

His interest in logic is limited. He has little use for logical subtlety or the rigor of proof. He considers them only insofar as he believes they are needed for the truth necessary to the tranquillity of the soul. Therefore, in logic, he is vastly inferior to Aristotle and the Stoics. He has been accused of logical superficiality. My reply: Epicurus understood that logic and objective cognition are not in themselves the ultimate reasons for the attitude toward life or the Existenz of man. They are essential only in connection with their significance for Existenz. Otherwise they are neutral, irrelevant, and, should they be elevated to the absolute as such, even ruinous. But the obverse, unfortunately, is that with his dogmatic unexamined thinking Epicurus has foundered. He appeals to what, in recent centuries, has been referred to as common sense, understood as man's ability to discern and judge. This ability is presupposed and in its simplicity taken for granted; it applies to the immediately given, smugly assured in the belief that it cannot be deceived and angrily reacting to what is difficult or sublime. It exerts the power of all that is roughly comprehensible and supposedly beyond doubt.

The end results are: First, the great truth that all that exists for us, that must become present and assume sensory form out of the most sublime thinking, is limited to the reality of sensory perception and pleasure; no question is asked as to the content of either. Second, Epicurus, ever intent on letting fictions go up in smoke, himself creates a world of fictions: the world of atoms. His critical intellect succumbs to a crude and impoverished self-enclosed fantasy world. By positing this world as the absolute, only authentically real one, he shuts out immeasurable realms of actualities. He is firm in the belief that, by means of his common sense, he has comprehended the theory of atoms as the only one possible, the one correctly demonstrated, the one deducible from nature. The source of this freedom from doubt on his part is not cogent cognition but dogmatic faith, which demands absolute certainty about Being itself. Epicurus formulates this by justifying the whole of cognition as merely a means toward tranquillity of the soul. The very fact that this basis of cognition is so questionable testifies to the nature of this insight as faith, in distinction from its alleged nature as knowledge.

D. Bios theoretikos

However, the meaning of Epicurus' cognition is not so easily exhausted. To him, the means to reach tranquillity of the soul is transformed every moment into a purpose complete in itself, cognition as such being the presence of the purest pleasure. The means to tranquillity becomes the content of tranquillity. "In philosophy, pleasure goes hand in hand with knowledge: for enjoyment does not follow comprehension but comprehension and enjoyment are simultaneous" (Fragments, B17).

Epicurus produced his voluminous opus by steadfast and many-sided application. A state of theoretical contemplation animated by thought filled the days of his life. Thinking itself was purest pleasure. It "enables one to lead a life complete in itself and has no further need of eternity" (N212–13).

When one differentiates the ways of life into a practical (acting, active) one, a creative one (poetic, artistic, literary), an observing one (contemplative, theoretical, cognitive), then each of these configurations of life in turn contains a multiplicity of motives, of interior states, of goals.

Epicurus exemplifies the *bios theoretikos* in a manner that is clarified when set in contrast to two other ways of life.

Epicurus' attitude differs from that of Democritus. Democritus declared that he would rather find one single proof than be king of the Persians. In such a dictum we may see the first burgeoning of the scientist's self-perception, which has come to full clarity only in the modern world. The scientist delights in factual cognition, which for him is a step on the path that leads to infinity. To have taken a step here that has not been taken before and to have advanced knowledge for all time is an experience of great happiness for the scientist. He can call his own a cognition cogent for everyone, a tiny place within all that is cognizable. He labors so that his successors may be able to progress on a path whose end he does not see and on which each follower in turn takes only one further step. Whoever wishes for perfection experiences the curse of this path: never to reach the finish line, either as an individual or as the totality of the generations of scientific investigators. But whoever takes part in this race is compelled by the task. He reaches out for the truth that is incontrovertible, and finds it. But he also realizes that one cannot ground one's life on the content of this truth, unless the scientific attitude proves to be indispensable for all authentic life.

Nor can Epicurus' attitude be likened to that of Anaxagoras. Euripides (perhaps with an eye toward Anaxagoras) writes: "Happy is he who has attained possession of knowledge. . . . Contemplating he regards the unchanging order of the immortal All . . . never will shameful scheming steal into the heart of such a man" (Fragments, 902).

Aristotle sees the apex of man's possibility in cognition. Reason is what is most divine. It has more permanence and gives greater joy than any action, and is sufficient unto itself. Thus it goes throughout antiquity. So with Cicero (*Hortensius de philosophia*): "If we were . . . permitted to lead an immoral life on the islands of the blessed . . . the cardinal virtues would lose all meaning there. . . . We would be happy there merely through the contemplation of nature and through cognition, which alone is to be praised also in the lives of the gods."[3] And in late antiquity, we read in the astronomer Claudius Ptolemaeus: "I know that I am mortal, a creature of this day, yet when I pursue, in thought, the orbit of the stars as they circle the pole, my feet no longer touch the ground: Zeus himself beside me—I am then nourished at the divine feast with ambrosia."[4] This attitude continues throughout the Christian world and

[3] Franz Johannes Boll, *Vita Contemplativa*. Heidelberg, C. Winter, 1920, 16.
[4] Ibid., 17.

has come powerfully to the fore since the Renaissance. For Pico, man's dignity lies in his having been created by God so that he may know the laws of the universe, and love and admire its greatness and beauty.

In this knowledge imbued with piety toward the world, the moral life is inextricably bound to awe before such order. "The starry skies above me and the moral law within me" (*Critique of Practical Reason*, Conclusion) are still complementary for Kant.

For Epicurus it is a matter of neither a discriminating, constantly probing scientific will to truth, nor of blissful, reverent contemplation. Scientifically, he is wholly uncritical and in no way an investigative scientist. As to the universe as a whole, he knows no reverence, neither love and admiration nor aversion and disdain.

He actualizes the possibility of detached observation when faced with matters of indifference to him. He does not react emotionally. He knows what the All is. It has no signification, no meaning beyond itself. All one needs to know is what it is. Observing in complete detachment leads to independence and peace of mind. Virgil is right in saying of Lucretius: "Happy is he who has been able to win knowledge of the causes of things, and has cast beneath his feet all fear and unyielding Fate and the howls of hungry Acheron" (*Georgics*, II, 1.490ff.).[5]

Neither the object nor the All and its order deserve our admiration; rather, it is the thinker who, by way of his alleged knowledge, triumphs over all adversity that might—but now no longer can—befall him. Truth as such or the content of actuality does not compel his interest.

But then, observation is satisfying in itself, a noble pursuit in our leisure time, since it is unalloyed pleasure without painful consequences; it is an activity providing a singular intellectual pleasure, in which content is a matter of indifference.

Yet the connection of reverent observation with the moral life takes on a form that, examined for its meaning, is somewhat less weighty and more trivial: "The greatest good is reason . . . it teaches that one cannot live pleasantly without, at the same time, living rationally, honorably, and morally; nor can one live rationally, honorably, and morally without living pleasurably" (B, Letter to Menoikeus).

Epicurus is neither scientist nor metaphysician. He belongs within the ranks of those pious toward the world, by virtue of his affirmation of his own existence within it—a world bereft of transparency or transcendence.

[5] *Virgil* with an English translation by H. Rushton Fairclough, Cambridge, MA, Harvard University Press; London, William Heinemann, rev. ed., 1950.

4. THE ORIGIN AND NATURE OF FREEDOM

1) There are two, opposing, positions in conceiving the course of events: "all is chance" or "all is necessity."

Chance: We are startled by the unexpected which bursts through natural necessity. Whatever is incommensurate, sudden, discontinuous, unforeseen, and incomprehensible is represented as an expression of acts of divine will and arouses fear.

Necessity: Knowledge of actual causes leads to the conception of necessity in all occurrences, owing to the unbreakable laws of nature. Everything happens within the continuous transition of becoming and growth. The necessity attendant to insight into specific natural causality is transferred and incorporated into the philosophical concept of the necessity underlying all things (the necessity of fate, of divine providence, both combined in *heimarmene* of the Stoics). Necessity invalidates chance. Chance is a deception due to insufficient knowledge. Everlasting necessity is implacable, we have to submit to it. Fear of chance yields to submission to necessity.

Epicurus denies both positions. Both lead the soul into servitude, either to the fear of terrifying chance or to the paralyzing burden of the irrevocable. Both exist, chance as well as necessity. Understanding them correctly leads man to freedom. Epicurus insists on chance but robs it of terror; he insists on necessity but robs it of the ineluctable.

2) Epicurus' way is an apparently insignificant correction of Democritus' atom theory, but in fact it changes everything. He maintains that variations in the falling motion of atoms are due to chance and not to law. This results, first, in the formation of small vortices from which worlds arise. These worlds are simultaneously grounded in chance and in necessity. The chance deviations are continuous for all time and part of all occurrences. For Epicurus such chance has a twofold significance:

First, chance, understood in this way, is "natural." "The wise man also does not regard chance to be a god, as does the multitude—for a god never acts senselessly—nor again to be an incommensurable causality" (N181). Since chance is not an arbitrary intercession on the part of powers, and is not dark destiny, and not the goddess Tyche, it has lost its terror.

Second, chance in the sense of the deviation of atoms at the most minute level makes our freedom comprehensible. It guarantees freedom against necessity, which would otherwise be immutable and oppressive. In this way freedom of the determination of the will is a universal attribute of all living beings. Thus the movement of their members follows the free impulse. The spirit within us is not hampered by inner compulsion. The fact that it is not condemned to endure and suffer is due to the deviation of the atoms, "which, no matter how minute, is not restricted in place or in time" (Lucretius, *De rerum natura*, II, 293). Absolute necessity would be ineluctable were it not for atoms breaking through it by virtue of their deviation.

3) The concepts of the deviation of atoms, the spontaneity of living beings, and the freedom of rational acts, though different in origin, seem to converge. However, Epicurus also differentiates chance and intent: "Everything happens according to necessity, chance, intent" (N195). Three reasons for the course of events are at play; the third is intent, our freedom, that which we make out of that which we encounter. Hence the wise man is superior through his insight, which he proves and which at the same time he secures for himself in life and in action: first, in that he can laugh at "fate (necessity), which many would admit as lord over all" because he has "explained" it; second, in "that only some things happen necessarily, others by chance"; third, in that "some things happen through us, because, while necessity is irresponsible, chance is unstable, and hence it lies in our hands not to submit to any lord" (N181, Letter to Menoikeus).

Chance, itself deprived of power, serves Epicurus to deny the power of natural necessity, which is unbearable to his consciousness of freedom. "It would be better to follow the fables about the gods than to be slave to natural law; at least the former grant the hope that one's prayers will be heard . . . while natural necessity is implacable" (N181).

The course of events partly follows from necessities and partly originates in chance. Epicurus seeks to ground himself in neither comforting necessities nor significant chance happenings. Both lack grandeur. Neither the divine necessity of an eternal order nor the miracle of divine intercession exists. The wise man relates to both by soberly comprehending their nature; he will then not let himself be disturbed by either. He realizes there is a third factor: freedom. This consists not only of intent—that is, practical decisions based on rational insight—but also of a condition that becomes a steady, reliable fundamental attitude.

4) Such freedom (*eleutheria*) is identical with purest joy, with tranquillity, with a state beyond confusion. It is the consequence of a life of self-sufficiency: "The greatest fruit of self-sufficiency is freedom" (N220; Fragments, 77). Necessity, chance, and freedom as intent are the three moments of existence that, if grasped correctly and followed correctly, permit the actualization of a condition that is the freedom of the wise.

5) Once such freedom is achieved, neither necessity nor chance can

be of moment to us. To be sure, chance as a rule leads the dance of great goods and ills. But for the wise, chance does not yield any good or ill that is essential for the happy life. Of course, to have chance on one's side is best. But since this does not by any means happen all the time, the wise learn "to accept the good that comes by chance without any excitement and to be armed against the apparent misfortune that derives from it" (N208). All fortune and misfortune of the many is a matter of the moment, but wisdom has nothing in common with chance. It is still better "to live rationally in unfavorable than irrationally in favorable circumstances" (N181).

5. THE PHILOSOPHICAL PRACTICE OF ACTUALIZATION

Cognition of the universe, insight into the nature of death, calculated guidance of bodily needs are insufficient for the actualization of pure joy. Those basic philosophical thoughts must prove themselves in practice in order to actualize their meaning. Since the human being is given to himself as a natural being and conjointly with others, he has to find what is right and fitting within these realities. The question "what ought I to do?" demands a concrete answer. Epicurus proceeds to offer it: first, he gives advice on how to deal with oneself (a psychotherapeutical technique), by means of rules for life and a calculus; second, he points to what above all else is essential for human happiness, namely, friendship; third, he supplies directions for dealing with the realities of human society, the state, religion, wealth, and poverty.

A. Rules for life

In dealing with ourselves, basic rules need to be set up. It is easy to formulate them in thought, but to actualize them is difficult. They require practice (*askesis*) if they are to be dominant in life. "One ought not to play the philosopher, but actually be a philosopher; for we do not need the semblance of health, but actual health" (N218; Fragments, 54).

To engage in practice it is necessary to emphasize the essentials, to impress them on our memory, to have them immediately available in succinct formulations whenever they are needed. Hence Epicurus formulated them in sayings, in incisive, simple, clear statements (*kyriai logoi*). He demands that they be memorized. It is in this form that he compiled his main doctrines. They gained their shortest form in the *tetrapharmakon*, mentioned earlier: "One does not need to be afraid before

god or the gods . . . death means absence of sensation and hence is
nothing to us . . . the good can be obtained easily, the bad can be borne
with ease" (N220).

What is practiced through constant repetition becomes the habit of
truth. Hence statements like: "Get used to the idea that death does not
concern us" (N176, Letter to Menoikeus).

Practice demands daily effort, but it can lead to a conclusion in which
the true, pure, pleasurable, reasonable attitude of life is attained. "One
must try to arrange the following day always better than the previous
one, as long as we are still on the way: but once we have arrived at our
goal we may embrace a measured cheerfulness" (N218; Fragments, 48).

Dealing with ourselves calls particularly for the calculation of desires,
which was described above.

Alongside these general rules for life Epicurus formulates specific
ones that arise from the underlying principle, such as:

"Doing good brings more pleasure than having good done to you"
(N209).

"Whoever worries least about tomorrow approaches it with the greatest pleasure" (N208).

"Do not do anything in life that must make you afraid of your
neighbor's noticing it" (N219; Fragments, 70).

Then Epicurus makes value judgments. He points to the warning
example of unphilosophic man:

"A small soul is made cocky by good fortune and downcast by
misfortune" (N208). "He is a little man in all respects who has many
good reasons for quitting life" (Fragments, B38).

"With most men repose turns into rigidity, mobility into abandon"
(N215; Fragments, 11).

Epicurus also observes the ages of man:

"It is not the young man who should be thought happy but an old
man who has lived a good life. For the young man at the height of his
powers is unstable and is carried this way and that by fortune like a
headlong stream. But the old man has come to anchor in old age as in
a port and the good things for which before he hardly hoped, he has
brought into safe harborage . . ." (Fragments, B17).

B. The essential good: friendship

Schooling oneself in the principles is the path "for you alone and together
with your peers" (N181, Letter to Menoikeus). The noble man "concerns
himself most about wisdom and friendship" (N220; Fragments, 78):

". . . no greater good than friendship, no greater wealth, no greater joy" (N209).

Why friendship? To begin with, Epicurus' answers are soberly evaluating, such as: "We offer, one to the other, a sufficiently interesting spectacle" (N210).

Further: friendship is useful and, at the same time, something fortunate. These two cannot be separated. We choose friendship for its own sake, "but its motivation is utility" (N216; Fragments, 23). Human nature "does not love for free and does not enter into friendships without benefit" (Us527).[6]

But later on, benefit recedes into the background: "We do not need friends in order to make use of them, but to be able to believe that we may make use of them" (N217; Fragments, 34).

In the end, benefit disappears in rendering aid: "Let us prove to our friends our sympathy not by lamenting with them but by caring with them!" (N219; Fragments, 66). In a situation of shared exigency "the wise man understands better how to give to his friends than how to take from them: such a treasure of self-sufficiency has he found" (N217; Fragments, 44). Also, the initial motive of utility is turned completely into its opposite: "Even though we enter upon friendship for the sake of pleasure, yet we assume the greatest pains for the sake of our friends" (N209).

The path of friendship: "One cannot praise either the one who strikes up a friendship too hastily or the one who hesitates doing so. One must be willing to risk something for the sake of friendship" (N216; Fragments, 28).

We gain our inner certainty from our neighbor and then "we also lead with each other the most pleasurable life in firm mutual trust" (N215).

For "lasting happiness in life," friendship is the greatest good. But only wisdom is an imperishable good; friendship remains a perishable one (Fragments, 78). But when the sage "has enjoyed friendship to the fullest, he does not lament woefully the untimely demise of a dead friend" (N215).

Only friendship gives us a happy life. "Friendship dances a round around the world, calling to us to wake up and praise the happy life" (Fragments, 52). If his words have come down to us in authentic form, Epicurus speaks about friendship in hymnic terms that are otherwise alien to him.

---

[6] References preceded by Us are to Hermann Usener.

C. Dealing with the realities of human society

State, religion, wealth and poverty are realities within which man on earth has been placed. For the philosopher they present the danger of disturbing his tranquillity. He cannot altogether withdraw, but must seek a way of reacting that makes him immune to them. Epicurus presupposes that only a tiny number of people are capable of philosophy. He does not mean that human beings and their institutions should be made philosophical. Rather, he ponders how, in this unalterable world, those few could actually be philosophers.

1) *The State*. Epicurus' advice is to stay away from politics. "The wise man will not participate in politics and will not want to be a ruler" (N199). "Whoever is wise does not pursue politics" (N208).

His further advice is: Stay clear of the many! Limit your contact with them to a minimum in order to be safe from them! "I never strove for the approbation of the many; for I did not learn what pleases them; but what I do know is far removed from their understanding" (N210). "Especially if you must live among the many, you must withdraw into yourself" (N210).

It might be thought that, according to Epicurus, the philosopher would have to strive for security in order to actualize his life in the world. The means of acquiring security in the world are power and prosperity. But this conception confuses two kinds of security.

To be sure, it is correct that power and wealth provide a certain security of existence, but it is paid for by a state of unrest in the gaining and maintaining of it; hence it is coupled with constant insecurity. Epicurus, however, has an entirely different security in mind, namely, the tranquillity central to his attitude toward life. This he is most likely to achieve under conditions of remoteness from the many and from the state.

Outward security of existence, not possible as such but even when achieved to a high degree, would not obviate the terrible insecurity that arises from the false representations of things above and below the earth, of the world and of gods. The philosopher desires the security of inner tranquillity. This is within his reach. He is responsible only to himself. Whether he is recognized by the world is no concern of his.

The material security of existence, which Epicurus by no means disdains even though he has no need for it, has nothing in common with the philosophical tranquillity of soul. But both are promoted if this advice is followed: "One must liberate oneself from the prison of daily routine and affairs of state" (N218; Fragments, 58). "Live in seclusion" (*lathe biosas*) (Us551).

Yet Epicurus wants to comprehend that which he does not want to participate in. As he comprehends nature, so also the state. Once he knows what they are, he can live out his life within them in tranquillity, no matter what happens. Hence his *theory of the state*: Whence the state and laws? What do they mean?

a) State and law are not established by nature. There is no natural community built on mutuality. To pretend otherwise is deception. All men, by nature, want to prevail with their desires and their will to power.

b) Instead, state and law arise out of a purpose by means of a contract and rest on regulation. There is no justice by nature. Laws are based "only on a contract" (N213). "For all those living beings who have not been able to enter into a contract providing that they will neither harm one another nor allow themselves to be harmed, there is no justice or injustice; the same applies to all nations that cannot or do not want to enter into a contract regarding this matter" (N213).

c) The laws are subject to change. What they have in common is their utility, what is special about them is how this utility is achieved in accordance with a particular time and place. "Under the aspect of universality, what is just is the same for all; for it is, in some way, advantageous to mutual association. Under the aspect of particularity, however, such as of a country and all other presuppositions, it does not follow that what is just is the same for all" (N214).

New conditions supervene. What was just by law because it was of benefit to the needs of mutual association is no longer just when this utility undergoes a change. For those "who do not let themselves be confused by empty words but look at practical matters" (N214), whatever, for a period in time, was in harmony with the concept of justice is so no longer.

d) Why does the individual obey the laws? According to Epicurus, not for reasons of inner conscience, or respect for the state, or awe before the gods. It is for fear of discovery. If there were no control of illegal activity "through the disciplinarians appointed for such cases," everyone would do what he wants. But since he never knows whether his illegal activity will remain hidden, he fears discovery. "Fear of the future prevents him from enjoying the present and feeling confident about it" (N209).

e) For Epicurus, state and law have a different purpose. The philosopher does not violate the laws, since all his actions are rational. "In regard to the sages, the purpose of the laws is not to restrain them from committing an injustice, but to prevent injustice being done to them" (N209). In his apolitical life, the philosopher acknowledges the requirements for operating a state; but, for him, the state's ultimate purpose is to secure the philosophers' right to live and think in freedom.

2) *Religion.* Epicurus says: "The sage will venerate the gods" (N199). By this he means the contemplation of the blessed figures who, between and beyond the worlds, lead their lives of immortality, oblivious of any of the worlds. The gods are nothing other than the self-sufficing condition of unalloyed pleasure. This condition the sage wants to achieve for himself. In the gods, he contemplates his own goal. Thus Epicurus promises to him who thinks, practices, and testifies to his philosophy: "Nothing, whether in your sleeping or waking state, shall be able to disturb you; rather, you shall live like a god among men. For the man who lives among imperishable goods is not like a mortal being" (N181; Letter to Menoikeus).

Such a view, however, is not to be mistaken for a religious one. No Epicurean religion exists. He has no wish whatsoever for ritual and prayer, for mysteries, for a religious-priestly community. He does not desire a community that is contingent on a god, but one that is philosophical and self-sufficient.

He combats state and national religion only in conjunction with his followers, whom he wants to liberate from the fears engendered by all deceptive religious representations. The actual religion of the people, he leaves untouched. Since he must live in the world as it is, he has to adapt himself outwardly, for the sake of peace. Epicurus does not take up cudgels other than in a combat of minds in the interest of his friends. Security and tranquillity in a withdrawn life is all he asks for. Hence he can participate in public rites without unease.

3) *Wealth and poverty.* Society allows for great disparities in property and wealth. These do not concern the philosopher. For, Epicurus says, the happy condition of man puts all that is truly necessary within easy reach, while making it difficult to obtain the superfluous. The wealth required for our natural needs is limited; that demanded for idle whims is limitless.

The philosopher should keep as remote from money-making as from politics: "When living a free life, one cannot acquire many possessions, since this cannot be done easily without subservience to the vulgar masses or the powerful. . . ." However, Epicurus in no way disdains riches: "But should one happen to accrue riches, it is easy to use them for the benefit of one's neighbors" (N219; Fragments, 67).

Epicurus likes to indulge in wordplay with the double meaning of "riches": riches in material goods and inner riches. "With animal-like bustle one accumulates a heap of riches while life remains poor"; "Self-sufficiency is the greatest of riches" (N207). "Happiness and beatitude are not obtained by means of heaping up money, by mighty influence, by offices and power, but solely by freedom from harm, by assuaging the passions, and by a mood of the soul that is mindful of the limits of the natural aims of life" (N209).

"Whoever does not consider what is his own as the greatest of riches would be unhappy even if he were lord of the world" (N207). "Nothing is enough for the one to whom enough is too little" (N219; Fragments, 68).

"It is better to repose with equanimity on straw than to lose one's peace sitting on golden cushions at a richly laden table" (N210). "There is something pious about cheerful poverty" (N207).

6. THE SAGE AS IDEAL; EPICURUS AS IDEAL

The philosopher who has become godlike represents the ideal. This ideal is attainable to man. Perfected wisdom is reached through practice. The following are the hallmarks of the sage:

First, unshakable certitude: "Only the wise man can maintain an unshakable certitude" (N211); second, the impossibility of his backsliding: "Whoever has become wise cannot lapse into the opposite mood of soul and cannot deliberately imagine it" (ibid.); third, freedom from anger and favor in his life with others: "The blessed and immortal nature knows no trouble itself nor causes it in others, so that it is never constrained by anger or favor. For all such things exist only in the weak" (B95); fourth, his life in the world: "We must laugh and philosophize at the same time, keep house and exercise our other faculties and never cease to give voice to the right philosophy" (N217; Fragments, 41).

Does such a sage exist? All Epicureans have recognized him in Epicurus himself. He was the realization and the ideal. The gods are distant, unapproachable beings, but Epicurus, the wise one in this world, is a palpable actuality. When gods do not care about us and we have no access to them, man alone remains.

Epicurus himself pointed this way: "We should choose an able man and keep him before us so that we live, as it were, within his vision and act as though he saw everything" (N210). "The admiration of the wise is of great benefit to the admirer" (N216; Fragments, 32).

By these precepts his followers are led to regard Epicurus as the uniquely accomplished sage and ideal, something that he himself seems to be hinting at:

Some, he says, have found their road to wisdom without anyone's assistance. They have paved their own way. For these he has the greatest praise. In this sense he referred to himself from the very outset as self-taught. Others, he says, need outside help. He seems to imply that we lack the strength to rise unaided from the depth of misery; someone has to reach out and pull us up. In speaking of such successors, Epicurus mentions Metrodorus: these are praiseworthy men. "Do not despise the man who can be saved only through the aid of others; merely to wish to be saved is in itself meritorious" (Us192). Another kind of person needs to be forced and urged in the direction of right, for example, Hermarchos. He merits greater recognition (while Metrodorus is, rather, to be congratulated). "Both attained the same goal. However, it counts more when one has had to master more recalcitrant material" (ibid.).

7. CRITICAL CHARACTERIZATION OF EPICUREAN THOUGHT AND LIFE

Philosophical critique can readily show the deception inherent in the claim of Epicurus' philosophy that it possesses the characteristics of a science. However, this is not really relevant. What matters today is to expose the content of the Epicurean life in its inadequacy, and to do so not by reasoning that appeals to our intellect but by questions addressed to our will.

A. The poverty of content

1. *Against the premise that pleasure is the highest good and the only goal:* What makes life worth living? Epicurus answers: Nothing other than this life itself. What is this life which is worth living? Epicurus: It is pure pleasure in existence. But is life not fulfilled by something more than life, by something that takes meaning from our willingness to sacrifice our very life for it? To this, Epicurus answers: These are fictions from which we must liberate ourselves so as to obtain the imperturbable tranquillity of the pure pleasure of existence.

To be sure, only that which is present in our existence becomes real for us. Life is diminished if it is considered as something completely divorced from its presence. We must not lose ourselves in the past or the future, must not adopt a life based on fictitious imaginings if our life is to be actual and true.

But is such presentness pure pleasure? What is decisive, pleasure as such or that which gives this pleasure? Is not pleasure so abstract a concept that in its generality it signifies no more than simply a "yes," whereas what matters is what we say "yes" to?

Epicurus answers: Pleasure is peace of mind, absence of pain, *ataraxia*—but devoid of content. Instead of saying "yes" to what is historically concrete, Epicurus holds to a vague notion of pure pleasure which is supposed to be happiness. Do I want to live in such a way that I make pleasure the ultimate goal of my efforts? Or is not "pure pleasure" much too little and, moreover, impossible?

2. *Against* ataraxia *as the meaning of life:* The tranquillity of pure pleasure allows all that to wither which normally is part and parcel of human life. Epicurus is not prepared to expose himself to calamity, to pain, to upheaval. He wants to deny their ineluctability. Though their causes are embedded in the natural course of things, they themselves are not inescapable. Epicurus refuses to accept them for himself; rather, by distancing himself, he endeavors to shut them out. Instead of entrusting himself to upheaval, he wants to escape it and thus avoid the experience of crisis, of limit situations, of shipwreck. He thinks them away. He refuses the experience that "suffering is the quickest way to truth," a thought that informs Greek tragedy as well as Christian mysticism. He has no inkling that man's greatness may lie precisely in the degree to which he rises to meet calamity rather than letting it overwhelm him in unawareness.

Independence, for him, means to remain untouched by what is terrifying. He is unaware of another independence, which, precisely because we do not hold back, makes us experience the possibility of our being given to ourselves as a gift. There is something heartless in Epicurus' imperturbability, as also, though in a different way, in that of the Stoics and Skeptics. Even friendship, for him, is conceived as a tranquil state; he forgets that friendship is a constantly active bond between human beings, who mature in loving struggle, enhancing in the process their capacity for true amity.

Epicurus does not want to assume risk. He teaches the peace of mind reached by detachment and not that peace based on being sheltered in the Encompassing by way of loving immersion in the world.

3. *Against seceding from the world:* Distancing oneself from all that is worldly is the precondition of *ataraxia*. Do not get involved with the real world, with affairs of state, or the amassing of wealth, but live apart

from all this—this is Epicurus' counsel. He circumvents existence in the world by merely watching it; observation, for him, equals comprehension. He keeps it at a distance. Life is reduced to peace of mind without content and to the private sphere, to a state of pure pleasure without any other goal, without task and without ties.

Epicurus' garden, in which he lives in harmony with his friends, like a large family spread over the world in unvarying configurations, cut off and independent of the surrounding world, conveys to many troubled people the enchanting picture of what had, to a considerable degree, actually existed.

4. *Against the lack of responsibility:* Living in the garden and looking at the infinite possibilities of innumerable worlds causes a person to miss the world itself. He forgets that man realizes himself only by participating in the world, by contributing to the development of this world of his, and on which, as the world shared by all, Epicurean existence is in fact also dependent. Epicurus keeps us from entering into the roles offered by the tasks of the world, into the reality of the state, and into shared history. He does not wish to experience its fate as a participant.

Cicero expresses this criticism in his search for the philosophy most fitting for the man active in practical affairs and for the statesman. Epicurus' philosophy he names the least appropriate for someone guiding the state. "Nevertheless no wrong will be done to that philosophy by us, for we shall not be debarring it from a position that it aspires to occupy, but it will be reposing where it wishes to be, in its own charming gardens . . . it appeals to us to abandon the platform and the courts and the parliament—perhaps a wise invitation, particularly in the present state of public affairs. . . . Consequently let us dismiss the Masters in question, without any derogatory comments as they are excellent fellows and happy in their belief in their own happiness" (*Oratore*, III.17).[7] After this skeptically friendly acknowledgment, however, Cicero continues: We merely want to warn them "to keep to themselves as a holy secret, though it may be extremely true, their doctrine that it is not the business of the wise man to take part in politics—for if they convince us and all our best men of the truth of this, they themselves will not be able to live the life of leisure which is their ideal" (ibid.). In other words: Being an Epicurean is possible only as long as the sociological conditions allow for such a garden existence, which, after all, together with the garden, always remains an existence within the world. The Epicurean owes the possibility of his existence to the regulation of the state, which is served

[7] Tr. H. Rackham. Cambridge, MA, Harvard University Press; London, William Heinemann, 1960.

by statesmen. Epicureans are not guilty per se, but bear the burden of their nonparticipation, since, in the event of political or economic catastrophe, their own existence is also affected and destroyed. Political action against Epicureanism is not necessary, because Epicureans neither strive for nor possess political power in the world but live in obscurity. They should be left in peace.

5. *Against peace of mind as reached by the idea of annihilation in death:* When Epicurus brushes off death as something that does not concern us, it cannot be interpreted as a means to comfort us. According to his philosophy, such comforting is not at all necessary. Epicurus does not take death seriously. There is no need to be deeply affected by death, be it the death of a friend or the thought of our own death.

Much of what Epicurus has to say about death is correct. But he eschews an essential element, namely, the fact that man living in his temporality is made desolate by the prospect of dying. Epicurus lacks any vision that goes beyond death, ignoring what he might have found in Socratic thought, and what, with insight into the phenomenality of space and time, had been thought in every age through the ciphers of immortality. Epicurus recognizes embodied representations of death as fictions, and rightly so. But his negations lead to banalities whose correctness has to be acknowledged, of course, but which, in the way he establishes them, do away with the point of departure for any transcending experience.

6. *Against the presupposition that true knowledge brings happiness:* For Epicurus, knowledge of the truth is the means to tranquillity because such knowledge eradicates fear and is itself the tranquillity of contemplating that which is. However, this presupposition of his does not have truth as its aim, but, rather, a posited truth asserted dogmatically, suggestive by virtue of an unexamined plausibility, and confirmed by means of rules. This *"theoria"* as calming contemplation is not cognition in the sense of scientific inquiry, but, in the garb of proofs, basically an unquestioning acceptance in the manner of faith.

The presupposition "knowledge is happiness" stands in contradiction to the proposition "He who increases knowledge increases pain." Hence the erroneous presupposition has to be changed into the by no means Epicurean decision: I do not want any happiness without truth.

Epicurus makes it the goal of science to do away with unease. This we could accept as correct only in the sense that knowledge of what presently is and what is potentially threatening does away with the unease of not knowing, and thus forces us to experience and to accept what is most terrifying as something we know. But Epicurus sees this quite differently. His thinking extinguishes the authentic will to truth in favor of a dogmatic knowledge that does not stand up to criticism. If, as in Epicurus, it is the goal of science to recognize that there is no reason for fear, then such a goal blocks the path of the desire to know. The primal desire to know constitutes a risk; it is the great risk taken by man and ever will be so. No one knows where it will lead.

7. *Against the substitution of the world of atoms for transcendence:* In place of transcendence Epicurus has put nothing but the play of atoms and the void. There is greatness in this total relinquishing of transcendence, in this sobriety—even though it is false because it is itself ensnared in fictions, neglecting the substance realized through the reality of human Existenz. Epicurus' greatness, however, consists in his complete renunciation of everything that goes beyond presentness. Thus he rejects the ciphers of many Greek philosophers; for example, the eternal periodic recurrence of the same, or the transmigration of souls. As the ultimate horizon he conceives only the endlessness of space and time, of the coming to be and the passing away of a boundless number of worlds, simultaneously and successively. This horizon lacks any feature of pantheistic animation. He surveys it without awe. There is no trace of cosmic enthusiasm. This universe of worlds is merely empty endlessness, held together by neither sense nor goal, only by the indestructibility of the innumerable atoms, their accidental and meaningless motions and realignments.

B. On a principle of Epicurean thought: explication of the higher out of the lower

Against the way of explaining the higher out of the lower, Cassius writes to Cicero (*Ep.*, XV.19): "It is difficult to persuade men that one has to strive for the beautiful for its own sake"; but it is evident to them that pleasure and imperturbability are the fruits of virtue, justice, and the beautiful. According to Cassius, Epicurus teaches that there is no pleasure without a beautiful and just life. Hence those who love pleasure are indeed lovers of beauty and justice. In its result, says Cassius, the life of the Epicureans is as noble as, for example, that of the Stoics. Yet their argument is paradoxical: The higher is explained as proceeding from the lower. In fact, this paradox pervades all of Epicurus' thought.

Some examples:

All things come to be out of the atoms and the void, but then become the magnificent configurations of the world, of living beings, of the soul, of reason, of the gods. Cognition comes to be a requisite for our happiness, but since it leads to tranquil contentment in the contemplation of the true (in *theoria*), it then is happiness itself. It is the purpose of morality to guide the appetites—which as such are to be affirmed—in a manner that leads to a maximum of pleasure; but then it is the nobility of demeanor which as such brings happiness. Friendship arises from a utilitarian motive, since it contributes to the security of our existence; but then it is in itself such great happiness that it justifies all kinds of sacrifices made for its sake. Religion grows out of the fear of all that is incommensurable and unpredictable; but then again the pure representation of the gods provides happiness. Happiness itself (*eudaemonia*) grows out of pleasure (*hedone*) and is then more than pleasure, namely, tranquillity, imperturbability, self-sufficiency, freedom (*eleutheria*). The development of civilization makes it possible for us to build, from necessity and utility, what protects and facilitates our existence and endures beyond necessity as a world of happiness within that civilization.

These inferences are informed by a power of persuasion that produces a realistic effect and repudiates all that is fictitious. Almost always there is in them an element of rightness; they display presuppositions whereby the higher actualizes itself out of its own lower source. Physical, physiological, psychological explications draw from realities that are conditions without which the higher cannot realize itself. But "condition" is not the same as "origin." Mistaking the one for the other is a fundamental error of Epicurean thought.

Occasionally the aggressive provocation in the Epicurean buildup of the human out of the nonhuman, the good out of the bad, the lofty out of the vulgar makes itself felt. But each time there is a leap: Something that has been explained as being the lower persists on its own as the higher. To be sure, the shadow of its origin in the trite and crude, in the mechanical and instinctual falls on everything that exists. But then the higher maintains its independent validity, though lacking an appropriate foundation.

Where do the reason and wisdom of the philosopher originate? Where the blissful gods? No answer is given unless we assume the .following to be it: The gods came into being through the accidental constellation of the most refined atoms, and independent reason owes its existence to the same accident.

True, the shadow cast by the origin of everything higher out of the lower seems eliminated in the actual practice of philosophy and in the course of a noble life. Now the higher seems to endure by itself. But its origin remains effective in an altered form: in the absence of transparency in all Epicurean experiences. The practical life stripped of transcendence is at the same time impressively powerful and yet paltry: the mere pleasure in an existence that is reduced as much as possible and without illusions (except the illusion that tranquillity and the absence of pain are possible), without the historical continuity of a life filled with content. Such a life is reduced to an existence between the void that was and the void that will be; it is the instant of pure pleasure.

8. HISTORICAL POSITION AND INFLUENCE OF EPICURUS

A. Ramifications of Epicurean thought in later times

Some features were taken out of context, robbed of their original sense, and thereby estranged from Epicurus, but count as "Epicureanism."

Physical pleasure becomes the main issue. A life of excess grounds itself in Epicurus, counter to his explicit teaching and life.

Abstaining from politics and advocation of the reclusive life that avoids the many are turned into the comfort of the philistine, who, in his private pleasures, yields to passivity.

Liberation from fear of the gods is turned into hostility toward religion, now practiced with a joyous aggressiveness that in this form is alien to Epicurus.

The pleasure of *theoria* is broadened to include the pleasure of spiritual life as it is found in the study of beautiful forms in poetry, literature, and art. Epicurus himself had no interest in this. But such broadening of his *theoria*, the basis for evaluating Epicurus—as was done by one faction within humanism since the Renaissance—was incompatible with his cast of mind. Nothing could be more alien to Epicurus, with his gravity of mind that informed every emotion, than the noncommittal character, the lack of consequences implicit in a spiritual world devoted uniquely to self-cultivation.

The ambiguous development of Epicurean philosophy began early. Epicurus was a contemporary and possibly a friend of the poet Menander. There exists an epigram by the latter (referring to the name of the fathers of Themistocles and Epicurus, both of whom were called Neocles):

> Hail to you Neoclides, worthy both. One freed
> His land from bondage, the other from folly.

Menander wrote: "I am a human being and I believe that nothing human is alien to me" (transmitted through Terence, *The Self-Tormentor*, I, 1, l. 25). Epicurus was regarded as one of the founders of "humanism."

Not Epicurus, but the Epicureans, such as Horace, embraced—as joyful living—literature, poetry, the aesthetic existence. Via that source many people of more recent times found their spiritual life in harmony with the Epicurean and renewed it in accordance with the Epicurean model. The high estimation of Epicurus proceeds from Lorenzo Valla by way of Montaigne to a few modern humanist philologists.

It is just as great an error to ground humanism in Epicurus as it is to believe him to be the founder of modern natural sciences. The rigor, clarity, and unconditional consistency of Epicurus bear witness to an existential energy that cannot be associated with aesthetic humanism. Montaigne, the great skeptic spirit, derives his mental energy from an entirely different source. The Epicurean element is frequently and mistakenly interpreted as a supplementary contribution of "worldly wisdom" to the humanist mode of thought.

Epicurus is strict, not lax; serious, not playful. His teaching is binding for all of practical life and is not spiritual enjoyment.

A distinction has to be made between unconditional, hence true, Existenz, which illuminates itself in Epicurean thinking, and the conditional, hence untrue Epicureanism of an aesthetic way of life. In Epicurus we see one of the powerful figures of Greek Existenz. Gravity prevails. Man is identical with what he says and does. Whether or not one follows Epicurus, on this one point he has undoubted validity: To live with such strength in existential congruence, that is, independent of content, becomes a negative yardstick for all that is yielding, halfhearted, mired in possibilities, changeable and tentative; that is, for the aesthetic life that negates man existentially.

B. Unanimous hostility toward Epicureanism

Almost all other philosophies as well as Christianity are united in single-minded indignant rejection of Epicureanism. This isolation, already beginning with the Platonists, Stoics, Aristotelians, and early Christian thought, sets it apart from all other philosophies. True, these others are in violent conflict among themselves and given to polemical excesses. But here one is faced with a unanimity of defamation. Obviously, spiritual forces that come from the core of being are unleashed. The enmity, we sense, is deadly.

Seneca, moderate by comparison, says: "I do not speak of that philosophy which alienates the citizen from his fatherland, does not allow the gods to concern themselves with the world, and barters virtue for pleasure . . ." (Letter 90 to Lucilius).

Diogenes Laertius, in his life of Epicurus, recounts the calumnies against him: erotic excesses, unbridled eating and drinking (he had to vomit twice a day), his lack of education and his ignorance. He is called a pornographer. "But these calumnies are mad," Diogenes concludes (X, 8), and goes on to describe the real man above reproach.

There are other exceptions. One is the affectionately respectful and objective criticism of Cicero. In more recent centuries the inaccuracy and injustice of the traditional evaluation of Epicurus have often been recognized. For example, Bodin, in his *Heptaplomeres*, has a participant in the dialogue say: "I have encountered many despisers of the gods, also many who could be distinguished from wild animals only through their shape; but I have not met an Epicurean, that is, a man who, without hope of reward, piously venerated the gods, lived very simply and abstemiously, who, like Epicurus, practiced continence, justice, loyalty, and integrity in his morals, though he believed the souls to be mortal; nor does he believe that there are laws imposed by the immortal God. In short, someone who posits the highest and ultimate good of man not in bodily lusts but in the serene tranquillity of a superior soul" (Book 1, 7).

C. Epicurus' polemics

It is interesting that the tranquillity of soul advocated by Epicurus and the Epicureans does not exclude extremely fierce polemics. This fierceness has to be understood as arising from the threat posed to tranquillity of soul itself, which casts a shadow over it. The polemic turns against religion, which, through its fictions, creates empty fear, and almost as fiercely against the Skeptics, who challenged the ground of this tranquillity of soul, namely, unassailable cognition impervious to doubt.

Ataraxia, the extinction of affects and passions, the tranquillity of soul of the individual, is the goal common to Epicureans, Skeptics, and Stoics. But Epicurus opposes the skeptical philosophy of man's essential ignorance and of accepting what seems to be given.

Seen here are the polemics of a philosophic faith that has firmly settled within the edifice of its dogma. This faith draws its life and its strength from an alleged absolute knowledge of the one and only truth. Hence it must defend its precious possession, this salutary knowledge, with such fierceness. Here it becomes evident that we are not dealing at all with a matter of scientific cognition based on cogent certainty and presenting itself calmly, conscious of its significance and its limits. Instead, it is faith in rational form, which, in its self-assertion, rejects Skepticism

and declares the altogether different, self-possessed tranquillity of the
Skeptic to be impossible.

Epicurus explains: Whoever believes that one does not know, after
all, does not know this either; he forgoes "starting a quarrel with such
sophists." The senses cannot be contradicted. To shake this foundation
of our trust destroys "the basic foundations of our life and salvation."
Not only every system, but life itself would break down. "If all cognition
is annulled, then every norm of the practical conduct of life is annulled
likewise" (N243, 183).

The Skeptic surrenders all ground of knowledge and yet places his
"faith" in the tranquillity of soul. This faith is supported by ignorance.
Epicurus' thinking has the strange form of total religious unbelief. De-
fying all criticism, it firmly adheres to the base of his absolute knowledge,
a knowledge of dogmatic faith that allows Being to sink to the level of
atoms of matter and mechanical occurrences.

Among Skeptics and Epicureans we notice an absence of philosophical wonder as well as of an original desire to know and an experience
of mystery and a substantive ethos. They remain static because they are
deaf to the meaning in the questions addressed to them. They seem
unconcerned, with an indifference linked to a paucity of feeling. They
let things go by, standing still themselves, neither alive nor creative.

But they can be a corrective—against illusions, by pointing out the
inevitable. They can offer a refuge in times when we fail to be wholly
ourselves, when the heart gets tired, when, as it were, we may be permitted to withdraw for the moment, always provided that the remembrance of what now is silent and absent does not disappear altogether.

Epicureanism turns against any other substantive philosophy. Only
atomism is true. One main opponent is Stoicism, whose philosophy—a
pantheistic faith informed by reason-nature—vainly promises tranquillity of soul. Whatever enters the field claiming to be philosophy is
critically dissected, despised, ridiculed. Epicurus alone, and exclusively,
possesses the truth. All the others are in error and in misery.

D. Unbelief and belief

Within the "unbelief" of Epicurean philosophy is found the "belief" in
salvation through pleasure in immediately sensuous presence; in other
words, the belief in unbelieving presentness of existence. Insofar as it is
confined to the immediacy of presence devoid of transparency, it is not
a faith. It is faith, however, as the power of a knowledge that, as knowledge, is not tenable.

This faith in the form of a knowledge knows an absolute, eternal Being active behind appearances: the world of atoms, their eternal, accidental, and necessary movements and configurations. Of course, we cannot declare a false knowledge as such to be a faith, but it can be so labeled with regard to the motive that causes this knowledge to be considered true. This motive is the need for something firm, the will to fix it in formulated doctrine. In Epicurean knowledge it works in analogy to revealed faith, which in theology clothes itself in intricate systematic formulation. Both erect dogmas that match their confessions.

Considered from the standpoint of empirical, critical knowledge, such knowledge is called "mere" belief. It is, however, "more than knowledge" because of the force with which it is held. In Epicurean unbelief it is the strength of the belief in the world of atoms, gratifyingly thought to be the ground of all givenness in nature.

This knowledge of Epicurus in no way corresponds to the great enlightenment that is man's portion and to his task to liberate himself "from his self-incurred tutelage," as Kant put it. This enlightenment, never completed but always in movement, proceeds by way of the sciences, in constant self-criticism, and destroys illusions; at the limits of such knowledge it experiences every mode of the presence of Being. Epicurus' sobriety is not that of philosophy, which needs and promotes the sciences as indispensable, and never contravenes scientifically founded knowledge; but it goes beyond them because of an origin out of which it first arrived at the sciences. Epicurus' thinking is, rather, a mode of false enlightenment, a believing knowledge alien to science that should be called science-superstition instead.

E. The type of a-religious philosophy

The a-religious faith of the Epicureans, limited to the individual and his friends, ignores the organized formation of community or Church or monastic orders; but it does create an analog to communities and churches within the circle of friends who revere Epicurus as the godlike savior and preserve unchanged the one and only truth as taught by him.

Comparison allows us to discern the type and significance of a-religious philosophy in other configurations. In the extremely effective Indian Samkhya philosophy is found: unpreparedness for the world and for action (life in concealment), disinclination for risk, experiment, adventure, for building in the world, and thus renunciation of all participation and responsibility and duty in the world; lack of transcendence; the Existenz of tranquillity before the void, coupled with consciousness of the pleasures of existence; the ethos of lovelessness outside the friend-ship of those of like mind and persuasion; the basic error of achieving knowledge through unscientific science.

Buddha's original thinking had this character at the outset (disre-garding all later development of Buddhism): redemption in the inde-pendent individual, indifference toward the world, association in monastic orders which, in harmony with their purpose, live apart from the world without task in the world, "atheism."

In spite of all their differences (Epicurus' pure pleasure against Bud-dha's Nirvana experience), particularly in their historical influence (in the remoteness from life—in Epicurus, within the circles of friends; in Buddha, within the monastic orders), one basic possibility for man can be seen: separation from the world. It is possible to live in this manner, but it is done mostly in a vague sort of way, without consistency, and always under the condition that existence be sustained either through property, no matter how small, or by begging.

In all instances, veneration to the point of idolizing an individual forms the core of the cohesiveness: Epicurus, Kapila, Buddha. Belief in the discoverers of unbelief is regarded as the most certain, most blessed, most human form of life.

We are not dealing here with a specific psychological-physiological constitution, or with a basic mood of temperament or character. Instead, what is conveyed to us is a type of meaning that develops from a deceptively personal atmosphere, since it is the single person that matters. Whether in optimistic or pessimistic mood, this way of thinking dem-onstrates an impersonal serenity that goes beyond psychological predis-position. It is achieved through thinking and practice in continuous effort.

F. Have we joined the anti-Epicurean front?

Are we now, too, with our critical remarks, part of the almost universal battle line drawn up against Epicurus by the history of philosophy? It would seem so, since we consider Epicurus' scientific knowledge to be only allegedly scientific; indeed, completely contrary to science. Also, it might appear as though we were saying that Epicurus' life of detached equanimity necessarily neglected all that gives human life substantive content. The tranquillity of pure joy brings with it a withering of the humanity of human beings. Epicurus refuses to accept the part of pain that reveals depth. He refuses to take the risk implicit in the historic immersion of Existenz. Instead of a richly fulfilled Existenz, we are left with the barrenness of a life of pleasure and tranquillity. By refusing to follow his road, to choose him as guide for our life, we appear to oppose him altogether.

But there are limits imposed on naysaying. The objection of a lack of clarity on matters of science applies, in some sense, to almost all philosophies; it has been only two centuries since insight, based on mental discipline, began to draw a line between science and other disciplines. The accusation of paucity of content is mitigated when we contemplate, in all its grandeur, this thought and practice, how consequentially it was carried out, its radicality, its harmony with itself. Epicurus will be a guidepost forever. Even if he is rejected as a permanent guide, there are moments in life when his philosophy can serve us as a refuge in times of weariness, as a respite in our weakness, as a transitory means to keep us going (as does, at other times, Stoic philosophy). This also always implies a shortcoming, the nature of which is brought home to us through Epicurus in all the seductive power of his reasoning and its consequences. Counter to his intention, Epicurus can help us by increasing our strength in the battle against the very tendencies whose nature he illuminated on the highest level. We enter the garden of Epicurus in order, overcoming ourselves, to abandon it once again.

Gnostic Dreamers

BOEHME

SCHELLING

INTRODUCTION

Gnosis is the name of a certain historical phenomenon arising in the centuries that surround the beginning of the Christian era. It manifested itself first outside Christianity, but then also achieved prominence within it.

But gnosis is equally the term for a way of thinking that transcends all ages, though it found its most prevalent and conspicuous expression at that period. It is, however, an objective type, an attitude on the part of the human spirit, manifestly innate from the beginning of all civilizations until today.

Gnosis makes known what really is, from where and how it has come to be, what can and will come to be, and which path is the path of salvation for us. We receive answers to the questions we pose to our existence: from where? to where? what for? why? In particular, the individual, his soul, derives guilt and what appears to be guilt, position, and task from this embracing whole.

Like every metaphysics, gnosis makes the supersensible turn into a determinate objectivity. Its hallmark, however, is that this is done not only conceptually but also by intuition turning into thought. The supersensible becomes temporal, spatial, and corporeal. Hence gnosis is differentiated from the speculative approach to transcendence, carried out in concepts, in a thinking that goes beyond and founders logically. For gnosis postulates supersensible worlds, regions, spheres, times; hence there is a supersensible history with events and actions on the part of personal beings, their apostasy and their liberation. What we are and what the present world of men is—this has its origin, place, and future within the framework of supersensible history.

The gnostic manner of thinking is characterized by an extraordinary wealth of imageries, apparitions, personages, happenings in the supersensible world. To be sure, all metaphysics needs ciphers and metaphors. Gnosis is distinguished by its reveling in these pictures, by the relish in endless invention and repetition. Gnostic life becomes a contemplative thinking of life in another world, from which the threads of what is immediately present are pulled.

Finally, the gnostic manner of thinking, as all philosophy, is characterized by the importance of thinking for Existenz. This unity of thinking and existing is termed "gnostic" when thinking comes to mean liberation and redemption, when thinking is initiation, is itself actuality. In gnosis this cognition has precedence of ethos, which is only the consequence of cognition. Gnosis means participation in authentic Being. This participation passes through the forms of *ecstasis*, of contemplative life, of seeing aesthetically and feeling intuitively. It may be so pervasive as to become the mainstay of life, or it may occur with no implied obligation, with virtually no consequences, as a mere way of experiencing.

What gnosis imparts has a dreamlike quality. For its imagination the inaccessible and supersensible realm assumes corporeality. This cannot be simply brushed off as nonsensical. Whatever has attained some reality within human history is never totally without truth. The meaning underlying gnosis must be clarified in the atmosphere of genuine science and critical philosophy. This meaning can be called a truth. Hence we call those philosophers who think intuitively in the form of embodiments "gnostic dreamers of truth."

Gnostic thought may be found in many other philosophies and in ordinary ways of thinking, but not as dominant as it is with them. Among the outstanding Western thinkers who effectively developed this thinking I have chosen Boehme and Schelling.

BOEHME

I. LIFE

Boehme was born in 1575 in Altseidenberg, Silesia, the son of a prosperous peasant. He learned the trade of a shoemaker, became a journeyman, and settled in 1594 as shoemaker in Goerlitz, married at the same time, and had six children.

What, through his immersion in the supersensory world, he spiritually saw and thought, he put down in a manuscript titled "Aurora," a copy of which, in 1612, reached the chief pastor of Goerlitz, who was outraged by its contents. Boehme was forbidden to write more by the pastor and the municipal council. For seven years he obeyed this injunction. But then he broke out; he wrote his numerous works in the brief span between 1619 and his death in 1624.

Up to 1612 he had practiced his craft successfully. After that it was interfered with by his persecution, and also neglected by him. Worries about his livelihood were allayed through the help of friends (mostly belonging to the nobility). In 1619 he still complained that he must, time and again, devote himself to his worldly affairs in order to "nourish the earthly body as well as wife and child" (VII, 377).[1]

In retrospect he wrote this about the injunction against writing and the persecution: I "had resolved, even after the persecutions [had ceased] not to produce anything further, but, obediently, to let God be quiet and let the devil, with his mockery, sweep over me. . . . But things turned out with me as when a seed is sown in the ground: it grows forth in all storms and foul weather, contrary to all reason . . . and returns with hundredfold fruit, moreover with still deeper and true knowledge and fiery force" (VII, 390). Of the chief pastor he said: "God made him into a mallet that must drive the machine. His blaspheming has been my strength and my growth" (VII, 319–20).

When, at the end of the year 1623, his friend Franckenberg printed

[1] Citations of Boehme's work are to *Jakob Boehme's Sämmtliche Werke*, ed. K. W. Schiebler. Leipzig, 1831–1847.

Boehme's shorter writings without the latter's knowledge, the storm broke out anew. Enjoined by the municipal council to leave the city temporarily, he spent a few months in Dresden, honored by friends and treated with regard by the Elector of Saxony. He died shortly after his return to Goerlitz.

His friend and biographer Franckenberg described his appearance: "His . . . external bodily form was one of physical decline and poor appearance, of small size, low forehead, elevated temples, somewhat curved nose, grey and almost sky-blue glittering eyes. . . . [He had] a short sparse beard, a weak voice, but he spoke in a sweet voice, was modest in his gestures, humble in his speech . . . patient in his suffering."

Spiritual origin: Boehme grew up in Lutheran-Christian piety, in consciousness of sin and redemption. He had not studied at the university, nor had he enjoyed a specialized theological education. But, as he himself said, he had read much, most likely the Bible above all, also medieval mystics as well as Paracelsus, Schwenkfeldt, Weigel.

Fundamental experience: Franckenberg tells of something that never appeared in his writings: how in 1600, at the age of twenty-five, Boehme was initiated into the innermost ground of nature through the sight of sunshine falling on a pewter vessel. Only when pure light meets with darkness does it become luminous. In that period of his life something extraordinary must indeed have been going on in Boehme. He wrote later: "In this my first so very serious searching and desiring . . . the gate had been opened to me so that I saw and knew more in a quarter of an hour than if I had been at places of higher learning for many years." And, further: "But something opened itself up in me from time to time: although I carried it within me for twelve years and was pregnant with it. . . ." After twelve years it overcame him "like a cloudburst: what it hits it hits" (VII, 400). He wrote it down. So it was "with the fiery urge, even though I did not intend at all that anyone should read it; I merely wrote down God's miracles for myself that had been shown to me . . ." (VII, 341). This was the origin of his first and, for a long time, only work: "The book Aurora or Sunrise was my childish beginning; hence I wrote down merely in the reflected light without reason, merely after beholding it in an almost magical way" (VII, 428). "To be sure, I saw into its innermost, as into a great depth, for I saw through it as into a chaos. . . ." Even afterward the sun "did shine for me for a considerable time . . . but not always steadily. When it hid itself, I hardly understood even my own work . . ." (VII, 400–01).

The content of the fundamental experience, symbolized by the brightness of the sun on the dark pewter vessel, is the unfathomable contrariety in all things. Boehme speaks of his melancholy. The latter, as well as the rapturous moods, surely overcame him often as simply given experiences. But he speaks of them as being grounded in meaning: "I have got into [a state of] sore melancholy . . . when I observed the great depth of this world, the sun and the stars and the clouds. . . . Thus I found there evil and good in all things, love and wrath in the irrational creatures as well as in wood, stone, earth . . . as well as in humans and in animals . . . that, in this world, the godless are just as well off as the pious and that the barbarian nations occupied the best-endowed countries. . . . For this reason I became melancholy. . . . The devil must have been overjoyed at that and often impressed on me heathen thoughts. But when, in such misery, my spirit . . . earnestly arose in God, to wrestle, as with a great storm, without letup, with the love and mercy of God . . . He shone brightly for me with his Holy Ghost so that I might understand his will and get rid of my sadness; then the spirit broke through. . . . But when I stormed so violently against God and all the gates of hell . . . my spirit soon broke through the gate of hell into the innermost birth of the godhead and was surrounded there with love. . . . But such a triumphing in the spirit . . . cannot be compared . . . with anything save with that where, in the midst of death, life is born. . . . In this light my spirit soon saw through everything and recognized God in all creatures, in herb and grass, who he is, how He is, and what is his will . . . thus years must have passed before the right reason was granted to me" (II, 212–13).

Boehme found God in the radical changes of his melancholic and euphoric moods. Out of these agitated states he read in the book of nature, recognized the *signatura rerum*, grasped the boundlessly terrible and the overwhelmingly magnificent.

The work. The work "Sunrise"—"Aurora"—stands by itself. All his other works were written in the brief space of his last six years, often in simultaneous production. Boehme believed that in his later writings he had achieved greater clarity than in "Sunrise." Although in Boehme periods of development hardly play a role (the expression "unground" [*Ungrund*] seems to have appeared first in the treatise "On the Incarnation of Christ"), a change becomes noticeable. What is considered greater clarity is also increasing schematization. The originality, the imaginative force of his language seems to wane. We might think here of an analogy to typically schizophrenic change. But we lack sufficient biographical material for such a diagnosis.

Though they deal with a variety of specific themes, all his many writings aim at the whole. This whole, however, is the vision in its modifications, and not a system. Boehme writes without discipline, without will or capability for form and structure, as if overflowing, losing himself, conceptually confused. For long stretches the reading is torturous. The gems are embedded in a jumble of texts. No one can doubt, however, the depth of his meaning, the force that uses and develops popular speech, unplanned and unaware, yet with impressive plasticity. No overview or mental discipline guides his pen. He is carried away. A good part of his writings remains unintelligible, especially if the reader is not sufficiently versed in the language and imagery of the nature-mystical tradition. He varies his manner of expression, his images, metaphors, schemata. The reader finds nourishment only where the original intuition is forcefully present and the basic dialectical operations are carried out in pictorial simplicity. These are high points from which the text quickly deteriorates again.

II. THE SCHEMA OF A SYSTEMATIC REPRODUCTION

To present in systematical form something that is not a system is misleading only in regard to the order and form imposed on it. In the case of Boehme, the substance is preserved in the summary given below, but beyond it, it exists also in endless variations and ramifications. Let us see how it can be presented succinctly, following Benz and Martensen.

What is God? Whence am I, whence the world? What has occurred that has made me the way I find myself now? Boehme answers this in three stages. He cognizes, first, God before creation; second, creation; third, the progress of the created world, the fall and salvation.

1. What is God before creation?

a) *The astonishing answer*: "The Nothing is God" (VII, 191), and "God has made all things out of the Nothing and is the self-same Nothing" (IV, 309).

But this Nothing is a strange Nothing. It is not Nothing altogether. What then? God Himself is "the seeing and feeling of the Nothing . . . and is called a Nothing (even though it is God himself) for the reason that it is incomprehensible and ineffable" (VI, 597).

This Nothing is touched by us in thinking when we think of God. God is the "unground." "The unground is an eternal Nothing" (VI, 413). There, within the eternity of the unground, there is nothing but stillness, an eternal quiet, no beginning and no end, no searching or finding, or anything that would be a possibility. The unground "is first and foremost a *magia*"[2] (VI, 245).

In the unground there is an eternal will. We recognize "that the eternal beginning in the unground is an eternal will in itself, whose primal state no creature is to know" (VI, 247). For "the Nothing is a desire for Something." The desire in the Nothing makes, "in itself, the will into something . . ." (VI, 413). "With the free joy of the Nothing [God] leads himself to desire; for in the Nothing there is an eternal will to revelation. . . . Will in free joy is named God" (VII, 191).

"The will in the unground is like an eye in which nature lies hidden; like a hidden fire that does not burn, that is there and also is not" (VI, 322). The eye "is a will . . . a yearning for revelation, in order to find the Nothing" (IV, 285). Its "seeing is in itself, for there is nothing before it that would be deeper" (VI, 332).

Unground, primal will, the unseeing eye, themselves nothing, yet they do not remain in the Nothing. They become manifest:

A "will is as flimsy as a Nothing, therefore it is desirous, it wants to be something so that it may be manifest in itself" (VI, 247).

However, the being "that, in the eternal unground, eternally emerges in itself and returns into itself . . . goes forth out of itself with what it comprises, manifests itself in the gleam of the eye" (VI, 333).

The eternal mind of the unground enters into ground and being, "as an eternal birthing and consuming . . . an eternal love-play, such that the unground wrestles and plays with the ground it has shaped, hence with itself. It gives itself to Something and again takes that Something into itself" (V, 22).

How does this happen? The Nothing itself "causes the will to be desirous." This desiring, however, "is an image where the will sees itself in the mirror of wisdom" (VI, 247).

The eye of God, the look into the depth, sees nothing as yet. That "is an eye of eternity, an unground-like eye, that stands or sees in Nothing" (IV, 284–85). This great tremendous eye in which all wonders, all shapes, colors, and figures lie hidden sees nothing in a vague, limitless infinity where it encounters no object.

The dark will for which nothing else exists wants to take possession of itself and its plenitude. That comes about through Sophia, wisdom, God's contemplativeness, the eternal idea which stands before God. By virtue of Sophia, the nonseeing look into the depth becomes the seeing

---

[2] "*Magia*" may be a neologism formulated by Boehme. The meaning suggested by Jaspers is that what "unground" refers to is not susceptible to conceptual thought, only to invocatory thought. —Editors' Note.

look. In the unground God would not be manifest to himself. "But his wisdom has become his ground in eternity" (VI, 251). Sophia is the virgin who in the dawn of eternity speaks before God, makes possible for him the revelation of himself before himself. She is called virgin because she does not give birth but merely receives the images and reflects them. She is selfless, without desire.

b) *Sophia* is—I list here only some of the images and concepts by means of which Boehme depicts her—the mirror of God. God sees himself in it as in a mirror. Through it, He is able to confront himself. Cognition first grows out of such a confrontation. Hence Sophia is called the image of God. In the image the incomprehensible becomes comprehensible. Sophia is called, further, the ob-ject [*der Gegenwurf*], the exhaled [*das Ausgehauchte*], the egressed [*das Ausgegangene*], the emanated [*das Ausgeflossene*], the found, the uttered (cf. Benz, 11ff.).

However, Sophia is not an abstraction. For Boehme, there is nothing spiritual without the corporeal, even if it is a suprasensory corporeality. Hence it is the corporeal form of the overarching will of God, the body of God, embodied configuration. It is "not a being which is conceivable as bodily . . . as we humans are, yet is essencelike and visual" (IV, 71).

Since it is the body of the whole triune God, it is also called the "house of the Holy Trinity" (VI, 340).

It is the garment in which God manifests himself to man. Without it his configuration would not be recognized. "For we human beings cannot, in all eternity, see more of the spirit of God than the splendor of his majesty" (IV, 71).

Through Sophia there becomes effective in God the principle of all revelation, of all becoming and life, the principle of opposites.

As the unity devoid of opposites, the unground is like the Nothing but is filled by an infinite plenitude and the urge to manifest itself. The will of the unground "is neither evil nor good but is merely a will, that is, a knowing without understanding for anything or in anything . . . and is neither desire nor joy; rather, it is surging or willing" (IV, 500–01).

But God is not the Nothing resulting from an absence of opposites; He is the unity of opposites. This is the *mysterium magnum* of Boehme. Duality in the unity, unity in the duality. God himself is the unity of opposites, is darkness and light, love and wrath, fire and light. Yea and nay are One Thing.

The sensing of its own self is the eye of eternal seeing, the eternal yea, the eternal unity. In the will it contracts into itself, is the eternal nay, the eternal ownness. The center of the yea is love, of the nay wrath (cf. Benz, 128–29).

In regard to oppositeness Sophia is the first principle of separability. This likeness "is the separator in the emanation of the will which makes the will of the eternal One separable: it is the separability in the will out of which forces and properties come to be." Hence "arises the multiplicity of the wills, and out of it also came to be the creaturely life of the eternal ones such as angels and souls" (VI, 469).

The will of the eternal One is without feeling, without bent toward anything; for it has nothing toward which it could incline except in itself (VI, 469–70). "Desire is the ground and beginning of the nature of sensitivity of one's own will . . . out of it the separabilities of the wills are brought to the sensitivity of a selfsameness" (VI, 469).

In summarizing his thoughts, Boehme expresses time and again what God is; for example: God "is the One vis-à-vis the creature, as an eternal Nothing; he has neither ground, beginning nor abode; and possesses nothing save himself; he is the will of the Unground, is in himself only One; he needs neither space nor place: from eternity in eternity he gives birth to himself in himself: he is like or similar to no thing, and has no special place where he abides: eternal wisdom . . . is his abode: he is the will of wisdom, wisdom is his revelation" (V, 7).

The reflection in Sophia allows the groundless will of God to find and grasp itself, but only as in an early-morning dream of eternity. It shows him the wealth of possible splendors but in outline only.

c) *Nature*. God becomes actual only through eternal nature. As a means of revelation it stands in opposition to the virgin, the eternal idea. God, who sees himself in the mirror, desires what he sees. It is to become actual. The pleasure of beholding and desire allow nature hidden in God to break forth.

But God remains as yet in the eternity of his life with this nature. It is not the nature present to us but the nature prior to creation. As this nature, will separates itself from the unity. It multiplies itself into an infinity of particular wills.

Concomitant with this breakthrough of nature, a darkening occurs. This is the condition for light to reveal its brilliance. All opposites now actualize themselves to full revelation. The yea of all things becomes manifest only through the eternal nay. Even though yea and nay are not two things adjacent to each other, but one thing that drives itself forth in the dynamism of its contrariety, they divide into two beginnings or two centers, each of which wills and works in itself (cf. Martensen, 49–50).

These two "centra" are the will of nature and the will of spirit, or the individual will and the universal will. In the eternal process of revelation, the will of nature subordinates itself to the will of spirit. It proceeds in seven configurations of nature. In the first three configurations there is a hostile relationship between nature and spirit; in the last three nature is the willing servant. The first dark triad (1–3) is followed by lightning (fright [*Schrack*]), and then by the light triad (5–7) (cf. Martensen, 51–52).

In the dark triad, nature shows what it is capable of doing through itself. Despite its tremendous power it still remains unsatiated, in wild unrest. It moves in three stages (cf. Martensen, 52ff.).

1) *Contraction:* It is the first act of will out of the Nothing. It is cold, hard, sharp, strict—it is salt, the power that is locked in itself, craving exclusivity and not tolerating anything beside itself.

2) *Expansion:* It wants to spread out, is desire directed outward, is urge into diversity—it is mercury. These two qualities are opposing desires: the one wants to include everything in itself, the other wants to pour itself out; the one to withdraw austerely into itself, the other fleeing out of itself. The one wants greater stillness, the other clamors and rages. These warring powers are inseparable, cannot let go of each other, but must wrestle one with the other. In the end this struggle turns into an oscillation comparable to the turning of a wheel.

3) *Rotation:* It is movement that cannot come to an end, because it has no goal; it is terrible restlessness and fear. It cannot remain where it is and yet does not move from the spot—it is sulphur. It is also called *centrum naturae*, wheel of nature, wheel of life, wheel of fear, the wheel of birth, of eternal fire.

4) There now awakens, in the fear of nature, *the yearning for freedom*. The immeasurable suffering yearns for deliverance. Before this yearning, love manifests itself, but becomes manifest only when there is something that desires it. Love lets its light shine into the darkness. A tremor, a terror (*Schrack*) passes through nature—lightning.

Fear is afraid of the fiery lightning. The darkness, the selfishness of natural desire is consumed by it. The dark and the light world, wrath and love separate. The configurations of nature turn gentle. Thus, whatever in God's life before creation is a prototype will return in all Being: Each life must be born twice, as is nature through lightning. The new light triad has these configurations (cf. Martensen, 54ff.).

5) *The light water spirit:* In it the powers are concentrated into a unity. Hostility has vanished, one power takes pleasure in the others, a

gentle love reigns, the strictness and sharpness of nature are muted and reshaped. Here lies the birthplace and the seed of all things.

6) *The comprehensible sound, the resonance:* The powers just collected are led forth in a comprehensible separation. They give sound and become clear. But no human ear can hear these celestial sounds.

7) *The harmonious whole:* It is the wisdom that has become actuality, life, and corporeality. It is called the uncreated heaven, the celestial hall, the kingdom.

As they are represented, these seven nature-configurations engender one another in turn. But they are not successive; rather, in movement, they are life in God, an eternal presentness, a whole (cf. Martensen, 56ff.).

d) This summing up cannot claim to be an accurate presentation of Boehme's teaching. He sees, thinks, and writes not only in endless repetition but also in endless variations and rearrangements. One scheme is merely one among many. To illustrate what such sketches represent and what meaning accrues to them, the following needs to be added:

1) *Nature furnishes the images.* But salt, mercury, sulphur; harsh, sweet, bitter; oil, water, fire are not ciphers, but the powers that manifest themselves in these actualities. Light is love, darkness hate, warmth wrath, salt covetousness, sulphur fear.

2) For Boehme, the method of thinking via images of nature is coincidental with *the divinity of nature.* To be sure: "There is nothing in nature that does not contain good as well as evil" (Richter, 89), but God himself is the contrariety present in him which, in him, is unity, is this dual possibility. "When God created this world with all there is in it, He had no other material to fashion it from than his own being, than himself" (III, 9).

Hence nature presents a twofold aspect. As the essence of this world it is "smoke coagulated from the eternal ether" (Richter, 90). But there is equally the magnificence of this world. God is in nature although "nature neither grasps nor comprehends him, just as air cannot grasp the radiance of the sun" (VI, 5).

3) *The seven configurations of nature* brought each other forth consecutively. Contraction brought forth its opposite, expansion; both, in wrestling with each other, brought forth rotation, the eternal wheel of the fear of nature. The desire for freedom from the wheel and for deliverance is answered by eternal love, in fiery lightning or fright (*Schrack*), in which what is mere nature is consumed. Now the light movement unfolds. At first the gentle docility of nature confronts the spirit. But it is spirit only in understanding one for the other, in consonance. In conclusion, there is total harmony.

What is presented in this form as the life of God prior to creation is an event not in time but in eternity. When we think it, we understand simultaneity as a succession. The illusion arises that a temporal story is being told. But in God all moments that, presented in separation, look like crises or incidents are held together by the eternal bond. Hence Boehme turns against his own description. He must speak "in the manner of the devil," as though God had a beginning. He, therefore, also turns against the compartmentalization (*Abteiligkeit*) of thoughts.

4) *The sequence of steps* signifies the inner revelation of God. What Sophia and nature are within God returns as the unfolding plenitude in creation, preconceived by him through the former. And finally it means the becoming visible of His plenitude to the thinking creature, that is, man (cf. Benz, 21).

To this corresponds the meaning of the "glance," of the eternal eye (cf. Benz, 36–37). God sees himself and his possibilities in Sophia. God sees man through Sophia. Sophia opens the eye of Adam, the primal man, so that God's plenitude becomes revealed to him. In the glance at Sophia there is the eternal glance in which God cognizes man and, correspondingly, there is in man the glance in which he cognizes God. In the eternal glance God cognizes himself, and in man—the image of the godhead—the glance is that in which man cognizes himself.

5) What Boehme calls the seven wholesome spirits and the seven properties are, in the godhead, *the eternal principles* of the formation of all things. The uncreated nature thus shown is the prototype and power in all created nature in which, therefore, these moments recur. The imagery of natural elements, feelings, moods presents Boehme's glance at the forces through which everything comes to be. Such a design is analogous to that of Hegel when he sketches the categories of his logic as *God's conceptions prior to creation*. But Boehme's pictorial intuitions greatly exceed the sparse conceptual guidelines, whereas in Hegel the pictorial quality, while he does not own up to it, is present though concealed, kept marginal, as it were, not altogether canceled in the sharp contours of his thought-configurations. In Boehme reason is veiled in imagination; in Hegel the imagination, in reason.

2. God and creation

God manifests himself not only in himself. He creates a world outside himself.

In the inward divine process arises the trinity of the divine processes and the seven configurations of the wholesome spirits of nature, both in the mirror of Sophia. In the outward divine process this—which, as eternal harmony, uncreated, is present to itself in the image—steps outside into the actual contrasts through space and time. Now that which was one is separate and consecutive.

Beginning, middle, and end, separated from each other, seek to combine. Everything created must go through a development from the incomplete to the complete. What, in absolute completeness, is eternal enters a process of relative completeness. What has thusly been created is life. It unfolds through continued births. God manifests himself at different times of revelation.

His creation is the world of the spirits and the natural world. God does not create them out of nothing, but out of himself. In eternal wisdom he has the forms; in eternal nature, the matter of creation. Everything that is bears the stamp of the Trinity. It wrestles in configurations of the seven well-spirits.

The world cannot be called God. The Son is not created but is God out of God. The world is created and external to God.

There is a radical difference between eternity in God and in creation. How the created world stands before God as possibility is expressed by Sophia in the Old Testament (Proverbs 8:22–31): "The Lord possessed me in the beginning of His way, before His works of old. I was set up from everlasting, from the beginning, or ever the earth was. When there were no depths, I was brought forth. . . . Before the mountains were settled . . . was I brought forth. . . . When He prepared the heavens I was there. . . . When He established the clouds above: when He strengthened the fountains of the deep: When He gave to the sea His decree, that the waters should not pass His commandment: when He appointed the foundations of the earth: then I was by Him, as one brought up with Him: and I was daily His delight, rejoicing always before Him . . . and my delights were with the sons of men."[3]

This passage is a major source for Theosophy. Schelling confesses that it acted on him like a fresh morning breeze out of the sacred dawn of the world; even if he had found it in a profane writer he would have considered it an inspired text. Boehme echoed this vision: Before the time of creation, God saw the created world in a reflection, as in a mirror. In it he saw, for all eternity, the idea of angels and souls as well as men, though as shadows, not as creatures.

How does the world, which is eternally in God, but only as a shadow and not corporeally, arrive at the actual condition of creaturehood? Why

[3] King James version.

did God create the world? By eternal fiat or his word as expression of
his will, through the "let-there-be! of the Creator" (Martensen, 137)?
But why this act of will? Boehme answered, approximately, that the
triad desired to have children in its likeness; out of love God formed
the idea of another existence which is not-God but is utterly in need of
God. What is decisive is: God created the world not out of necessity but
through free decision. In spite of Boehme's affirmative formulations, this
decision remains an impenetrable mystery for him. "Even though we
know the fiat, we do not know God's first move toward creation. We
know no cause to explain how that which had stood in its nature throughout eternity (without beginning and unchangeable) has come into motion;
for there is nothing that would have stimulated it" (VI, 50; cf. Martensen,
140). As God moves toward creation a beginning is posited. But how
can something begin in the unchangeable, in which there is no time?
"We are not supposed to know the reason and cause, and God has
reserved it for his power . . . we are also not to reason further about
this for it disturbs us" (VI, 159).

Hence it "is the greatest miracle brought about by eternity that it
has worked the eternal into a corporeal spirit which no reason can grasp
and no sense can find" (VI, 49). "No created spirit can posit itself and
hence it cannot fathom itself, either. To be sure, we see our potter . . .
but we do not see his creating. . . . The soul grows forth like a twig on
a tree of humanity; but the first movement toward creation is not to be
known by us. It is a secret which God has reserved for himself" (VI,
49ff.; cf. Martensen, 141–42).

3. The course of the created world

a) *Exposition:* With creation the bond is dissolved that holds together all
forces and configurations in God's eternity. Each force is set free so that
it may move according to its own will. But as yet there is no strife
between the innumerable particular wills. Everything is still in a state
of balance that is maintained through the unity of eternal wisdom.

The primal state of creation is the life of the angels in a marvelous
natural world that by far surpasses our earthly world in its perfection.
It is a realm of pure spirits of light: within it are the realms of the three
archangels Michael, Lucifer, and Uriel, surrounded by a host of angels.
The lives of these beings are not bound to the limits of space and time.
To be sure, they have locality, but they can be where they wish. They
know neither proximity nor distance. They live in the communality of

love in common joy. The content of their lives is the adoration of God
in the cycle of eternity. Though created, they constitute a second eternity,
as it were, a condition they share with all of creation.

But this changes. The angels have to pass a test, with the view of
strengthening their relationship to God. Not all pass this test. Lucifer,
the most powerful of all created spirits, held sway over a—for us—
indeterminate area of natural worlds to which our earth also belonged,
at that time resplendent in beauty and magnificence. Lucifer's temptation
was: He saw his beauty, for he was wonderfully beautiful; he saw his
power, for he was a most mighty lord. He directed his imagination onto
himself, his ego, and became ill-disposed toward the Son of God, who
was more beautiful and mightier than he. He thought that he could
himself become like God and rule in all things through the power of
fire.

He opened his *centrum naturae*, his fiery ground, and thus caused
his light to go out. He became dark. The fundament of hell, which had
been hidden since time eternal, was now unveiled. He awakened the
principle of God's wrath, the first three configurations of nature. His
torment consists in a constant climbing in order to raise himself above
the heart of God; but each time he sinks back once more into the deepest
abyss.

Why did Lucifer fall? Lucifer, says Boehme, knew well that he was
not God, and he foresaw God's judgment and his fall; but the fall was,
for him, not a feeling, only a knowing. As to his feeling, he had in
himself the fiery lust, the fire-root. The latter now burned in him, goaded
him on to want something totally new, to raise himself above all king-
doms and above all divinity. He had the illusion of not having been
created. He was conscious that God could not kill him. "But God has
created him into his harmony, such that he wanted to play with him in
his spirit of love as on the stringed instrument of his revealed and formed
word, and this his own will did not want" (V, 41).

Lucifer draws the natural world which is subject to him into his fall.
Previously there existed a magical connection between spirit and nature.
Now a terrible *turba* (confusion) enters into nature. The bond of the
forces is truly dissolved. Instead of acting together in harmony, the egoism
of all the particulars now falls into conflict and confusion. The consequence is a state of chaos. God's wrath becomes manifest in fire, ma-
terialization, darkness, and death.

This happened at the beginning of creation. This fall within eternity,
which could still contain creation itself, first brings about our temporal

world. From the beginning the latter has shown itself as a shattered, broken, disturbed, disordered eternity. The dawn of creation is heralded by a great catastrophe.

But God does not want the destruction to be final. He initiates the reaction. He puts everything under water. His purpose is the re-formation of the earth. Only now does that which is told in the Mosaic story of the creation begin. The six days of creation are stages in the battle between the forces of God and those of darkness. Only now does that which we call time begin.

The earth was unformed and void (*tohu wabohu*). It was necessary to rebuild the world that through Lucifer had become a ruin. The end was the creation of paradise, of the perfect abode of light for the creature of light, man, the first man. In paradise everything was in a state of balance, but not so in the rest of the world. Man was destined to extend paradise over the whole earth. What happened?

To understand this, we must first know what Adam, the first man, was.

The first man was One, unity without multiplicity.

The first man was endowed with spirit-corporeality as his heavenly garment, and was not yet clothed in incarnate corporeality. The heavenly body of Adam could pass through all things, and things through him, without laceration. His corporeality is that of the angels (cf. V, 47ff.). External things do not harm him; he is impervious to frost, heat, thorns. He is free of sickness and death. He neither knows nor needs sleep. He breathes not air but the divine spirit of life. He has no bowels and needs no material nourishment. He drinks from the fountain of eternal life that is hidden in the earthly water source and does not need to drink water. He is androgynous, without sex; procreation occurs through inner imaging; this self-imaging takes place by means of loving contemplation of the divine image. Begetting and giving birth are one and the same act (cf. V, 54–55).

The first man was microcosm. He contains the three principles of the macrocosm: first, the principle of fire, the eternal father, as the soul of man; second, the principle of light, the eternal son, as the spirit of man; third, the sensuous world of things, as his transitory corporeality. In Adam the principle of light is dominant. Therefore he possesses the clear cognition of divine, natural, and human things. He understands the language of God as well as the language of nature. For him, all that is visible is irradiated by the invisible. For Sophia is his bride as she is the bride of God. He is, after all, God's image. Adam, the first man, is put to the test and tempted, as was Lucifer before him. He allows himself to be awakened to false pleasure by the Devil. He is tired of his being in God. The unity becomes boring for him. Adam becomes "tired and blind to the kingdom of God" (III, 190). He no longer wants to receive things out of the hand of God, but wants to experience them by himself, wants to "try out how they are in themselves" (Benz, 61). He wants to know the multiplicity of things not in the unity of God but in their selfness and separateness. He wants to taste how it is when the balance is dissolved.

"That was the real test, what the free will of the soul would do, whether it would want to . . . enter into selfness" (V, 99). Adam failed.

Because he turned away from God, the world gained power over him. For "he led his will and desire from God into selfness and vanity, and broke it off from God" (V, 101). Therefore nature overpowered him, the forces of the world gained mastery over him, he became a slave to the elements and the stars. The complete transformation of his nature becomes evident in the following actualities:

He is overcome by sleep. The eternally wakeful First Man becomes subject to nature. "Thus he fell victim to the Magia and that was the end of his glory, for sleep hints at death" (VI, 178). First Man had lost his immortality.

There follows "the transformation of the spirit-corporeality of celestial man into the incarnate corporeality" of earthly man (Benz, 76).

This loss of power was, further, First Man's falling prey to sexuality. The oneness turned into the duality of gender.

Boehme understands the fact of gender to be of supersensible origin. Originally, First Man had an androgynous nature, which man will again assume in his future perfection. This is grounded in the nature of God. God is androgynous; he is his unity with the celestial Sophia (cf. Benz, 23ff.).

Sophia is female and she is a virgin. Wisdom is called the bride of God, God's playmate. She is "the mother in which the father is active" (VII, 99). Boehme speaks of the marriage of Sophia with God. She could not give birth unless the spirit of God were active in her. She is called the "eternal mother," the "one who gives birth to all things" (III, 47).

The relationship of the divine will to itself is called "lust." Its desiring is "a grasping of itself" (V, 8).

This androgynous self-relation and this self-cognition do not split unity apart. For this reason Sophia is called virgin. No desire originates in her. She is the unblemished mirror. She "is a virgin and has never given birth . . . goes out from God and not back . . . rather, it is her will to open up God's miracles" (III, 153).

The androgynous character of complete First Man corresponds to the androgynous nature of God. The magical birth of First Man is the image of the primal act of self-cognition on the part of God in the mirror of Sophia. In Adam there was the androgynous unity of the male fire-soul and the light-body of Sophia (cf. Benz, 66).

Hence the fall from the unity is thought of as adultery on the part of Adam. "And here Adam lost his chaste love-play and his virginity" (VII, 241).

As of that moment he can no longer be alone. The phrase "It is not good for man to be alone" refers to the fallen Adam. God creates Eve out of his body. His no longer being able to be alone is the punishment for that first rebellion against God.

His eternal playmate, Sophia, vanishes into the ether. That is, consequent upon his hunger "for earthliness," "the celestial picture of the angelic world" faded for Adam (V, 101). Or, to put it another way, he lost his unity with the divine consciousness. Or, the state of balance was dissolved; opposition and strife dominated.

Adam's fall constituted a repetition of Lucifer's fall. But there is a difference between the two. Lucifer was in total opposition to God, and meant to put himself in God's place. Adam's fall was merely a half-measure; he wanted only possession and enjoyment of multiplicity, diversity, finitude. He was smitten with the world of the senses.

This whole story of the fall of First Man is alien to church dogmatics. Ecclesiastical doctrine begins with the fall of man in paradise. In Boehme this is only a second step in the progression by which Adam and Eve enter completely into the calamity of earthly existence (cf. Benz, 74 ff.).

After his fall Adam fell asleep in the divine world. He awoke and found himself in the external terrestrial world. His eating the fruits of the tree of the knowledge of good and evil actualized what previously had been desire. Now the "vanity in the essence of the flesh awoke entirely" (VII, 242).

But a dim memory remains. From afar, merely surmised, Sophia shows herself to man in his fallen state. The goal of all love is this lost unity. That eternal, sexless, wakeful bond of the One with God, that harmony of the androgynous is what man desires in sexual love. But this goal cannot be reached. Rather, the attempt to regain the unity leads to propagation, toward multiplicity (cf. Benz, 68–69).

Now we have reached the world in which we find ourselves and which we ourselves are. Its basic character is its state of total contrast.

Contrast has its source in God. It showed itself as indispensable for his revelation to himself. This contrast in its character as the principle of all life, all cognition, and all illumination permeates all modes of Being. As the basic form, it returns everywhere. But contrast assumes a different configuration in consequence of the fall. The contrarieties become independent; the bond of unity is loosened. The movement becomes a torment in which the prototype, the unity of opposites, is sought but not found in time.

Boehme's work is dominated by this fundamental idea of opposites. It is effective through the relentless emphasis upon this phenomenon in its terrors and its chances. Everything moves in contrasts: no life without death, no pleasure without fear, no peace without struggle. All things are divided into Yes and No. Darkness is the enemy of light but also the condition of its manifestation. Consuming fire brings forth gentle light. Out of wrath grows love. All opposites, however, constitute a unity in the primal ground and in completeness. In the absolute itself the unity is preserved while manifesting itself in opposites. In the absolute, infinity does not exclude the finite, love does not exclude wrath, eternity does not exclude time. In the fallen world, however, the bond is broken; unity is not present but must be pursued.

"Reason asks: Why did God create a life of pain and suffering? . . . Why does he tolerate the will that runs counter to his? Why does he not abolish evil? . . . The answer: No thing without something countervailing may become manifest to him." If there is no resistance, everything pours forth out of itself without returning into itself. Without countervailing there would be no sensibility, neither willing nor effecting, neither understanding nor knowing. For "a thing that has only one will has no discernment" (VI, 454). It stands still, knows nothing other than the One, knows neither evil nor good. In a unitary will there is no self-knowledge. "But when there is such a discernment in the unitary will," there grow from it ungrounded and innumerable wills, like branches from a tree. Thus speaks reason: "What is the benefit . . . of there being an evil together with the good? —Answer: Evil . . . brings about the good as the will, so that it will again . . . strive toward God and . . . be desirous of the good; for a thing which, in itself, is only good . . . does not desire anything" (VI, 455).

This state of the world and our present life are not final. The process continues. As God saves the world after Lucifer's fall, so God saves it again after the fall of Adam.

In Christ becoming man, the new Adam enters the world. From now on man can be reborn. Conciliation and salvation will proceed.

Boehme describes heaven and hell, the unchangeable will after death, the magical state after death in the in-between region of spirits in the sidereal body, the completion of all things.

Hence the total picture presents itself to him as follows: at the beginning the pure world of the angels; at the end the complete spirit-world; in between, temporal existence. The last has eternity behind it and before it and all around. In this temporal history the angels, who themselves have no history, play a role as the servants of God.

b) *Discussion:* This gnostic total view of all things in their ground requires critical characterization.

First: Any effort to present Boehme's thoughts in a framework of order and clarity leads to misrepresentation. Boehme proceeds imprecisely, indeed almost arbitrarily, changing directions, realigning and altering the configurations of thought. For these reasons a conceptually more precise exposition must necessarily give a false picture, because of its very clarity. It separates what converges into one flow. It constructs an ordered whole which is only partially and at that fleetingly present in the texts. Nonetheless, the exposition is not altogether false, since such clear outlines are present in Boehme as possibilities. We are justified in distilling the core from an impenetrable mass of repetitions and confusions. This core has appealed to many, but not even this core can be determined unequivocally.

In this core there appear necessary and relevant contradictions. On the one side there is the emphasis on ignorance, the rejection of the desire to know, the awe before the mystery: "for I have never desired to know about the divine mystery, much less have I known how I might seek or find it . . . I sought only the heart of Jesus Christ, in order to hide myself in it before God's fierce wrath" (VII, 399–400). On the other side there is knowledge overreaching itself, with its emphasis on God's demand to be cognized, the certainty of knowledge about all Being as grounded in God himself, the total knowledge of the course of things from eternity to eternity. On the one side Evil is a necessary aspect of the process manifest to God, and on the other side Evil is the accidental moment of Lucifer's and Adam's acts of freedom, through which Evil first breaks into the magnificent creation. In other words, we are gripped by the intuition of evil in the primal ground of Being (wrath is the root of all things), and we are constantly called upon to battle for good against evil and, for our salvation, to participate in the choice of a path that leads away from evil. And again: The God of heaven and the God of hell are like two powers, and yet they are not two gods but one God. Everything, so also God himself, becomes manifest through contrast.

Without revelation God would remain unknown to himself. Thus God stands counter to God in himself. But the contrast is at the same time the unity. In the oppositions the One speaks for itself and with itself.

Boehme's method is an ancient one, which is common to all early civilizations; it used to predominate in the common consciousness but today plays only an incidental role. In essence, this enduring element is not myth, but cognition by means of analogies, correspondences, identities, meanings in intuitable generality. Such cognition is impressive where it presents itself with meaningful vividness; it is then original and alive. But when it is rationalized in concepts and schematisms that lead to interminable thought operations, it sinks down into arbitrariness without persuasive power. Bereft of the forcefulness of pictorial language, thoughts become mere assertions.

In reading Boehme's texts, we have a confusing experience: The impressiveness of the images and the arbitrariness of the points of departure, the seeing of meanings and the lack of comprehension, the plausibility of a game and the total lack of evidence—one seems to cancel out the other. But, oddly, in spite of all this the fundamental questions remain meaningful.

No matter what the scientific exploration of the world asks and answers, it does not penetrate to those fundamental questions and to speculation about them. Scientific research produces specific answers to specific questions referring to the realities in the world, a progression of questions and answers that is endless.

Boehme did not grasp the relationship between the exploration of the world and speculation about Being (or between science and philosophy); it did not become a problem for him.

Wherever a contradiction arises between visionary answers to the question of Being and the results of scientific inquiry with regard to questions of reality, it is science that is correct. But this contradiction does not pertain to where philosophizing, in regard to the fundamental questions—whence, whereto, what for?—carries out its own independent thinking. There, science is merely a means.

Such means can be applied in a manner that is philosophically false. If, let us say, we apply a stage of scientific research that has been proven correct up to this point in order to fill the gaps within a line of thinking of an entirely different derivation, or to buttress the content of a philosophic thought with a scientifically obtained justification, this is scientifically unproductive and philosophically meaningless. An example: interpreting statistically obtained atomic processes as acts of freedom supposedly already demonstrated at the very basis of the processes of

matter. Or, let us say, if the convergence of scientific calculations concerning the beginning of the world-process—as it appears in the cosmos,
in the planetary system, in the earth's history—is conceived as pointing
to the act of creation, which is supposed to have taken place approximately five billion years ago.

It is a different matter when gnostic thinking, looking into the core
of things, tries to let intuitions that arise at the cutting edge of research
be articulated in the same way as intuitions of nature. The teachings of
Copernicus implied—because the parallax of fixed stars could not be
measured on the basis of the earth's orbit—an infinite distance of the
fixed stars. Boehme must have heard about this. He stands by Copernicus.
"The sun has its own royal *locus* and does not stray from the place where
it has first come into being. But some believe that it circles the earth
day and night. . . . This opinion is false. The earth turns around and,
together with the other planets, circles the sun" (II, 297). But for Boehme
the desire to measure the world, to determine its size, to ascertain the
distance of the fixed stars is altogether a different matter. "No one knows
the depth or the breadth of the *locus* of this world, and even though
some physicists or astrologers have dared to measure its depth with a
compass their measuring is merely nonsense or is a measuring of our
conceptions, as if one wanted to catch hold of the wind" (II, 292).

Surely Boehme did not understand the method and meaning of
astronomical research. He dislikes measuring and counting. But from
the very beginning he senses that his intuition of nature is beyond the
reach of scientific research and instinctively grasps the infinity manifesting itself in nature as the language of the world through which God
speaks. "I have read about the order of the seven planets in astrological
books, and find it all right; but the root, how they have become and
where they have come from, I cannot learn from men, for they do not
know it. Neither was I there when God created them" (II, 295).

The drama of cosmic history, above all the dominating and all-
determining role of contrasts, has to be understood as the objectification
of Boehme's own experience. He himself points to this. What man
experiences is the ground of things itself, analogous to the process in
God and in the world. The objective is the mirror of the subjective and
vice versa.

The source for this insight is Boehme's experience of the turnabout
of the basic inner mood. There is much in Boehme about melancholy,
both subjectively in his own life and objectively in Being. Boehme called
his sadness the black devil. He describes the boundless happiness when
joy is triumphant, and knows this joy only as born out of dejection.

"Overcoming is joy" (V, 306). "We recognize . . . that every life arises in fear, as in a poison that is a dying, and is yet also life itself, as it can be recognized in man and in all creatures. For without fear or poison there is no life . . . especially in man" (VI, 254). "For each life comes to be in torment of fear. . . . For everything that is in nature is dark and in fear" (VI, 370).

In considering method in Boehme, we have to realize that it cannot be grasped by way of reason. But his clarity is astonishing when he expresses himself on a few decisive points of his procedure which, in its execution, is so confused and uncontrolled, and equally when he discusses the origin and meaning of his insight:

1) The source of his insight is not thought but immersion in its immediacy. "Most likely you say that I was not present at the creation of the world and hence may not write about it. But the spirit which is in me was present there and makes it known at this time" (Martensen, 17). Boehme states that he sees the truth inside himself, but at first as in a chaos where everything is densely packed. Only gradually does it arrive at greater clarity (cf. ibid.).

This immediate immersion presupposes a rebirth. God cannot be cognized without God. No matter how natural man may twist and turn, he cannot escape being caught up in the world. The fall of man brought about by Adam and his rehabilitation in Christ is a process repeated in each individual.

2) For Boehme, this occurs wholly in the present and not through the guidance of a tradition, a doctrine, or a church. For him, Jesus as a historical figure is of small moment. Boehme abhors the historical view. It is not the knowing and hearing about something that is helpful; rather, it deceives: it leads to confusion. One is saved only by one's own actions and experiences, by certainty in the manifestation of the divine essence, by beholding the *signatura rerum*, without scriptural proof (though Boehme does quote the Bible occasionally), without dogmatic reference to the illumination through the holy spirit while reading the Biblical texts. Only the immediate, which manifests itself unhistorically, eternally, is valid for him. "Even if I had no other book than my book which I am myself, I would have books enough; the whole Bible, after all, lies in me. As long as I have the spirit of Christ . . . As long as I read myself, I read in God's book, and you, my brethren, are all my letters which I read within me" (VII, 132).

To be sure, Boehme has a positive relationship to the Bible, is at home in it. But he recognizes the harm of serving the letter. What is important is not the letter, but the living word. "Letter-brokers" (V,

262) do not understand the meaning. "A true resonance belongs to it that is in concord with the resonance in the letter" (V, 190).

Current faith is merely historical knowledge. "Oh, how dead is today's faith! It stops with knowledge: one believes that one speaks about God when one knows much . . . that this is the way to eternal life. Oh, no, none of that helps, let me tell you. . . . True faith in Christ is something wholly different. . . . True faith is the true will" (IV, 212–13). "It depends . . . not on any historical opinion but on being well-intentioned and on doing good" (IV, 88). It "must be earnest. . . . Your will must turn completely with all your reason and senses toward the will of God" (IV, 214). "The world, after all, is filled with books and talk about the fall and the new rebirth." But for the most part "only the history is described, namely, that it happened at one time" (III, 18) and will and shall happen again. Hence Boehme chides the "history-scholars," the "history-mongers" (cf. Elert, 55).

3) However, imparting the tremendous insight creates difficulties that lie in the nature of things and cannot really be overcome. When translated into the temporally manifested language of partitioning, of sequentiality, of finite formulation, the divine insight takes on a misleading appearance. "If I had the tongue of an angel and you the understanding of an angel, we could understand one another. But I must speak in an earthly manner with my half-dead understanding; and since I am merely a spark, a particle . . . of the whole, I cannot describe the entire Godhead in a comprehensive manner all at once. I must grasp the one after the other: thus you shall see the whole at last. Indeed, I must at times speak in a devilish manner, as if the light would be lit out of the darkness, and as if the Godhead had a beginning. I cannot teach you differently. God has no beginning, or, more correctly, he has an eternal beginning and an eternal end. Therefore I exhort the reader not to understand me in terrestrial terms but to comprehend everything in a high and supernatural sense" (Martensen, 40).

III. BOEHME'S ETHOS

The ethos of Christian virtues—humility, self-surrender, love—is valid also for Boehme. However, it is not characteristic for him, nor does he give it prominence even though he often expresses the following demands: Do not quarrel with anyone; in all external matters, surrender calmly as to the will of God (VII, 405). When Boehme formulates what man ought to do, he responds to his own vision of the nature of man.

This is how he sees him: God has made man the lord of all creatures, has endowed him with senses, reason, and intellect, and especially with language, so that he can differentiate, tame, and utilize all. Still "higher . . . cognition did God give him so that he can see into the heart of things . . . into earth, stones, trees, herbs . . . also into stars and elements so that he knows their nature and power" (III, 1).

Man's first task is to know himself. Nothing is more useful for him than "that he learn to know himself properly: 1) what is he? 2) out of what or whom? 3) for what purpose has he been created?" (III, 1). "Without which reflection we are all blind and have no true cognition of God, but move about like dumb animals and look at ourselves and God's creation like a cow at a new barn door" (III, 3). But as man "now knows himself properly he also knows God his creator, together with all creatures" (III, 7).

Man has his great task because of his extraordinary nature. He feels in himself God's "magnificent power" (IV, 71). More than that: "God is himself the essence of all essences, and we are in him as gods through which he reveals himself" (IV, 86). But Boehme also writes: ". . . in this world a man should not crave to know His sanctity" (Elert, 48).

The great task may be defined as the adoring cognition which is the wellspring of true life. Man can cognize God "because this visible world is the expressed and formulated word according to God's love and wrath . . . but man's soul a spark from the eternally speaking word of divine knowledge and strength, and the body . . . a being of heaven after the manner of the obscured world: he thus has the power to speak of the mysterium magnum out of which all beings have come to be" (V, 4).

The life growing out of adoring cognition presupposes the authenticity of the cognition. Knowing adoration brings about inner movement and action in the world consequent upon it. It is the great question of all philosophy: What happens to me when I pursue such thoughts and speculations and visions, when I live in such a vivid world of thought, when my certainty in it becomes the ground of my consciousness of Being?

Boehme says: No speculation is of use to man if he does not apply it for his salvation. "What good is science to me if I do not live in it? The knowledge must be within me, and also the willing and doing" (VII, 410). Together with intuition of the depth and the ground of all Being, there comes also assurance of the ethos. Each being yearns "for that out of which he first originated" (Richter, 90). If he reaches it, he attains all truth, that of knowledge as well as of action.

If we ask Boehme why he writes at all, he replies, in accordance with this sense of his knowledge, which is also his ethos: "I write only for the purpose that man get to know himself, what he is, what God, heaven, angels, devil and hell, as well as God's wrath and hellfire are. . . . Therefore consider well, you human being, in this time, what you are! Do not value yourself so little, as so trivial, and do take care that you remain in paradise and do not put out the divine light in you" (III, 36–37).

The reader must be ready: "My writings do not serve the full belly, but a hungry stomach; they belong to the children of the mystery" (VII, 384).

To those who seek guidance he says: I do not know "any better advice to give you than to show you the path on which I myself travel, and thereupon the door was opened to me" (VII, 407).

In an age of fanatical religious battles, Boehme was an early proponent of tolerance, with thoughts that were not new. It is characteristic for his nature that he stood up for it. God is not only the God of the Christians, but also that of the Jews, the heathen, the Turks. God reveals himself to each people according to its peculiar nature. The root of the quarrel lies in the fact that we cling to images and letters rather than to the spirit. If one could do away with the images, the one living word would speak. But it is couched for us in various images. We quarrel about images.

IV. CHARACTERIZATIONS

Boehme epitomizes the substance of his work in the sentence "I have merely written down what nature and man are" (VII, 320). Indeed, nature in the magnificence and the terror of its inexhaustible phenomena; the infinite immeasurable vastness of the world; man in his questionableness; good and evil; the love and the fierce strife in nature, history, and every man—all this stands in the foreground.

Boehme's self-confidence was considerable, as is obvious in the very humility of his behavior; when the chief pastor threw his slipper after him, Boehme picked it up and put it down at the pastor's feet. He was completely self-assured. Through his message of the great *mysterium*, he believed himself to be an event that would change the world. The title of his first book, *Aurora*, denotes the rise of a new hour of the Reformation.

His meekness does not exclude polemical fierceness. He rejects all educated classes, universities, theologians, jurists, physicians. He calls his opponents liars, thieves, murderers, great whores. Expressions such as the following are no rarity: I "close my book with a solid wall and a bolt before such idiots and wild devil's calves" (III, 7).

V. BOEHME'S INFLUENCE

Boehme, for his part, held fast to the Lutheran Church on principle. He was not the type of enthusiast who establishes sects. Even though, throughout the centuries, his adherents formed societies, the Boehmenists did not become an organized sect even as time went on.

His influence, however, was considerable. The physician Walter, who in his last year in Dresden became Boehme's friend, named him the *Philosophus Teutonicus*. The name stuck. Hegel confirmed it: "As a matter of fact, it was first through him that philosophy in Germany emerged with the character peculiar to it" (Hegel, XIX, 300).

Angelus Silesius, the mystic and poet, responded to Boehme with love:

> The fish lives in water,
> the plants in the earth,
> the bird in the air,
> the sun in the sky;
> salamander must keep in the fire.
> God's heart is Boehme's element.

Boehme's works arrived first in manuscript form, later in print, in Holland, England, and France. King Charles I of England praised them. Leibniz and Newton valued them highly; the Enlightenment held them in contempt. Novalis and Tieck renewed interest in them. For Baader and Schelling he became one of the most important philosophers. Hegel respected him: Boehme, he said, deserved neither contempt nor high honors; he thinks in the form of intuition and feeling, but the truth of philosophy lies in the concept. On that score, Boehme is a barbarian; yet "a man who, in spite of the rough manner of his presentation, possesses a solid, deep heart" (Hegel, XIX, 297). Hegel specifically judged him as follows:

About the forms of Boehme's thinking: ". . . he looked at all concepts within an actuality; or he uses actuality as concept." Thus "Boehme's great mind is locked into the hard gnarled oak of the sensuous." "One gets a sense of his wrestling . . . a battle of his . . . consciousness with language." He makes use of "the Christian form as the form of the idea"; "he tosses and turns himself around in several forms because neither the sensuous nor the religious one can suffice." "But it is a form one cannot reconcile oneself to and which does not allow for a definite picture regarding the details" (Hegel, XIX, 301–04, 327).

About the deepest content of this thinking Hegel says: "In the background there is the most speculative thought, which, however, never comes to be presented in a manner appropriate to it." The "content of the battle is the deepest idea which shows us that the most absolute opposites are to be reconciled. . . . It is a tremendous, wild and rough exertion from within to pack together what lies so far apart in form and configuration . . . thus he wrestled to comprehend, to grasp the negative, the evil, the devil in God" (Hegel, XIX, 303, 327).

About Boehme's personality: ". . . his pious nature . . . deep and tender to the highest degree." His life was founded in the Protestant principle "to immerse the world of the intellect in his own heart and to look at, to know and to feel in his self-awareness all that was beyond it otherwise." He represents "the German, the heart's depth that communes with the innermost" (Hegel, XIX, 327, 300, 304).

SCHELLING

Editors' Note

Friedrich Wilhelm Joseph von Schelling was born on January 27, 1775, in Leonberg, Germany, the son of a learned Lutheran pastor. He studied theology at the famous Tübingen seminary, where, with his older friends Hegel and Hölderlin, he lived through the stirring events of the French revolutionary epoch and the classical age of German letters. At twenty-three he became a professor at Jena. There, he had tempestuous friendships with Fichte and the circle of Romantic writers, including Tieck, Novalis, and the Schlegel brothers. In 1803 he married Caroline Schlegel. He taught at Würzburg, Erlangen, Munich, and was invited in 1841 to the University of Berlin to fill the chair left vacant when Hegel died in 1831. Schelling died in Ragaz, Switzerland, on August 24, 1854.

This chapter is a translation of Jaspers's lecture, "Schelling: Grösse und Verhängnis," at the Schelling Centenary Conference held in Bad Ragaz, Switzerland, in 1954. It was published in his *Aneignung und Polemik*.

WORK

1.

What is philosophy? Schelling answers: Philosophy is "throughout a work of freedom." It cannot be comprehended from the outside. One has to enter into it. Hence he considers as valid the circle: "The idea of philosophy is none other than the result of philosophy itself" (II, 11).[1] It cannot be defined from the outside, for there is "no concept of this science other than through itself" (XI, 360).

[1] Citations are to *Sämtliche Werke*, ed. by K. F. A. Schelling. Stuttgart and Augsburg, 1856–61.

143

Schelling never gives up the independence of philosophy. Even in his old age he said "that we would rather give up the thought of philosophy if it were not possible to think of it as a wholly sovereign science" (XI, 301). There is no higher authority to limit it. Schelling's philosophy of revelation too turns, in the mode of thought, toward the facts of history and not, in the mode of submission, toward revelation and dogmas. "He who desires and is able to believe does not philosophize, and he who philosophizes proclaims, precisely in this way, that for him faith is not sufficient" (XIII, 135).

Since philosophy is a work of freedom, it is essentially volition. "He who attacks another's philosophical system attacks, at bottom, not only his intellect but also his will" (XIII, 201). Philosophy demands courage, above all the courage "to take hold of that which one doubts only because it is too transcendent for our familiar concepts" (XIV, 16).

Who can do justice to such a high demand? Schelling answers: Philosophy cannot "be everyone's thing." In order to be able to philosophize, one has to be a certain kind of person. The demand made by philosophy contains something "that excludes certain people for all time" (I, 417). Philosophy, though imparted to the public through the works of the philosophers, is yet an "open secret." It is comprehensible only to those born to it; for the others it is an eternal mystery (I, 314).

When the many speak of philosophy, when philosophy is presented as readily available knowledge among a great many other things, when those of poor understanding give the name philosophy to empirical psychology or logic, Schelling has this to say: "Misusing a word that designates a specific thing by giving it the meaning of lesser things cannot cancel the thing itself" (II, 60).

But Schelling, whose work echoes with the *odi profanum vulgis et arceo* (V, 5), has also given a contrary answer to the question as to who could satisfy the high demand. He calls philosophy not only "the highest" but also "that which is of greatest concern and most desired by all men" (VIII, 84). Philosophy must enter into life. That applies not only to the individual but also to the condition of the time, to history and to humanity. The power of philosophy must penetrate everything, because one cannot live without it. Can the esoteric, which at first presents itself to every man as an open secret, in the end reach everyone after all? Can it, issuing from the seclusion of an aristocracy of philosophers who keep remote from the world and rule over nothing, become that which rules over everything? Is, in the end, every human being called to philosophy?

Schelling seems to affirm this. The individual arrives at freedom only in the freedom of his world. He who wants to be free wants everything around him free. "Philosophy which becomes life is that which Plato calls the *politeuein*, that is, life with and within an ethical totality" (VI, 576). But this totality is possible only by way of philosophy. "Human affairs cannot be ruled by means of mathematics, physics, natural history, poetry, or art. Only the right metaphysics gives us true understanding of the world" (XIII, 27).

2.

Only through metaphysics does the center of the All become present. Only from there issues true guidance of insight as well as of action. Without metaphysics there is only dissipation and ruin.

How does philosophy get into this center? Intellect and sensory perception are not the origin of philosophic insight. These put knowledge at the disposal of everyday concerns, in a clear form as the knowledge of the sciences, which is cogent for everyone and equally valid for every intellect. Philosophic insight has a different source. Only if we feel confirmed in our innermost being and answer with what Schelling calls intellectual intuition can we understand philosophy.

What is intellectual intuition? Schelling has a variety of answers.

The most simple approach is to certify intellectual intuition through the way in which we are conscious of ourselves. In being conscious of myself I am both subject and object. In the I, that which thinks and that which is thought are the same. If we consider as clear only that which is before us as a sensuously intuitable object, then the I is indeed a mystery. The I is I only because it can never become the object of sensuous intuition. Hence, Schelling concludes, it can be determinable only in an intuition which intuits no object at all, which is not at all sensuous, namely, in an intellectual intuition (I, 181).

This simple undebatable puzzle implied in the fact of the consciousness of the I was merely Schelling's starting point. What he means by intellectual intuition goes much farther. It is a matrix of construction for speculation, as space is for geometry. It is a condition which he compares with sleep. It is an act of freedom through which alone I can be convinced of the authentic existence of whatever is. It is liberation from being tied to objects. It is, however, not subjective, but is the "indifference" of subject and object, encompassing both. It is the standpoint of "absolute reason," in which time ceases to be and all things are seen merely as the expression of absolute reason and not as objects of reflection. It is the standpoint of the absolute. Whereas in his ordinary state of consciousness man lives outside the absolute, bound to objects, in time, entangled in finiteness, intellectual intuition lifts him above all this to the plane of eternity. In this sense it is ecstasy. It is a state that allows man to attain authentic reflective awareness, whereas in the natural state he lives without reflection.

Thus we see in how many different ways Schelling speaks about this origin of philosophy: condition and free act, guideline of speculative construction, and place prior to all consciousness. It is always a matter of something to which we want to rise, of the place out of which we think as we philosophize. On that plane what is, is close to us, present in us, is not remote, not elsewhere, not outside us. It is the place where what authentically is, but never is object, reveals itself in original experience. From outside or from below intellectual intuition, neither it nor that which manifests itself in it can, in thinking, be seen, much less comprehended as an other.

What Schelling characterizes as intellectual intuition with the words "pure thought," "ecstasy," "absolute reason," "construction" is an extensive area held together solely by one purpose: to see in it the origin or the experience that precedes all philosophical thought, supports it, fulfills and guides it.

We should never fail to hear, should never forget what Schelling demands here: that of which one speaks when philosophizing. Measured against the standards of scientific research as posited by the intellect— the area of object-boundness—it is nothing. Philosophical thinking requires a radical redirection. If this is forgotten and the yardsticks of the sciences are applied, then philosophy appears to give only examples of objectlessness, that is, within this particular horizon, absurdities.

We must be grateful to Schelling that he, who in his old age allowed himself to be considered the spokesman of ecclesiastical orthodoxy and of restauration, in fact never denied the high rank of philosophy, nor its sovereignty or that independent origin he circumscribed with the terms intellectual intuition, absolute reason, pure thought, ecstasy.

But does all this not leave us with a sense of dissatisfaction? Is there something that grates? Is this way of discussing the encompassing origin of intellectual intuition not somewhat impetuous, uncritical? Does the opening up of a world of supersensual intuitions perhaps follow from the objectless presentness within the consciousness of the I? Or is Kant right that the I, since it is not the object of intuition, also is not determinable? And are those apt formulations advancing the earnestness of our philosophizing not also shot through by something disconcerting, something exceeding human possibilities, something arrogantly aristocratic and forcefully despotic? But let us first listen to an example of Schelling's lofty speculation.

3.

Schelling's work is pervaded by the age-old fundamental question: What is Being? In various ways he leads us to a thinking experience of the most extreme sort, to the place where what is must become manifest. I shall try to present one of these ways (IX, 214–21):

Schelling almost never takes the direct way of approach. He likes to proceed from a familiar premise that can be presumed to be shared by all. Only after this preparatory step can we grasp where he wants to lead. His preparation takes the following form:

a) In examining the statements about Being which have arisen, I perceive the contradiction in which each incipient reflection soon finds itself; next I see the contradiction also of the systems in which such reflections of the knowledge of Being can each find completion. This original lack of system in human knowledge impels systems to arise, albeit as the idea of a higher whole. Within this whole the antagonistic systems, by their very coexistence, create that superior consciousness in which man is again free of all systems, stands above all systems.

This higher whole—which is again a system, but the one that precludes conflict with any other system—can be realized only in a series of stages. While the stages conflict with each other, each is true, though not at the same but at various points of the development. The philosophy that wants the truth of the whole must become genetic.

In such a genesis all contradictions cease because each position taken in thinking, each mode of Being has its truth in actuality, hence is preserved; and each is also overcome because it becomes untrue if it claims to be the whole. But this genetic movement can, as a whole, be truth only if the subject of this movement is only a subject that pervades everything and is not arrested in anything. "For wherever it would remain, life and development would be inhibited. Pervading everything and being nothing, that is, being nothing in a way that might allow it also to be something else: this is what is required."

Thus the question about Being has become the question about the one subject that pervades everything, about this subject that is all and yet is nothing of all that.

b) But we still have not arrived at the question to which we should now give an answer. A new preparatory step is necessary. Schelling, reflecting, says we must first query the question. The question "What is this subject?" presupposes the question about the meaning of this question itself. The accepted way of thinking leads to false expectations when this question is asked. Because in answer to the question "What is something?" we expect a definition. But here, when the question applies to the pervasive subject of what is, we must understand from the outset that there cannot be a definition. A definition as answer would effectively cancel the meaning of this question. Why?

"Nothing can be defined that is not, by its nature, confined within definite limits." But, in any questioning about a pervasive subject, that which is being asked is not confined within such limits. Hence I must "make the indefinable, that which cannot be defined in the subject, itself into the definition." The subject of philosophy, to all intents and purposes indefinable, "is nothing—not something . . . but it is also not nothing, that is, it is everything. It is only nothing singly, in an arrested state, particularly. . . . There is nothing that it is, and there is nothing that it is not—the incomprehensible, the truly infinite."

It is remarkable how Nietzsche answers the question about the Being that would not be a special Being, not a merely interpreted Being, but Being itself: "It would have to be something, i.e., not subject, not object, not power, not matter, not spirit, not soul: —but would I not be told that something of this nature would be the spitting image of a chimera? I believe that myself: and a pity if it did not! To be sure: It must also be the spitting image of everything else there is and could be, and not only of the chimera! It must have the great family trait in which everything recognizes itself as related to it —."[2]

These are answers to the question as to the meaning of the question what is, or, what is the subject of all configurations of Being. The uniqueness of the question, the difference between it and all other questions, has first to be made clear.

c) Does Schelling supply the answer? He does not. An answer cannot be reached by means of a statement involving a concept. What is necessary is an act of freedom on the part of the entire being of the thinking person. Something must not only be thought but also be an inward act. This is how Schelling describes it:

"Whoever wants to master the completely free, self-productive philosophy must rise up" to the incomprehensible, indefinable. What has to take place? "Here all finitude, everything that is still something that is, must be left behind, the last attachment must vanish; here one has

[2] *Nietzsches Werke*, ed. Elisabeth Förster-Nietzsche. Leipzig, C. G. Naumann, 1899—, XIII, 229.

to leave everything—not only, as one is wont to say, wife and child, but also whatever is, even God, for, seen from this standpoint, even God is merely something that is. . . .

"The absolute subject is not not-God, and yet is not God; it is also that which is not God. Hence, in this respect, it is above God. . . .

"Thus he who wants to position himself at the starting point of truly free philosophy must leave behind even God. . . .

"Only that one has arrived at the ground of his self and has recognized the whole depth of life who at one time had left everything behind and had himself been left by everything, for whom everything had gone under, who had seen himself alone with infinity. . . .

"But he who wants to soar up into that free ether must leave behind not only the world of objects but even himself. . . ."

Schelling describes the state that now sets in: "He who truly wants to philosophize must be rid of all hope, all desire, all yearning; he must want nothing, know nothing, feel himself wholly bare and stripped, must give everything away in order to gain everything."

Here too the older Schelling reminds us, as so often at the high points of his thinking, of the philosopher who had inspired him throughout his life: "How high Spinoza rises when he teaches that we are to sever ourselves from all particular and finite things and rise up to the infinite."

d) The preparatory thought operations, followed by the instructions for "leaving be," are an appeal to the thinker and a circling around what is being thought. Now we are ready. Now that which authentically is should become evident. Might it be sufficient to negate all finiteness, to have merely negative concepts of the absolute subject? No, says Schelling, "we strive in all ways possible to attain to its affirmatory concept." And, as a matter of fact, he has given us not just a great design, but a series of designs, a world rich in concepts of Being itself, and of the history of Being, as well as of our being-human within it. How does he get there?

After all, the principle was: In that absolute subject nothing is to be posited in such a manner that its opposite would not also be possible. That is: Nothing is so indefinable that it cannot also become something definable, and nothing is so infinite that it might not also be comprehensible. But what is the meaning of these strange sentences? That this absolute subject is altogether free. It is free to enclose itself in a configuration, or not to enclose itself. It does not lack form or configuration but does not remain in any configuration, is not chained to any. By assuming a configuration it can victoriously step out of each one. It would not be free if it had not been free from the beginning either to assume a configuration or not to assume it. Freedom is the essence of that all-pervasive subject, or it is itself nothing other than eternal freedom.

But if it has assumed a configuration out of freedom, it is not capable of breaking through again immediately into its eternal freedom, but can do so only by passing through all configurations that necessarily result.

The content of philosophy is now the process of Being and of the world: how it is grounded through not-to-be-predicted acts of eternal freedom and then takes a necessary course; or: how eternal freedom encloses itself in a configuration and, due to the world-process, finally breaks through again, back into its eternal freedom. This philosophy sees, in the whole of the process of Being that leads from eternity back into eternity, the wrestling power that again consumes every form, rises up again out of each like a phoenix, is transfigured through fiery death.

Can we be persuaded by this task of philosophizing and by this total aspect of Being? Up to the moment of the highest question and of the insight that no determinate answer is possible, we can concur. But when Schelling answers that it is the "eternal freedom," at that very moment a collapse of thinking seems to occur, comparable to Nietzsche's idea of the "will to power." In the objectivizing of freedom, both took a perilous leap.

Philosophical criticism that draws assurance from the origin runs as follows: The fundamental experience of freedom takes place in relation to transcendence, through which it knows itself as a gift to itself. It amounts to a denial of the essence of existential freedom and to a violation of transcendence, if freedom is ascribed to the latter as its essence. "There is no freedom without transcendence"—this is the experience, to be sure, not of arbitrariness but of every substantial freedom. But what becomes of transcendence if we attribute to it what only in relation to it is the essence of finite Existenzen?

I would gladly bring to mind a second example of the great speculations of Schelling, namely, his unforgettable question: Why is there anything at all, why is there not nothing? He posed this question early and repeated it well into his old age, in various connections and with varying answers. But such an account would be too space-consuming, and, in the end, would return to the very same point, namely, the total intuition of Being, which we reached before. From the sovereignty of the philosophical thrust toward the ultimate, and from the power of illumination reached in pushing to the limit, Schelling retreats to narrow quarters—the intuition of Being as eternal freedom and its passing into the world-process. How did this happen?

In transcending, Schelling arrives, appropriately, at thinking Supra-Being, which neither is nor is not, at the Being of everything, at the unthinkable, which he expresses in forms that appear similar to the lofty Asiatic speculations—above all, Buddhistic ones. But he relinquishes such transcending—which shatters determinate categories, this thinking in categories that goes beyond categories—in favor of a fixation of transcendence. He thinks transcendence itself, that is, as freedom, as master of Being, and he defines this freedom as being able to act or not to act, hence as arbitrariness, as the form of freedom that is the worst for us. His use of the idea of freedom makes him speak of possibility and capability. Using the categories of possibility, actuality, necessity—the categories of modality—he thinks first an inner-divine life, and then the theogonic and cosmogonic processes. If this whole can be termed an ontology, then it is an ontology of freedom and an ontology of modality.

We ask about the existential truth contained in such an ontology of freedom. The position that freedom cannot become an object for us and yet is actual within us became a guideline for Schelling in determining Being itself, which also can never become an object. Freedom, instead of being illuminated philosophically in its existential significance, becomes a supersensual object. Once more: Freedom, existentially actual only in relation to transcendence, is transferred to transcendence and thus robbed of its meaning; it becomes an arbitrariness of transcendent Supra-Being.

What happens here is what happens whenever Being itself, or Supra-Being, or God is to be brought into view as an object in analogy to our experience, rather than approached by means of a transcending thought in which logic breaks down. No matter how grandiose the concepts appear, they are doomed to a terrible breakdown, since they turn into what pretends to be knowledge. For Asiatic as well as occidental thinkers the philosophically perennial command remains valid in its Biblical formulation: You shall not make for yourself an image or a likeness.

If we accept this premise, then what about the question Why is there anything at all, or why is there not nothing? Why do we ask this question?

Posited as a question to the intellect alone, it is trivial, frivolous, a joke, unanswerable. Schelling has raised the question to the level of deeply moving philosophizing. In his inability to provide an answer he has expressed a depth of experience. But precisely at that point he wants an answer. This answer becomes central for him; that standing-at-the-limit becomes a merely transitory, though always repeated, moment.

Why does he so urgently want this answer? He says, for example

(XIII, 7), that, in view of the bleak drama of history, of man who, unaware of his purpose, is swept away by this never-resting movement of history toward a goal that he does not know, the experience of a world that is nothing but vanity inescapably leads us to the conviction that all Being is ill-fated; and that then and therefore we are forced to ask the final desperate question: Why is there anything at all, why is there not nothing? Only the answer to this question can deliver us from despair. No science other than philosophy can give the answer. "If I cannot answer that ultimate question, then everything else sinks for me into the abyss of a bottomless void."

Is that true? Is it not possible to stand at the limit with this question, without answer but also without despair, and not plunge into the bottomless void? This is possible when this question, though not answered, but thought through in all possible ways, results in the philosophic thrust into the earnestness of Existenz; when, within the realm of ignorance, we take hold of life in its relation to transcendence, ambiguously illuminated through a world of possible ciphers.

Here it is not a matter of rational decisions. Schelling's true insight that philosophy is volition is inescapable. Our thinking will says: An answer such as that of Schelling's gnosticism is untrue for philosophic cognition and disastrous for Existenz. The resulting calamity must be shown as the necessary consequence of such a way of thinking. But a knowledge capable of answering those questions is by no means necessary for the salvation of man's Existenz. It is perhaps necessary, however, that the answer eludes him in time, so that he can walk in honesty. The path is accessible to him here and now.

I wanted to bring to mind examples of Schelling's speculation, but I would need a long time to reproduce this world of thought adequately: his speculation about unity and duality, his grasp of personality, his notion of actuality and his illumination of the historicity of all that is actual, his speculations regarding time (perhaps the most significant contribution to the subject following Augustine), and especially his philosophy of mythology. Even today his critical lectures (XI, 1–252) about all possible ways of interpreting myth are the most beautiful introduction to the understanding of its historical actuality. He forces us to attain the height at which alone it is meaningful to speak about myths.

4.

Yet, no matter how philosophically exciting Schelling's thoughts are, the descent from peaks always leads to failure. A leap has taken place that can give the impression of Schelling taking himself by surprise. A fog arises in which spirits and ghosts are potentially present. Is there something associated with the first origins that has resulted in the inversion? Is there perhaps the intention of showing, in principle, the wellsprings of the untrue? Is there something inherent in the nature of this fascinating philosophizing that results in allowing its own truth to go astray—not, to be sure, through logical errors, but through a radical inversion of the great beginnings? I shall attempt three points of view.

First: To an almost unprecedented degree, Schelling's philosophy is a *philosophy of reflection* that aspires to overcome itself as reflection. Reflection is meant in every sense of mirroring or bending back. Reflection means the movement of thought which regards, asks, comprehends, and goes beyond the thought itself. Reflection means echoing: I think the thoughts that have already been thought, which reach me out of my surroundings, out of history; they take place within me as if they were my own. Reflection means the pleasure that is no longer the original pleasure of experiencing and acting, but is pleasure in this pleasure of bringing to consciousness that and how it is. The connection within this threefold meaning of reflection is such that it may be captured with the word "reflexivity."

Reflexivity belongs to being human. But the mastery of reflection over authentic originality, over possible Existenz, over the actuality of self-realization is something new. Reflection, when it becomes absolute, takes the place of substance. We must inquire of Schelling whether and to what extent he is the great philosopher of that reflection which penetrates to the ground of Being.

From the beginning he thinks, by means of philosophy, a philosophy of philosophy. With him, philosophy sometimes appears to be sublated into the consciousness of it. In his studies Schelling hardly ever moves ahead by primary research, but through the reflective grasp of what has already been discovered. He recognizes the actuality of his thinking and living in its reverberations from past history. Occasionally it may seem as though he were resurrecting ideas and making past greatness visible again. He tends to consider himself as part of the historic forms of greatness, hallowed, as it were, by the reflection from the past. The greatness of what has been becomes his own greatness by being seen and expressed. The interpretation he gives to unfavorable criticism bears this out: In a letter as enraged as it is self-pitying, he likens the treatment he received to a repetition of Christ's Passion.

Schelling makes reflection the subject of his philosophizing.

He knows: Philosophy arises through reflection. This is its inescapable path. "As infinite science it is, equally, the science of itself" (II, 11). Reflection, at the origin of philosophy, is an act of freedom. It springs from a dissatisfaction with natural being. Man is not brought to reflection by nature. He has to desire it. "Nature does not release anyone voluntarily from its tutelage, and sons of freedom are not born" (II, 12).

But taking hold of reflection by way of freedom presents a risk and a danger. For if reflection becomes its own purpose and goal, then it is deadly. This is how Schelling sees it: Reflection confronts man with himself. The most noble activity, however, is one that does not know itself. "As soon as man makes himself the object, it is no longer the whole man who is acting." The original balance between powers and consciousness is sublated through the freedom of reflection. "Mere reflection is a mental illness that nips man's higher existence in the bud and kills his spiritual life at the root" (II, 12). Schelling poses the task of overcoming without destroying what must be risked in reflection by the thinker.

Reflection is, indeed, the means of becoming master of one's thoughts. It is by virtue of reflection that Schelling perceived the sovereignty of philosophy. Philosophy takes its distance, once again, from all thoughts entertained by it.

Here, then, is the question addressed to Schelling's philosophy, which cannot be answered by a thought, only through familiarity with Schelling's work and nature. Who is the master of the thoughts—what is there, where does the guidance come from?

Could it be that Schelling did not become master of reflection because it arrogated dominance to itself? Did the genius of the spirit replace original thought in Schelling?

Externalized reflexivity is called gesture. It is actuality, but is intentional, demanding, unstable actuality. Schelling loves the grand gesture, the solemnity of appearance, prophetic dignity. He presents himself as someone unique, as someone endowed with extraordinary knowledge. This is how Schelling projected himself and how we see him to this day.

With Schelling, a new tone entered the history of philosophy. This urgency, this intensification, this emphasis, this heightened sound played on an organ, as it were, intends effect. We are forced to listen. The aristocratic gesture is twisted into philosophic demagoguery. He claims a certain nobility for himself and yet may lack an unfailing nobility of the heart. He knows about the nobility of the spirit without being truly noble himself. He presents himself as an exception, yet fails to be so. He presents himself as a victim, and this too is gesture. The grandeur of elevated perspectives leads him to the limits where kitsch begins.

Schelling exemplifies the consequence of a position of total reflexivity, which, ultimately, is untransparent even to itself. This paradigm derives its greatness from the inspired idea of philosophizing-as-echo. Schelling unfolds a speculative virtuosity that, in spite of the diffuseness of deceptions, yet achieves wonderful insights. With Schelling's deep aesthetic sensibility, something is activated in him that may be likened to an earnestness within a lack of earnestness because the potentiality of earnestness is present. If there is an echo, it is an echo that is grasped and gripping. It is as though the thinker in his sensitivity would glean from not-being-himself the ability to express all the more clearly what has been experienced only as an echo. It is as though, in his self-delusion about what is actual in himself, he is enabled to say what philosophy is, what it could be and should be. But if one's own substance—this constant criterion of philosophic truth—is absent, what is left is mere gesturing, mere thought-play, even nonsense. And yet there is significance in all this. In his capacity to attract and repel, Schelling remains exciting for us. Even in his mischievous absurdity, we view him with amazement, attributable to our awe before greatness. But on the other hand, there remains the lingering question, even as we address his profound thoughts, whether they are not already vitiated by the worm causing their deformity. It may appear to us as though from their very inception reflection cast a shadow on even his most elevated thought forays.

A directionless reflexivity must lead to a pervasive ambiguity concerning Schelling's knowledge about what is philosophical and his non-realization of this knowledge. He knows about the philosophy that he does not actualize. He demands so much that is right, and yet he does not fulfill these demands. But he comports himself as if, by having formulated these demands so clearly, he had already fulfilled them. Since he does not follow up on his knowledge about the essential, that knowledge is obscured again. Hence the break occurs: measured by the yardstick of his own philosophizing, he seems to be actual neither in his philosophy nor in his life. His philosophizing first appears as the knowledge of how things should be, and subsequently like the forgetting of this knowledge.

Thus we seem to sense in Schelling a responsiveness to an experience of possibilities. And yet this is thought that, far from being the unfolding of originality, soon shows itself to be forced construction. It is not the power of the essence that prevails without need of noise or violence either; rather, it shows itself in the form of dictatorial demands. Neither is it the quiet self-assurance of greatness, but restless sensibility. And neither does it show character determined by the reliability of a transcendentally grounded will, but a softness characterized by swings from boasting to reticence. He is a master of gestures, as well versed in the mannerism of the philosopher's tranquillity as in that of the prophet's thrust.

He stands in stark contrast to earlier philosophy, to its deeply moving unpretentiousness, to its concealed manifestation, which Schelling himself saw and pointed to. Schelling no longer matched the clarity, purity, and moderation of Kant. He is not yet aware, as Kierkegaard and Nietzsche will be, of the new call for honesty that arises in the medium of infinite reflection. He lacks the firmness, the marvelous unreflectedness despite all reflection that we see in the great metaphysicians, such as Spinoza, Anselm, Plotinus.

Second: We cannot think without *thinking an object*. Whoever philosophizes must also *objectivize* as he thinks. But philosophy gains its truth by melting down the objects. It loses its meaning, on the other hand, by becoming fixed to objects whose permanence may even turn them into the object of philosophic research.

Schelling recognized this in his earliest writings and repeated it up to his last ones: Being cannot be an object. The young Schelling recognized the principle of the enthusiasm that he rejected (I, 317–26): It arises "when one considers the intuition of oneself to be the intuition of an object external to oneself, and the intuition of the interior intellectual world to be that of a suprasensual world external to oneself."

The older Schelling repeats: "All disregarding of our present state, all knowledge that is not pure development out of what is present or actual is . . . reprehensible and leads to enthusiasm and error" (IX, 20ff.).

Yet with regard to the development of his philosophy of nature, which according to him is possible only if, in intellectual intuition, we abstract from all customary intuition, Schelling says: As *my* construct it will always be comprehended in my intuition, and I know that I am dealing throughout only with my own construct" (IV, 91).

When he speaks in laudatory terms about how "pure intuition long ago invented symbolic language," he immediately qualifies: "Every audacious formulation in philosophy borders on dogmatism, since it attempts to represent something that can never be the object of representation. It symbolizes what it cannot explain by reference to sensation. If one takes the symbol to be the object itself, then a philosophy comes into being that sounds even more fantastic than the religion of the ancient Egyptians" (I, 405).

The old Schelling still reiterates: "It is a contradiction that eternal freedom is to be cognized; . . . as an absolute subject, it cannot possibly become object." Though Schelling later spoke of the absolute subject in terms of capability, volition, and desire, he says: "Eternal pure capability evades everything, it is nonobjective, is absolute inwardness. The same applies to pure volition and desire."

However, Schelling forgets this clear insight, though on occasion he recaptures it momentarily, to the very end. The range of his work presents a cognition that he has declared to be impossible. For he develops at all times an objectivity, that is, a history in which that which is, is thought objectively: as the history of self-consciousness in the stages of knowing and acting consciousness, as the history of nature in its stages up to man, as the history of Being as a whole, of the theogonic, cosmogonic, mythological, and revelationary process.

Surprisingly Schelling believes he has overcome the ties to the object, as well as dogmatic thinking, solely by thinking Being not as object but as becoming. But becoming is no less objective than being-object, the system of becoming no less objective than the system of unchangeable Being. To be sure, his philosophizing is genetic, but that which is thought genetically, although it is not an objective thing, is an objective suprasensuous-sensual process.

The pattern of genetic philosophizing remains constant in Schelling, no matter whether the content is transcendental consciousness or nature or the being of God or myth. These contents need not contradict one another. Rather, they come together in Schelling's last comprehensive intuition: his negative and positive philosophy.

Again and again Schelling executes his perilous leap. This he can do only by becoming the "enthusiast" whose principle he himself had unmasked. To this corresponds also his early and late profession of loyalty to the enthusiasts, whether Boehme or Baader or even Swedenborg.

This leap is not an act of volition. It is not immediately noticeable to the reader. Schelling grounds his actions in intellectual intuition, by means of which man is in the center and the origin of all things. The self-recognition of eternal freedom, presented as a process of Being, is our own consciousness. Reflection is the driving factor in Being itself. Or, conversely, our consciousness is self-recognition of eternal freedom. We are ourselves that process (IX, 225ff.). Hence our ability to recognize it.

What tremendous enhancement of man by Schelling! "In man alone we find again that unfathomable freedom; in the midst of time, he is outside time; it is granted to him to be again the beginning, hence he is the restored beginning." And without hesitation he ranges himself among the enthusiasts. "A vague memory of having once been the beginning, the power, the absolute center of all is evidently active in man."

What motivates this leap to the objectivization of the cognized suprasensible? Aside from the theosophic intuitions, which were ever-present second nature to Schelling, it may have been the reflexivity of his mode of thought and existence.

If undirected, unlimited reflection threatens to become philosophy itself, then the question arises: How does the road lead from unlimited reflection to earnestness? Or from thought to actuality? Or from philosophizing to Existenz?

All philosophy, as configuration of thought, as work of the mind, has an exposed flank. It is incomplete. To achieve wholeness it needs to be completed. This completion may be an ecclesiastical faith; philosophy may become the preamble of such faith and thereby cease to be philosophy. This is not a possibility for Schelling, just as it is not for any other philosopher.

Instead, Schelling sought that completion in a second philosophy, brought forth by him for the first time. This philosophy is to take hold of what is positive, of actuality itself, and thus overcome for all time reflection and what is negative in philosophizing.

As a matter of fact, philosophy—as the human achievement of thinking—needs to be completed in actuality, albeit in the actuality of man, in his possible Existenz, which the individual actualizes but does not recognize historically. Then the answer to the question of the completion of philosophy will not be given through knowledge, but through this actuality of philosophy itself. Philosophy can illuminate only indirectly, can encircle, call attention, arouse.

Schelling perceived the inadequacy in the reflexivity of philosophizing, and perhaps in the reflexivity of his life altogether. He sought deliverance from reflexivity without recognizing his own reflexivity, without inquiring into the question of deliverance. He sensed that with all the reflections and even with the overcoming of the movements of reflection in the system we can never reach actuality. He experienced the negativity of all rational philosophy. What reason recognizes is everywhere the "what it is," the possible, and not the "that it is," the actual. In order to reach actuality and thus to assure to the seeker repose in the end, he invented positive philosophy. However, in Schelling this positive philosophy is merely the latest configuration of his objectifications of the suprasensuous, which, contrary to his own insights, he pursued throughout his life.

Based on this interpretation we may say: Schelling answered the question How does the path lead out of reflection into the earnestness of Existenz? not through methodical development of the modes of thinking that signify what makes Existenz philosophically possible, but through the transition from reflexivity to concrete objectivity of knowledge of Being.

To be sure, Schelling did not pose the question in this form of an alternative. But his metaphysics is a de facto answer. Here he commits an existential error as well as an error in thinking. He wants to find the leap to earnestness itself through philosophy regarded as the thinking of an object, that is, of actuality that is not excogitated, so that what is essential may again become an achievement of thought.

Schelling knew and did express this. It is astonishing to see him demanding and carrying out the absolute dominion of philosophy—by distancing himself from everything that, in methodical consciousness, is thought in the philosophy of philosophy—and see him subsequently falling prey to objectifications, and subordinating himself to schematisms, systems, and configurations of thought. We see a constant alternation between deep insight and objectifying fixation, between methodic insight and contravention of his own insight.

It is hard to find a philosopher who expressed with such lucidity the selfsame critical thoughts that invalidate his thinking as he carried out his metaphysics.

To repeat: Schelling confounds conjuring something up in order to make it present with objectification, or illumination of Existenz with gnosis.

By this process he neglected the task to which his insight actually led him, the task of testing all thinking against the existential meaning of its performance and contents. The objectifications would have to be tested as to their possible meaning for the illumination of Existenz or as ciphers of transcendence. The impetus, no longer capturable through any act of thought, would have to bring about, in Existenz, the response to philosophy.

Is the manner in which Schelling takes hold of intellectual intuition to blame for his errors from the very start? Might it be that he demands too much of it; above all, that he does not differentiate between intellectual intuition as a mental tool for creating pictures and thoughts and the experience of possible Existenz; that he allows the profundities of all philosophic truth to be mingled in a murky multiplicity?

In his passionate struggle for actuality, Schelling neglects the task of arriving at actuality by the way in which he thinks actuality. His failure consists in his persevering in "the pure ether of thought" and in being satisfied with the noncommittal intuition of fancies, fixating the objects in the bottomlessness of such fantasies. Yet this is something which both the young as well as the old Schelling had rejected as the original sin of free philosophy.

The following citations are the historical testimony of truth and its corruption in Schelling: When the young Kierkegaard heard the old Schelling in 1841, he commented, at the start of the lectures: "When he used the word 'actuality' . . . the fruit of my thoughts leaped with joy in me, as in Elizabeth," only to add a few months later: "Schelling babbles quite unbearably."

Schelling's leap into the ground of Being may be seen as a forced leap ending in a fall into bottomlessness, while he conjures up phantasmagoria. Or we may liken his ascent to Being to the flight of Icarus ending in his downward plunge.

And yet these attempts stand the test of truth as long as, issuing from the situation of our existence and consciousness, they serve to support the basic operations through which we become aware of this situation, reach and touch the limits. Hence the study of Schelling remains worthwhile. But to appropriate his thought may be likened to climbing a mountain, where every false step leads to a philosophic plunge. Philosophical life continues to be a matter of journeying, provided its impulse is grounded in a deliberate, fundamental decision at the core of one's philosophizing. It is the decision between alternatives: Either we elect to stand at a point outside and to speak from there, over and above the actuality of what is present, disdaining criteria, making use of an intellectual intuition that becomes questionable, and satisfied with gnostic cognition; or we remain within the orientation of our world and carry through with what we are and the reality we find ourselves in (all the modes of the Encompassing). Then, also in union with Schelling, we pursue the questions to the limit and urge them to that upward plane where there is no answer, where, rather, the questions become the speculative counterthrust into the earnestness of Existenz, into the actual presentness that we are and can be. We then recognize that those overleaping objectivizations cannot be carried out and hence are illusions of which it can merely be asked whether they achieve the meaning of ciphers, authentically carried out, or whether they are simply nothing.

Third: Schelling's undoing in failing to master reflexivity and in falling prey to objectivizations reaches its culmination in his *consciousness of his mission*. His reflection on his age poses this tremendous task within the perspective of world history. The objectivizations put him in possession of a knowledge it is incumbent on him to proclaim. Schelling had a consciousness of his mission early on, preceding all content. Knowledge of the task and possession of the true philosophy must then be seized upon in this consciousness of mission. He feels himself superior to all others, the only one who is called, in the flux of time and carried along with it, to be the guide and to bring about eternal truth.

The present and history are seen according to the old schema: Everything is undermined; the convulsion is a total one. The new is approaching; dawn is breaking.

Philosophy is destined to save the times. In his youth Schelling wrote: "The philosophers have often complained that their science has little effect on human volition and the fate of our whole race." How could it be otherwise? "They complain that a science which, as such, exists nowhere, has no influence." To be sure, there were basic principles, but only a part of mankind considered them to be true. "Who will follow the guidance of a leadership which does not yet dare to think of itself as the only true one?" (I, 112).

He feels himself to be the one who will be the bearer of this philosophy. He has started to teach it, but it is still incomplete. To the very last his high demand is upheld: the rejection of all previous philosophical thought, his appearance as the bearer of the one, true, new philosophy. "No philosophy up to now has reached the matter itself, that is, has become true science; instead, it has always remained mired in its preliminaries. In particular, recent German philosophy resembles an endless preface, whose main text one still awaits in vain" (XIII, 178).

In no period has this authentic philosophy been as urgently needed as in the present declining era. It alone is "the means of healing the disintegration of our times." But Schelling adds: "Of course I do not mean by this a feeble philosophy, not a mere artifact; I mean a strong philosophy, one that can compete with life, that takes its strength out of actuality itself and then produces something effective and lasting" (XIII, 8–10). Did Schelling from the very beginning raise the level of philosophy so far above the measure of human things that its toppling was unavoidable?

Measured against the magnitude of his claim, the actual Schelling is shamefully inadequate. Even though he senses the crisis of world history in the situation of his time, he is not involved in it with his whole being.

His discussion of the crisis and his response to it originate in reflection. In spite of all his radical statements he is able to live calmly and unquestioningly in the continuity of the traditional order. Also, because for him it was merely a matter of reflection, he did not, in any practical fashion, take the road into a new age. Rather, his thinking must be assigned to the modes of obscurantism of an earlier age, to a way of salvation that leads not to rescue but to deceptive reassurance.

Schelling is convinced that he is the bearer of a philosophy that will save us. He arrogates to himself the kind of professorial claim of preeminence that is based on being a knower, proclaimer, and prophet. From this position he demands a predominant role at the university, as befits the charismatic spiritual power with which he was endowed. Schelling's demands when he was called, for the second time, to the University of Jena in 1816 are one example. Goethe, with his sure instinct for limits and his sense of reality, prevented the appointment of his friend because of these demands. A more telling example is Schelling's acceptance of his appointment to Berlin by the king of Prussia as "teacher of the Age." Such a figure was then widely admired. Among the professors, an instinctive mimicking of Schelling's attitudes became noticeable. I myself, on attending Kuno Fischer's lectures, felt as though I detected in his speech a last faint trace of Schelling's manner.

All this accords with the strange nature of his self-assurance. In the brilliance of his intellect, the self-certainty of his abilities, the enthusiasm of his basic philosophical insights, the young Schelling stands before us as unshakable. Caroline Schelling called him "granite." But he turned out to be anything but granite. When, as early as his Jena years, his high claims failed and his first great success did not endure, his self-assurance turned into self-importance. His devotion to the cause became entwined with an egocentricity that clouded everything. With disillusionment came self-delusion. The almost constant polemics, the restlessness, the absence of constantly watchful critical examination made his self-assertion seem forced. He fell out with most of the great minds among his friends—Fichte, Hegel, Baader; he held almost everyone in contempt, regarded those of whom he approved as his pupils and judged them according to their loyalty—Steffens, Schubert, Beckers. His self-assurance was shaky and hence enormously sensitive. He courted effect; he acted grimly proud, denying himself to others; he became taciturn. But he continued in the conscious display of his superiority. Wherever he appeared as speaker, he held his audience spellbound, until this too came to an end, and he withdrew completely from public life during his last years.

One symptom of Schelling's three inversions is the extent to which he was mistaken about realities. He disregards them or misjudges them, while at the same time he has ambitions to penetrate the depths of actuality with his thinking, and indeed succeeds in doing so conceptually.

It is easy to discern to what degree he misunderstood his age. His lacunae become evident by comparison with Kierkegaard, with Marx, with the political thinking and the political events of his time, and subsequently with Nietzsche. If we compare what he thought with these great minds steeped in actuality, it is clear that Schelling was ignorant in the ways of the Romantics.

It further becomes clear that he had no conception of the meaning of the natural sciences and their achievements, that philosophically as well as scientifically he made foolish assertions with regard to matters scientifically verifiable. He would come up with ingenious theses such as: The creatures of earlier epochs studied by paleontology never lived at all; they were created as they are now, as also was the mammoth embedded in the Siberian frost, that is, from the very act of the world's creation they were created as something past (XI, 499).

Further, Schelling's estrangement from the political realities of his time has to be shown. Again, without having observed them properly, he develops ingenuous constructions in disregard of the realities. For example, in the revolutionary year of 1848 he proposes to the king of Bavaria, as best fitted for that role, that there be an elected emperor who, through the sovereignty of all the ruling princes, would unite Germany as a nation of nations, including Prussia and Austria.

Finally, to what degree Schelling was a stranger to actual religion needs to be stated. In his construct of "the philosophical religion" he propagates a new, historically necessary Johannine Age. He misunderstands the independence of religion as manifested in cult, rites, laws, community, in sacred places and ages, in the authority grounded on God. He knows that all these religious manifestations are not based on an error on the part of humanity which can be psychologically or sociologically explained. He considers philosophy to be a superior authority, enabling us to see through the various religious phenomena to guide religion and to found it anew. But the independent authority of critical philosophy is valid only for the manner in which philosophically grounded Existenz relates to religion. To be sure, it can question, limitlessly, the religious actuality, though it cannot appropriate it. Schelling wants to control religion philosophically and tell theologians how to think. He, who seems to take the historical reality of myths and revelations so seriously, appears blind to the actuality of religion.

Each of the three inversions—arising from reflexivity, from objectification, from the consciousness of mission—is grounded in a truth, a
truth that should not be lost as we reject the inversion.

Reflection ought to remain unlimited. Whatever we think in philosophizing must be brought to consciousness through methodological
deliberation so that we come to be masters of our thoughts and learn to
evaluate their meaning and their limits. But such dominion also includes
an awareness of the guidance within us that, though eluding our cognition, is part of our human responsibility and sets us limits. Wedded
to this responsibility, we are, beyond the realm of comprehension, given
to ourselves as a gift in our freedom and all its manifestations. Keeping
attuned to this guidance means refusal of a meaningless infinity, of
arbitrariness instead of sovereign reflection.

In thinking, we objectivize. *Objectivization* is essential. But it must
be carried out philosophically, that is, in such a manner that what is
objectified remains in suspension, that it is always only a foothold in a
movement that lets it disappear again. Hence philosophical formulations
are so irritating to whoever wants to grasp the content objectively as a
fixed possession: to him, it appears as though something is given with
one hand and taken away with the other. But we are spurred on precisely
when we are touched by whatever communicates itself indirectly in the
objectifications.

Being *conscious of one's task* is part of the responsibility of philosophizing. However, if it becomes a consciousness of mission its truth is
vitiated at its very root by the will to be recognized. As philosophers we
are individuals among millions. If we remain true to truth, then we
uphold something indefinable, as Schelling well knew. This is the unconditional point that supports the thinking and acting and the whole
life of the humblest as well as the greatest person. It does so, however,
only in the form of demands upon oneself, demands that comprise
modesty in one's demand on others.

5.

Schelling's immoderate claims for his philosophy imply a premise that
many before and after him also posited: There exists the one and only
true philosophy, which is valid equally for everyone and which therefore
rightly claims dominion. Hence arises the further presupposition: This
philosophy can originate and come to completion in the head of a single
thinker. He himself then becomes the movement of history in its entirety,
the turning point, the founder and ruler of his age.

Counter to this claim is the other presupposition: Such sovereign rank must not be granted to any man, not even the greatest in all the millennia (nor has a great man ever claimed such a rank for himself; it has always been imposed on him by the loyal faithful), because no one can possess the true philosophy. Everybody remains a mere human being. Man's life, looked at in honesty, is set within a realm of forces that cannot be exhaustively surveyed by any human being. We never stand outside. It is from within that we look for the opponent through whom we first define ourselves, and for the line of battle in which we find ourselves. We do not see them with any finality; hence the insatiable desire to communicate. Even what is most alien must be allowed expression and be heard. Whatever men are, think, and do concerns me without my having to become and think as they do. I want to be questioned and challenged so that I may deceive myself less. I want to question what is alien in order to force it into the open so that I may find out what is behind its assertions. I want to convince and be convinced. And I would like to acknowledge differences and be acknowledged by them. Only where there is the will to communicate can alien elements come together, can they define themselves in the encounter. Such communication is not the destructive battle in which the intellect serves as a weapon for the self-assertion of existence, rather than as a means for bringing about community. Instead, communication is a loving struggle. If darkened by hatred the lines of battle cannot be clearly drawn. True, hatred sharpens the eye for weaknesses, but it blinds it to the substance. In confrontations of hatred the antagonists can only repel each other without coming to know one another.

Since truth is possible only in communication, the real and worst enemy is he who turns a deaf ear to communication, to being questioned and called into question; who evades what he proclaims to be a hopeless lack of understanding; who refuses to answer; who demands, as preliminary to any discussion, belief in a certain something, be it man or thing. This resistance to communication constitutes the most profound rupture between men. It amounts to a betrayal of our very humanity. What happens in the intellectual sphere has repercussions in existence. As its ultimate consequence, the breakdown of communication leads to a state in which human beings can only avoid or kill each other. One criterion of truth, however, is whether it enables us to live together. That is true which unites us.

Fuzziness or half-measures have no place here; no unilluminated feelings must be left in control, such as, for instance, positing as a scientific truth a universally valid philosophy which, in deceptive garb, constitutes the last attenuated claim to domination. Such presuppositions harbor a radical alternative for philosophizing.

As we investigate Schelling's stand, some passages in his work permit us to claim him for our own. But mostly, indeed dominating everything, there is to be found in him the alternative premise. It forces us into profound opposition.

6.

Schelling's philosophy is ambiguous. The treasures embedded in his thinking are indeed precious. But his opus makes one think of a mine in which the veins of ore and precious stones have to be searched for laboriously, or like a jungle hiding marvelous blossoms in its luxuriant tangles. In dealing with Schelling we must be prepared to appropriate and reject, to alternate between gratefulness and irritation, to feel close to him and yet end up at the farthest distance.

We have a responsibility that cannot be satisfied by our intellect; it draws on our substance, for which intellect is only an instrument. In dealing with Schelling, who would presume to claim universal validity for his judgments? But whoever takes his philosophical purpose and himself seriously is seeking clarity. In compliance with Schelling's dictum that philosophy is essentially volition, he must know what he wants. By expressing what he considers to be true, the philosophizing interpreter of Schelling's work engages in open-minded battle with other admirers of Schelling of equal seriousness, those who do not indulge in the arbitrary limitlessness of mental operations growing out of a depersonalized moment of nonbeing.

Schelling can be helpful to us. He acknowledged and brought to our consciousness the high level of philosophy realized by the great thinkers of another rank, such as Plato, Kant, Spinoza. He awakened our sense of greatness in philosophy. He made us humble, provided we do not succumb to the temptation of pride in our participation in philosophical thought, for we have gained only a measuring rod, not a possession.

Schelling's thinking frees us from the accepted commonplaces. He leads us to the comprehension of the finite as finite; he shows how we gain assurance in the speculative ascent of Being. As long as we avoid slipping into the entanglements and bewitchments of his concrete intuitions about nature, myth, revelation, we arrive at the wondrous possibilities of philosophy.

Ultimately, Schelling's importance lies in his actualization of seduction itself. A great error, committed in grand style, has become visible once and for all, so that it will not be repeated. Because he fell into it, those coming after him can study in the light of his example what they are now able to avoid. Again and again we are exposed to the temptations to which Schelling succumbed. He shows them to us in grandiose style, alerting us to them for all time. His misjudgment accrues to our benefit. Schelling's succumbing to temptation has the exemplary character of a warning.

Philosophy is of such awesome effect and its seriousness so momentous that I would be despicable if I did not respond in kind. This is the path to which Schelling guides us and intends to guide us. However, as I have tried to indicate, the truth he postulates turns to a still indeterminate degree against his own work and even his nature. Hence he harbors in himself both greatness and undoing, and we have the task of orienting ourselves by his greatness while resisting what is his undoing.

Criticism of a great thinker must not be regarded as rejection. Criticism allows what is great to shine all the more brightly, even the greatness inherent in the error. My presentation here grows from my sympathy for Schelling over the decades during which I constantly wrestled with this sympathy. What unites us is Schelling's quality as a great philosopher who cannot be bypassed. I hope to have demonstrated my respect for him in the compass of my struggling with him. No one possesses the truth, the unlimited, complete, unalloyed truth. It suffices if a portion of it reaches us, reflectedly, as a stirring, glorious radiance.

Constructive Minds

LEIBNIZ

LEIBNIZ

Editors' Note

Gottfried Wilhelm von Leibniz was born in Leipzig in 1646, the son of a professor of moral philosophy. His precocious mind had absorbed much of extant European learning by the age of twelve. From 1661 to 1666 he pursued studies in law, mathematics, and philosophy, and received his doctorate in jurisprudence from the University of Altdorf in 1667. Instead of an academic career, he chose to serve princely patrons in more directly practical capacities. Both his practical career and his philosophical thought were pervaded by a kind of "diplomatic spirit" of harmonious striving.

After serving as secretary of the Rosicrucian Society in Nuremberg, he worked in legal reform and diplomacy in Frankfurt. From 1668 to 1673 he served the Elector of Mainz, and was sent to Paris to allay a French move into German and Dutch territories. He remained there until 1676, studying the new Cartesian philosophy with Nicolas de Malebranche and pursuing physics and mathematics with Christian Huygens. In Paris he also perfected his multiple-function calculating machine. A sojourn in London as attaché put him in touch with chemist Robert Boyle and the British Royal Society, to which he was elected in 1673.

From 1676 Leibniz served the house of Brunswick-Lüneburg as privy councillor, judge, librarian, and dynastic historian. On travels to Amsterdam, he met Spinoza, and studied the latter's still-unpublished *Ethics*. He played a crucial role in building an institutional framework for scholarly interchange in Europe, founding the Berlin Academy of Sciences in 1700. He also advised Peter the Great of Russia on educational and scientific reforms. Confined in his last years to ceremonial posts, he continued his varied researches with rigorous zeal. He died in 1716.

1. BASIC THOUGHT

Leibniz's development shows that the essential elements of his thinking, adopted from the tradition, are present even in his first youthful attempts.[1] From Aristotelian-scholastic thinking he takes the thought of the independent and authentic actuality of the *individual*, which cannot be deduced from the universal. It is something positive and is actual neither through negation nor through privation of the universal. It is not comprehensible through contraction of the species to the specific difference of the individual. Rather, the ground of individuality lies in the totality of positive determinations of substances. Each individual is individuated by virtue of its entire beingness (*entitas*). This traditional thought, adopted by Leibniz at seventeen, was deepened and reshaped throughout his life, leading him far beyond his beginnings.

Leibniz also took over the *mechanical* interpretation of natural occurrences, which, from the time of Democritus, assumed many forms and was brought up to date by Gassendi and Hobbes and the natural scientists of the time. Even late in life Leibniz remembered his decision to drop Aristotelian-scholastic forms of explaining occurrences in nature and to change over to mechanistic thought, which was proving itself so fertile in factual cognition. Leibniz soon took the next step. He not only limited the mechanistic interpretation to corporeal nature, but also transcended it with respect to the world as a whole through the notion of purposeful structure, the teleological order of things, which uses mechanism as a means, and reintroduced substantial forms in a new, altered configuration.

A third basic thought adopted by Leibniz is that of the *infinity* of the universe and of each thing, as it had its last great formulation in Cusanus. There is no smallest and no greatest, because we can always think something still smaller or greater. Everything is divided, into infinity; worlds are hidden in the smallest, worlds in worlds. The thought of infinity becomes fruitful for Leibniz in all areas of cognition through the bridging of opposites (rest is infinitely small movement; the living organism is a machine with a purposefulness reaching into infinity, as differentiated from the finite purposiveness of the machines produced by man, the finite parts of which are no longer machines). The notion of infinity gives depth to Leibniz's thinking, as well as contradictoriness and the means for solving the contradictions.

[1] Cf. Willy Kabitz, *Die Philosophie des jungen Leibniz.*

A fourth basic thought Leibniz accepted is that of the *harmony* of all things.

From the very beginning, all of Leibniz's thoughts are grounded— a grounding that remains unquestioned throughout his life—in the premise that the universe is completely in accord with reason, and hence it can rationally be cognized; that through God the essence of all things is rationality. This too is a time-honored idea: *nihil sine ratione*.

What is peculiar to Leibnizian philosophy is, first, the concatenation of all these basic thoughts, which, in themselves, are not original. Beyond that, it is the fertility arising out of this concatenation and the consistency with which it brings about—in the almost incalculable multiplicity of specific cognitions—a unity in thinking and a whole that can be presented as a system: the system of monadology and preestablished harmony.

Our comprehension of Leibniz's complete work would be restricted if we were to reduce it to one principle, for example, to logic and its presuppositions; or to the dynamics in physics through which mechanism first becomes possible as a real mechanism; or to mathematics, especially the theory of numbers, since Leibniz sees everything according to this paradigm and the structure of all things according to Pythagorean tradition; or to monadology as the final configuration of the metaphysical principle of the existence solely of the individual.

We may with equal right maintain that from the very beginning all of Leibniz's movements of thought are grounded metaphysically, and that monadology represents a convoluted structure resulting from logical inferences. We can speak of a basic frame of mind that resides in the notion of harmony, in intrinsic accord with the will of God, in the trust that everything is in order; and we can say right away that this basic frame of mind is precisely the ineradicable certainty of the rationality of God and the universe and that, therefore, rational cognition is the only way into the ground, and that, therefore, from the very beginning rational construction from logical premises was, for Leibniz, the form of his philosophy. The motifs of his worldview are expressed from the outset as such constructions. Construction is not empty for Leibniz, since it carries much weight in his metaphysical thought.

The conceptuality that forms the content of this construction is closely bound up with the ground of things itself. It aims at the most extensive, encompassing breadth, refuses to leave anything out, wants to combine everything, since it is already present in the ground of things and only as such becomes clear to reason. Leibniz's intellectual stature allows him to forge ahead, in his constructions, to depths that cannot be derived from the traditional elements of his overall thinking. But their metaphysical importance remains limited, since the rational premise of this form of faith in reason comprehending the ground of things lacks, as such, metaphysical depth.

The metaphysical impetus of faith in God's rationality lends a heightened importance to all rational activity. But then the independent interest in inventing, the pleasure of operating, making, and creating as such (whether a calculating machine or a mine, whether minting or political action) gains the upper hand. Leibniz concerns himself with everything, takes on almost every task, always by rational means, his *ratio* grounded in God; but the question arises as to what degree the original motive remains powerful and effective, to what degree it is lost in constructions and procedures, or to what degree it is presented in the infinite actuality of thinking or is flatly contradicted by it, leaving the merely constructive.

Leibniz's first great development out of the basic motive took place in Paris from 1672 to 1676. Especially through his contact with Christian Huygens, he became the great mathematician who, in connection with the thought of infinity, succeeded, in 1676, in discovering the differential and the integral calculus. This achievement has remained to this day his most famous, since it has been of immeasurable importance for the mathematical sciences. Leibniz never ceased developing new ideas, though none of them equaled the aforementioned in specific scientific relevance. He discovered ever new means of promoting his fundamental task, that is, to grasp the world in its rationality through the instrument of one's own reason.

2. THE MONADOLOGY

a) *Physics and metaphysics—science and philosophy:* We shall endeavor to comprehend the monadology critically by looking at its characteristics.

1) To be sure, Leibniz differentiates between physical research and metaphysical foundation. But in his thinking he does not keep them apart at all. In him, the metaphysical foundation itself assumes the form of a scientific theory of the underlying ground. The physical principles are posited as metaphysical ones grounded purely in thinking.

Thus, in Leibniz, the law of the "conservation of energy" is quite distinct from the same principle in modern natural science, since Leibniz intends it to be valid only in general, without application to or demonstration in natural phenomena by means of scale, measure, and readings.

As a result, such theses as: the mind is always thinking, even when we sleep without dreaming, unless it is devoid of all consciousness; or, the body is never without motion; rest is a minimum of motion; or, a substance is never without activity—all have an ambiguousness that on the one hand expresses mere metaphysical postulates, and on the other promises application to practical research, without, however, delivering on this promise. Here Leibniz's constructivism is akin to that of Descartes and Hobbes, as opposed to Galileo, Kepler, Newton. In distinction from these natural scientists, those philosophers think, to be sure, in mathematical terms, but without the mathematical method, which is considered fruitful only as it proves itself in experiment or measured observation.

Such constructivism is to be understood as metaphysics and must not be confused, even in its fundamental attitude, with science, in whose garb it appears.

2) A superficial indicator of the difference between science and metaphysics is that only the natural sciences allow for a genuine battle over priorities. It is characteristic that Leibniz could claim priority for many of his thought-constructs without eliciting any reactions. Over the invention of the differential and the integral calculus, however, a bitter battle of priority lasting for decades raged between Leibniz and Newton. For only here had an actual, weighty, solid discovery been made. Concerning philosophic thoughts there never was a battle of comparable significance. For in philosophy there is no actual priority, because there is no actual theft, either—except when texts are copied; here there is only originality of thinking, which cannot be repeated in identical form as is possible with the content of a scientific discovery.

3) Leibniz himself called preestablished harmony a hypothesis, even if an extremely certain one. He treated his monadology like a scientific theory of underlying Being, of objectively thought Being-as-such. He constructed this theory in its ramifications. At specific points he illustrated rather than proved it by means of facts. The whole is neither gnosis as it is found in theosophic tradition, nor illumination of Existenz as great philosophers carry it out by referring their metaphysical vision to man's entire conduct of life as well as to his decisions. Herder called Leibniz a "poet in metaphysics," Schiller spoke of preestablished harmony as a "humorous idea by an excellent mind, which he himself never believed," Hegel spoke of a "metaphysical novel."[2]

b) *The truths found on the way despite the absurdity of the whole:*

[2] Johann Gottfried Herder, *Andrastea*, in *Sämmtliche Werke*, Berlin, Weidmann, 1885–86, XXIII, 482. Friedrich Schiller, "Philosophie der Physiologie," ed. by Oskar Walzel, in *Sämtliche Werke*, Stuttgart and Berlin, J. G. Cotta, 1904, XI, 21–23. ¶2. Hegel, *Sämmtliche Werke*, XIX, 454.

Although the whole of monadology is invented as objective machinery of the universe, this thought-configuration gains its depth through the concept of infinity, and its effectiveness through Leibniz's ever new ideas regarding the details. Even if, as a whole, the thought-configuration is completely implausible, the questions it poses in the development of its thoughts can point to mysteries that, though not solved, serve to deepen world-consciousness. Leibniz, who, overall, seems so absurd, manages in particular instances to be to the point and almost always informative. He opens up categorial spaces, as it were. Though taken aback by the overall absurdity, we are yet enthralled.

We can find in Leibniz much that is positive—above all, certain points of view that supply the conceptual bases for further inquiry: the differentiation of "conscious" and "unconscious" and related concepts; the question of the unity and continuity of all things. In all this some sort of philosophy is operative "nonetheless," despite the form of scientific theory and manner of proof: The idea of individuality as monad contains existential possibilities; his intuitions garnered by means of the idea of infinity contain metaphysical ciphers.

c) *Aspects:* The meaning of monadology exhibits several aspects, depending on what we allow to affect us.

1) Logically, by its extreme complication, it gives the impression that it was constructed for the purpose of forcing the solution of all difficulties. Seen in this light it seems artificial, and absurd in its character as objectivizing hypothesis.

2) Then it can suddenly strike us as a great vision of Being, especially in the vision of nature awakening from sleep and coming to itself out of unconsciousness, of a world-event as a whole and in its details, in which the infinite wealth of a creative possibility, infinite by virtue of unceasing activity, manifests itself, as well as in the positing as absolute of infinite, wholly independent individualities.

3) Finally, monadology appears to be the expression of an attitude of life that understands and confirms itself in it, not only through its own unflagging activity, but also primarily in the serene belief that, basically, all is in order, and that this unbounded activity derives meaning from a constantly actual fulfillment, which is the unity and the peace of pure cognition behind all that is obscure, confused, violent, irrational, but is merely the foreground. This is like a faith.

Yet we cannot recognize a metaphysics in Leibniz's monadology as we can in Spinoza, Bruno, Plotinus, Plato, and in a few pre-Socratics. For, despite its other aspects, its effect is, as a whole, that of a construction. It does not become convincing, but fascinates as an intellectual game.

3. SHIPWRECK OF THE RATIONALITY INHERENT
IN THE UNIVERSAL

Leibniz never acknowledged the irrational and the antirational; but he did, from early on, keep his eye precisely on that which prevents the dissolution of actuality into the condition of being completely cognized, that is, into reason: the actuality of individuals and of chance, the factual. It was precisely this that drove him to seek the universal rationality in which the individual as well as chance would become rationally comprehensible. Through this tension between the universal, and as such inactual, and the individual, and as such the alone actual, his task was further deepened, since his thoughts went radically into the fundamental on both sides.

Against his attempt to achieve this cognition within *scientia generalis*, we can readily argue that such universal cognition always finds its limits in the axioms that are its starting points, to which particular cognitive structures are bound, but which themselves are not cognized in their ground; and, second, such cognition finds its limits in an actuality that never completely fits the universal forms and cannot be derived from the universal. Leibniz does not deny this, but he seeks to comprehend in an all-inclusive metaphysical construction why this is true for human cognition, whereas in divine cognition everything is resolved in rationality. He further means to see that and to what extent we participate in such divine cognition through the idea of the *scientia generalis*.

What he wanted to achieve as all-embracing, all-penetrating *scientia generalis* was possible only for divine reason, for which the infinite is completely cognizable—a knowledge out of the reach of human reason.

Yet only because our thinking is qualitatively identical to divine thinking, but quantitatively infinitely different from it, could the idea of the *scientia generalis* originate in the human mind. (Those human beings that arrived at perfect illumination in cognition, that is, completed monads, would be "small gods.")

There is another objection raised against Leibniz: Though, to be sure, he speaks of the individual in principle as well as most impressively, he does not in actual cognition pay attention to what is individual, does not lovingly indulge the particular, unique, irreplaceable individual. This objection is justified, and makes comprehensible that the tendency of Leibniz's works is so completely oriented toward the universal.

Another objection is: His *scientia generalis* does no more than generalize mathematics to apply to all cognition. Mathematics, it is said, is not only exemplary for, but the source of, all cognition. This philosophy, it has been claimed, is an absurd product of misunderstood mathematics and misunderstood reality. We cannot simply brush aside that many of his texts invite this stricture, but, in Leibniz, motivation lies instead in the opposite direction: From his metaphysical stance grounded in faith in reason, arises, first, his use of mathematics and its potentialities, and, second, his use of *scientia generalis*, of which mathematics is merely a shadow.

Against the construct of the universal cogitated by Leibniz, we can object that he drains what is thinkable to the point where contradiction is eliminated. He is stranded in the formal. But—wherever there is cognition—what is thinkable is the fulfillment by content of the merely logical form. If our thinking were not a thinking that structures intuitions and by means of its operations creates actualities in us and outside of us, it would be adequately apprehended in the theory of logic (which is called formal symbolic logic today), but would, at the same time, be recognized in its total emptiness and ineffectiveness. But that was not at all Leibniz's intention. There is no doubt that, in his intention, logical calculus has foundered, whereas, as modern formal symbolic logic, it is no longer what Leibniz was working toward.

What Leibniz knew, and Pascal before him, is that all logical thinking is suspended in the void, as it were; it can neither prove its specific beginning (the axioms), nor attain actuality. Leibniz believed he could overcome the suspension with regard to reason in God. Modern formal symbolic logic either has arrived at the "unphilosophy" of a rational game of correctnesses—and thus at what is endless, inapplicable, fruitless, and hence indifferent—or it has, it seems (in Wittgenstein), a great philosophical trait in that it brings to consciousness the foundering of knowledge that is absolute and, at the same time, unequivocal, and reveals, with maximal transparency, its radical opaqueness. Modern formal symbolic logic is far removed from Leibniz on both counts.

4. CHARACTERIZATION OF THE PERSONAL ASPECT

We are inclined to measure intellectual greatness against personal greatness. In Leibniz the disparity between the two is characteristic. His mind is broad, rich, inventive, clear, inexhaustibly productive, of universal capacity; his personality is faceless, as it were. Not that he was evil or mean-spirited; he was most likely decent and average, great neither in good nor in evil. He gives the impression not of concealed profundity but of an indecisive character. We encounter the mind of a giant in a human being devoid of pronounced personality. No other modern philosopher achieved such versatility of occupation, such plenitude of interests, topics, inventions; yet hardly any other philosopher seems so shadowy to us. The work is always clear, almost always interesting, has its distinctive style; but the man never becomes a person for us, devoid as he is of either greatness or style. What a baffling discrepancy between knowledge and mental capacity and personal nature!

Not even his contemporaries knew who he really was. Their mirror does not project his image down to us. He was admired without being liked. His fame is enduring, but his personality sheds as little light today as it did in his own time.

It is unique as well as symbolic for him how little he published in his lifetime, how almost all of his philosophy was channeled into his letters to scholars, how unconcerned he was about the fate of his literary remains, though he collected and preserved them neatly; that he allowed his major works simply to lie there, works that reached the public only half a century or longer after his death, and that even today by no means all he wrote has been published. The new publications have had considerable effect on mathematical, logical, and metaphysical thinking, but even they have failed to alter or deepen the image of his personality.

Given the great wealth of topics he was able to treat so substantively—his rational political ideas; the occasional glimpses he gives of being profoundly affected; what he is able to express authentically and forcefully, especially in the German language—Leibniz himself lacks contour, and what he actually discovered and experienced remains unclear. The matter-of-factness of his writings has nothing in common with the metaphysical presence of Spinoza or the ethical power of Kant. What he writes is always clever, based on observation, occasionally wise, and above all carries the full weight of logical thought as such. His thought and work as evidenced in his letters and writings testify to a grandiose objectivity such that Leibniz's person no longer seems to matter. Here a mind had put such distance between itself and the world that all interest save that in the subject discussed may safely disappear. The realities of his life do not allow us to discover the personality we expect to find. Yet philosophy (in contrast to scientific research) does not permit such impersonality.

5. CHARACTERIZATION OF THE WORK

The very greatness of Leibniz's mind leaves no room for any doubt about it. Even a brief reading is convincing, and more protracted study increases our admiration. It seems as if Leibniz could not write a single line without immediately being engrossing, inventive, astonishing. His bent is toward previously unthought possibilities; he discovers propositions and categorial determinations which, because of their essential nature, are indelibly imprinted on our minds. In his constructs the wealth of ideas seems inexhaustible. Leibniz's simplicity, clarity, conciseness, and the rapid yet unbroken progression of his thought are admirable. His critical sensitivity rejects the trivial and lets even the absurd appear ingenious. He is always lively; he discusses, develops, modifies, and stays in motion, refusing to be fettered automatically by his own categories, allowing everything to be carried along by the fundamentals of thought and his own unique attitude.

Wherever we open his writings we are met by clear air, the serene mood of the desire to know and the gratification afforded by the profound possibilities of thought and questioning, and of the marvelous things in the world. In whatever he encounters, he immediately discovers an inherent problem.

Thought, with him, is transmittable; it is everything, is simply explicit and hence without the slightest tendency to indirect communication. But the transmission of this overwhelming multitude of ideas raises severe difficulties once we attempt to gain an overview.

Historians of philosophy have tried to overcome this by an exposition of the Leibnizian system.[3] But the question is precisely whether, in the case of Leibniz, we have a closed whole, a total knowledge intended as such and free of contradiction, or whether, taken as a whole, this thinking is from the very first riddled with insoluble contradictions. Expressed differently, the question is whether the will to conciliation and to a universal complementation actually brings all opposites to a unity of knowledge that is not only grandiose but also convincing, or whether the will to unity achieves a mere semblance of such unity that is constructed by means of efficacious principles (development, complementing the one-sided, continuity, infinity, and so on) and their artful combination. Expressed still differently: We ask whether in Leibniz an integral

---

[3] Johann Eduard Erdmann, *Versuch einer wissenschaftlichen Darstellung der Geschichte der neueren Philosophie*, repr., H. Glockner, ed. Stuttgart, F. Frommann, 1932, Parts 1–2, vol. 4. Kuno Fischer, *Gottfried Wilhelm Leibniz, Leben, Werke und Lehre*, 5th ed. Heidelberg, C. Winter, 1920. Eduard Zeller, *Geschichte der deutschen Philosophie seit Leibniz*, 2nd ed. Munich, R. Oldenbourg, 1875.

whole is operative that is constant, unshakable, and true, a whole that enables him to speak in terms of the concepts and notions of opponents, adapting himself to them in order to lead them to understanding, yet without losing himself in such adaptation; or whether this might entail what in fact is accommodation and thus a shifting of his fundamental ideas so that the religious forces of his age, the political motivations, as well as the tasks imposed on him would overwhelm him for a time and push his statements into the iridescence of multiple possibilities.

These questions cannot be answered, since for Leibniz there are no such alternatives. His manner of thinking remains unchanged. By its nature it is capable of adopting the aspects of either of those alternatives. His projected systems, in particular the system of monadology, are not absolute positions but hypotheses, that is, procedures of cogitative inquiries. To be sure, his systematic thinking is familiar with the idea of a whole, especially of methodical knowledge gaining ascendancy through the *characteristica universalis* and the logical calculus. However, he does not recognize a system in actual fact in which all that exists has its place. Yet historians of philosophy have attempted time and again to represent Leibniz's system. Up to now these attempts have failed. Leibniz's way of thinking does not accommodate itself to a single seamlessly constructed thought-totality comparable to those actually and deliberately created by Hegel and Thomas Aquinas. If, using their work as a standard, we attempted to derive such a construct for Leibniz, as though it lay concealed in the innumerable letters, notes, essays, and writings, it would call for certain requirements, and certain discoveries would have to be made.

The first requirement would be a creative architectonic force comparable to that of the aforementioned great system builders. Second, such a project would need illustrative material, which Leibniz, despite his universal knowledge, never provided. Third, this project would most likely fail, because if it were to succeed, it would not produce the Leibnizian system—which does not exist—but a new system occasioned by Leibnizian thought.

Such an attempt would demonstrate that Leibniz actualized a way of thinking totally different from that of the great systematizers. If their systems are used as a standard, then Leibniz achieves less than they. In other respects he achieves more.

This becomes clear if we use another method of presentation. Such a method stresses what would not be included in those systems, that is, what for a system would be extraneous and trivial and hence not worthy of attention. The format of systematic exposition evidently obstructs our view of Leibniz's inventive, universal, and constructive thinking. We would prefer to see how Leibniz actually worked, something that is of interest to everyone. Such a method would reveal the abundance of topics taken up by him. He would be seen as wearing many hats: mathematicians, logicians, physicists, biologists, historians, geologists, and others would find matters of interest to them.

We have now pointed out what is instructive in Leibnizian thought and also its limit. So many rational ideas and methodical procedures, so much fertile experience in thinking and investigating make his work a treasure trove of great resources. He is instructive as regards particular topics, specific lines of thought, categorial possibilities. But his power to stimulate us is essentially different from, for example, that of Plato or Kant. Leibniz does not lead us into the innermost core of philosophy; he does not bring about a transformation of our consciousness of Being or our approach to life; he does, however, provide us with the means of thinking.

6. THE EXISTENTIAL QUESTION

After we have reviewed Leibniz's thought, no matter from which perspective, we are inclined to ask about the existential import of his philosophy: What motives lie behind all his interests? How are so many interests interconnected? Whence this universality? These questions are not easily answered.

We might say: It is the mode of thinking that determines the basic features of all categories and methods of rational thought. The universality is not universal curiosity, but the will to participate in divine reason, a reason that grounds and permeates everything. But as we try to come to grips with this subject in Leibniz, we find that he treats it as a separate topic.

Or we might say: It is the attitude of a will to universal conciliation distinct from and opposed to confining and burying all things in a system. Actually, we find in Leibniz deep insights into the possibilities of rational communication, but none into the authentic problem of communication, since, by means of the clarity of reason, he meant to be in possession of the substance. The will to combine everything is not the will to communication.

What is the basic philosophic stance that underlies all Leibniz's ways of thinking, or the basic conviction through which he addresses us as Existenz? One answer to this question is: Leibniz's trust in order, reasonableness, the harmony of all things. This trust seems to be absolute. It is expressed everywhere. There is harmony between the physical realm of nature, with its causality, and the moral realm of grace, giving meaning and purpose. God is one and the same as the architect of the machine of the universe and as monarch in the spiritual city of God. The paths of nature lead of themselves to grace. No "good deed" remains "without reward, no evil one without punishment." The good people, that is, those "who are not malcontent in this great state . . . take comfort in what God permits to happen through His secret, consistent, and decisive will." It would be impossible "to make things better than they are, not only with regard to the great whole but for ourselves in particular."

The great wealth of his knowledge and abilities is at the service of an outlook on life that itself lacks greatness. It lacks the element of protest and even a rudiment of despair. It lacks a sense of the tragic and the overcoming of it. Leibniz never speaks seriously about tragedy. His metaphysics is comforting; it does not arise from a sense of dread nor from mature reflection, and is not revealed through inner action. He speaks of dread only in general terms, such that the Gorgon's head is simply veiled for him. Leibniz appears to unite wisdom and contentment. But we are entitled to ask whether such an attitude might not explain and justify an existential indecisiveness that stands in clear contrast to Leibniz's decisiveness in his specific rational thought. It is an attitude of a basic weakness of character originating in a lack of capacity for despair. His thinking shows the way toward accommodation with any government and church, with any baseness and calamity. It exhibits the activity of making, inventing, working, rather than that of a supreme, existentially responsible will in the face of the ultimate, of transcendence; it cannot be likened to the free creativity of the poet and artist, or to the creative invention of a metaphysics great in its substance because it fulfills Existenz.

Leibniz represents no positive philosophic force, no existential possibility, no resolve in decision, but, instead, the possibility that even in the presence of universal knowledge and great talent in thought and invention, Existenz can be lacking. For this reason his worldview cannot convincingly be reduced to one type. He cannot be made to stand in relation to others, not because of his being an outstanding personality but because there is nothing decisive about him, nothing definite or integral. The many independently valid insights as well as the grandiose absurdities seem to hide a deep groundlessness.

His doctrine of the absolute independence of individuals in particular must not deceive us on this point. Leibniz's notion of individuality is an

objective one. The diversity of unique individuals, each in its own originality, is seen by him purely as an observer. All are monads, not only
the human spirits; they are differentiated only according to the degree
of clarity in their thinking. The only impulse emanating from his teaching is directed toward rational clarification; he does not address himself
at all to possible Existenz, at risk because it stands between losing itself
and gaining itself. All existential questions lie beyond the range of his
otherwise universal thought.

There is a connection between this existential lack and the absence
in Leibniz of the whole spiritual realm of *Verstehen*, the great hermeneutics of all possibilities of meaning which, later on, would become the
impetus of system building in Hegel's philosophy. In Leibniz, universality
is specific, not total. For an individual mind, to be sure, the idea of
universality can be only a fundamental task, one that cannot be carried
through. But Leibniz's great lacuna lies in the very foundation of his
thinking, a lacuna not filled by the manner of his historical investigations.

Creative Orderers

ARISTOTLE

HEGEL

INTRODUCTION

Editors' Note

Jaspers distributes those great thinkers who are properly called "philosophers" among four main groups:
  Seminal founders of philosophical thought;
  The original visionaries (various types of metaphysicians);
  The disturbers ("Probing Negators" and "Radical Awakeners");
  The creative orderers (builders of all-embracing systems). The given sequence accords with the intrinsic logic of Jaspers's distinction, as he makes clear in the following introduction and his appraisals of Aristotle and Hegel. The reasons are, in brief, that the creative orderers mean to comprise both the affirmations of the original visionaries and the negations of the disturbers; and that the creative orderers are at the opposite pole from that of the seminal founders. The founders open up the range of philosophical thought; the orderers gather all thought and bring it to a conclusion.

Hence Jaspers's project, uncompleted, of "The Great Philosophers" was to follow that order, and the orderers would have been presented last, after the disturbers. For technical reasons, however, it was felt that, in dividing the material into two volumes of approximately equal size, the large group of disturbers should be presented in the same volume, that is, Volume IV. This was possible only if the orderers were placed in Volume III.

Jaspers describes the philosophers discussed in this part as "creative orderers." However, the reader of the following introduction will notice that he does not refer to them by this designation. Rather, he talks about "great systematizers," "creative systematizers," "builders of systems." The reason is that "ordering" is the type of thinking that characterizes their greatness, while comprehensive "system-building" is the way in which they present themselves and exert influence on the history of thought.

Every philosophy that is serious and not merely an operation of the intellect is the foundation of a life. But in its historic configuration each is a special one. No matter whether we are dealing with metaphysicians whose original thinking penetrates into the ground of things, or with metaphysicians given to panoramic designs, or with thinkers who question and disturb, each one is limited in his own way. They do not take hold of the whole of God, world, man, in its actual scope, but concentrate on what to them seems to be the essential, such as a cause, a procedure, a form of life. If the content of their thinking has a universal resonance, this is due largely to happenstance and not intended on principle. Each is distinguished by his vision, originality, and inventiveness.

Not so with the great systematizers. They present an all-embracing system of Being filled with content and intended to take hold of all knowledge and fit it together into a whole. They want not only to attain a fundamental knowledge, not only to carry out operations of thought, not only to turn a specific content into the main focus of interest to which they cling. Instead, they want to appropriate everything thought prior to them and use it as building material and construction technique for their own edifice. They would like to take up even the disturbing thoughts of the probing and awakening philosophers. By depriving the disturbers of their dangerous sting, they turn them into moments of the great all-embracing movement within the system.

The greatness of the systematizers, however, does not lie in collecting and amassing, or in the universality of their material. This would be the way to compile encyclopedias (and, finally, lexica), which constitute the uncreative counterpart of the creative systematizers. Their creativity is contained in the concept of order itself. I am not speaking here of a partial aspect of this group. What is meant is that through them the vision is widened: not only do we see what has already been thought, but we see more, see something new everywhere. This systematic thought becomes creative in its own right. Furthermore, it is not something discovered by the great systematizer but, rather, is brought forth by him. This thinking is not confined to expression as a solely intellectual content of cognition but has to be experienced in its power, which builds as it discovers.

The great systems exude tranquillity. In the original metaphysicians this tranquillity is attained in transcendence. It is radiated by their very nature. The great systematizers take up this tranquillity as a moment of the tranquillity constituted by the harmonious whole of everything there is. The excogitated order of everything that is actual, that can be experienced, thought, executed, also presents the factual order of all things. Tranquillity is the result of everything being in order. Tranquillity in transcendence is transformed into tranquillity in the All of harmonious order.

I shall attempt to depict the three great systematizers: Aristotle, Thomas,[1] Hegel. Their achievements are almost beyond comprehension. Their enormous scope, the thoroughness of their information, their concentration on the particular—wherever it was within their reach—are just as astonishing as their steadfast adherence to the whole. They did not allow the immensity of material to overwhelm them, but appropriated it creatively. They managed to live in the tension between the plenitude of things and the unifying nature of their grasp, or between apparently abandoning themselves to the plenitude and the center from which the plenitude was drawn.

1. What the great systematizers had in common

a) *The All:* In distinction from systems that objectively have a specific character, the great systematizers desired to bring the All of things, actuality in all its ramifications, into a thinkable whole in which nothing is lacking, nothing left out. The entire world and meta-world are captured in their thoughts and crystallized in a doctrinal system. Few principles and methods govern throughout the whole, which becomes a unity that grasps the richness of Being. In the finished work it becomes actual as a known.

b) *The universal reception of tradition:* The great systematizers knew what preceded them. They consulted the texts of the ancients insofar as they were obtainable. They purposefully cast their eyes over all of history. But they differed in their attitude toward the ancient thinkers. Those not engaged in philosophical inquiry are primarily interested in deciphering the correct meaning of the ancient texts, but keep their distance, as it were, remaining "objective" and uninvolved, except for correctness of interpretation presupposed as a possibility. For them it did not matter whether what was understood was true or false, essential or inessential. Philosophers, by contrast, desire to understand by partaking of the blood of ancient philosophy, by bringing back to life what once had been. This is where philology and philosophy part company. The philological approach fails because ultimately the understanding of earlier forms of

---

[1] The essay on Thomas Aquinas, because of its fragmentary state, is not included in this volume.

thought is possible only in one's own philosophizing, as determined by the truth of the thought. Philosophical appropriation fails when it leads to a transformation exceeding and missing the correctness of understanding of the intended meaning.

In the case of the great systematizers, misunderstanding is inseparable from their appropriation, intended to create order and wholeness. What is appropriated is changed to a degree that amounts to cutting the heart out of the original philosophical life and leaving a structure of lifeless organs and limbs as the building materials of a new edifice. The thoughts are grasped and shaped by the new rationality of the systematizers. The seriousness peculiar to the ancients is lost in the new seriousness of the system. The pervasive seriousness of the ancient past no longer weighs in the detachment of relative comprehension of thoughts that have become objective.

The new systematic ways of thinking fixate and structure the multiplicity of antecedent thought, placing what went before on the one level of their own rationality, ironing out differences. The new systematic thinking often eliminates the authentic meaning of prior thought, by blurring the view for what the system is not able to appropriate. (Thomas, for example, does not understand Anselm's proof for the existence of God; Aristotle does not understand the pre-Socratics, whom he calls physicists; Hegel does not understand Kant.)

What original thinkers created and wove together and meant to awaken through their testimony becomes dismembered in the objectivity of systematizing thought. This dismemberment is now regarded as lucid thinking, which, however, can keep its meaning only if it leads back into the early unity of that fabric. That unity is incorporated into the new unity of the systematic whole. This is the order (*sapientis est ordinare*, as Aristotle and Thomas express it) that is arrived at on the basis of differentiations (*distinguendum est*, is Thomas's formula).

But these procedures by the great systematizers are themselves means within a new productivity, even if fatal for the greatness of the others. The immediacy of their vision, their perception of the world, their tremendous sensitivity to the appearance and meaning of all things is the ground from which the whole of tradition is put into service to enhance what is their own.

c) *The power to form schools:* The great systematizers were great teachers. Their thinking exhibited a power to form schools, not only in the sense of attracting a temporary group of disciples, but also as an educational force, which continues to influence thought. The stamp of their thinking and the solidification of their conceptions have determined the character of whole eras. Subliminally, their thoughts have entered our thinking up to the present. Within the narrower circle of deliberate philosophical education, they are a source of philosophical teaching. They provide the firm substructure for methodical learning, teach conceptual thinking and methodical order.

Through their claim to all-inclusiveness, the school is made, if unintentionally, the means of transmitting the material they deal with. They are indeed capable of expanding the realm of thought to its farthest reach, but are not able to ground or awaken the seriousness of Existenz.

Their activity breeds inexhaustible discussions of concepts, teachable applications, and extensions of thought, but in a manner that encases the breadth of such instruction within the totality of what is thinkable, resulting in a sense of completeness and peace. Within such systems institutions and the various states of a community are given the sense of orders destined to be enduring ones. The schools have carrying capacity. The thought structure becomes a sturdy scaffold.

Methods are developed to elaborate philosophical texts valid for generations to come. The universal validity claimed for this manner of instruction equates philosophy with science, the one science of the one truth. All problems lie within the common totality of this system. The system itself is not problematical. As the generations succeed one another, the method of planned learning usurps the place of original thinking.

d) *The pact with the world powers:* The great systems are well suited to be the tools of the power structures of this world. They confirm thereby their own sense of duration, by way of education and justification for the existence and actions of those powers. Intellectually, the range of their intuitions and methods allows them to deal with and rationalize anything whatever, imprinting and even drilling minds. Opposition of any kind is extinguished by incorporating its meaning into the tremendous intellectual structure; if it understands itself as the system understands it, it is opposition no more.

The will to power combines with the will to system. Everything is spiritually overwhelmed and subjugated by the process of integration. Another component of the system is injustice toward everything original. It is considered only as revolt, obstinacy, arrogance.

Aristotle was not in league with any worldly power. But his terminology, his differentiations, and his conceptions gave a scholastic mold to the thinking of the Western world as a whole and to the Arab world as well. Once integrated into Thomas's thinking, Aristotle was allotted the role of teacher in the thinking of the Catholic Church. By way of Marx, Hegel became determinative for the thinking of a third of hu-

manity: Thomism and Marxism are the only philosophies that—by
molding future generations through education—have the character of
worldly powers.

Manner as well as content of their effect fundamentally differ, of
course, with each of the three great systematizers. Aristotle's influence
is based on education in thinking, on the apperception of an eternal
order. Thomas works his effect through the ideal of order in a given
social actuality, that is, the Church. For the Hegelians, the master is
effective as a restorative force, and Marx provides an operational means
to the will to power which in conditions of mass desperation aims at
bringing about a new order by force.

2. *The limit of the system*

Representatives of great systems consider them as embracing all of philosophy. Whatever remains outside them is either incorporated as a
moment of the system or considered obsolete, erroneous, or negligible.

The system stands firm against any truth that cannot be incorporated
into the totality of the one whole. Such a truth disturbs not only the
unity of what is true in the system, but the peace grounded in it as well.

The system, when turned toward the past, aims at preserving this
peace (and then has a restorative effect); when directed toward the future,
it aims to bring about this peace through planning (and then has a
totalitarian effect). In both cases the system does violence and closes off
human possibilities, though in opposing ways. Ultimately, both forms of
peace would result in the peace of the graveyard, the death of the spirit
as well as of existence.

Mankind inclines toward systems. Our reason feels impelled toward
them. The organization of everything thinkable, known and knowable
in a systematic whole is not counter to truth in its origin.

But it becomes evident that every system has foundered. The very
idea of infinity—implying that it cannot be mastered by thought, neither
the infinity of the actual nor that of possible creations (as distinct from
the infinities of mathematics and logic)—leads to the insight that systems
are impossible. They have to leave out what does not fit into the whole,
what cannot be integrated, just as they leave out any future experiences
and creations, all that may already be present without having been noticed
by the system, that has been belittled or ignored by it, while being open
to the perception of any original thinker.

This antinomy cannot be transcended: the system and the breach in
the system are correlated. To deny or dispute either would be tantamount

to an evasion of the antinomy. The historic process of illumination in human thinking evolves by keeping this antinomy alive.

Ultimately, schools lead to restrictive rigidification, which in turn demands breakthrough. This breakthrough finally leads to the chaos that demands order and system. Hence there remains the impulse toward the system as well as to the breach; there remains danger in both, which keeps temporal man from attaining the tranquillity of the ultimate.

The circumstance that systems are unavoidable demands that the system be transformed by the breach. The final transformation would have to lead out of the self-contained unity of one work into the idea of a unity constituted by the communication of all, outside the purview of a single individual but providing a space that must be entered. In such circumstances the systems would transform their meaning. True, they would dissolve in regard to their absolute claim to universal validity as the one truth. They turn into dwellings into which we move without being tied to them. They no longer overarch the one whole as its firmament. For if we live within the idea of communication, we are nowhere at home absolutely. In our encounters we are on a journey in which the bonds of fidelity unite us historically but do not permit total knowledge to become the one and only objectivity. The systems themselves become functions. They exert their attraction, but we do not have to yield to them. They themselves are, as a whole, historic ciphers, which for others have been clues to reality. We may perceive them, they may touch us to some degree, but never assume the importance they had for those who produced them or followed them as the only valid ciphers.

In polar opposition to the great systematizers stand the creative, seminally effective, never-ending thinkers, such as Plato, Augustine, Kant. The seminally effective thinkers are also systematic to a high degree. But they do not generate a system of Being. They liberate those who follow them, arouse their own originality, know schools only as preparation.

The systematizers, no matter how irreplaceable for forming the instruments of thought as a schooling for all time, seduce us to come to rest in knowledge. Established as sole authority, they render new, original thinking ineffective. They do not stimulate independent creation; rather, they present what can be learned as a possession to be accepted.

Relinquishing systems of Being excogitated in a single work implies, for the progress of thinking, that systems become ciphers and that there may be several of them. But doing without them altogether implies, primarily, that our thinking poses questions—including the most essential ones—that are impossible to answer. Recognizing that impossibility sublates the question by transforming it into an inner attitude of thought. The attitude intrinsic to the system, however, presupposes that all substantive questions have been answered. The aporias lie within the system. They have only intellectual importance.

The great systems are an extraordinary historical actuality and the form through which philosophy has had the widest effect.

Closing one's eyes to the systems and refusing all knowledge of them makes one vulnerable and defenseless in philosophical encounters. Today's superiority of Thomist and Marxist minds in debate is a sign of impotence due to a lack of philosophic education. To be sure, philosophy in its substance is far more and far more profound than what can be taught and learned, since it illuminates the seriousness of Existenz. But without philosophic training as transmitted by the systems, such Existenz remains nebulous. It cannot demonstrate to the systematically schooled adversary what is truly accomplished by such thinking, and it fails to communicate its own thinking. This is one more reason to study the great systematizers even if ultimately we do so because of their greatness and the truth residing in them, despite their limits.

If the spiritual spark breaking through these systems were not preserved, the spirit, in some way, would die. The very descendants of those schools of thought live by the appropriation of new possibilities, the very possibilities they reject in their ordering totality. They provide an indispensable counterweight.

ARISTOTLE

Editors' Note

Aristotle was born in 384 B.C., of Greek parentage, in Stagira, a colony in Macedonia. His father, Nichomachus, a member of the medical guild of the Asclepiadae, may well have transmitted to his son a carefully observational, scientific way of thinking. At the age of seventeen, Aristotle became a pupil of Plato at the Athenian Academy, where for twenty years he broadened his interests to embrace the humane subjects of ethics, aesthetics, and politics. Inspired by the guiding notion of overall systematic order in the world, but dismayed by the Platonist preoccupation with mathematics, he went to Mysia, in Asia Minor, where he continued his biological studies and, from about 342 to 335 B.C., tutored the young Alexander of Macedonia.

In 335 B.C., Aristotle returned to Athens to found a new school, later known as the Lyceum and renowned for its peripatetic mode of instruction. When public sentiment turned against the Macedonians following the death of Alexander in 323 B.C., Aristotle was compelled to leave under suspicion of impiety. He died in 322 B.C. in Chalcis.

Over the centuries hundreds of works have been attributed to Aristotle; of these, perhaps twenty-five can be authenticated as actually written by him or under his direct influence. His writings, which have come to define much of our way of looking at the world, can be roughly separated into five areas: logic and knowledge (epistemology); physical nature and being as such (physics and metaphysics); living nature and "soul" (biological and psychological science); ethics and politics; rhetoric and poetics.

1. FIRST PHILOSOPHY

The topic Aristotle addresses in the metaphysical as well as in parts of the physical writings concerns, first, the ultimate principles of all that is and of all cognition; second, what pervades everything and supplies the means for grasping all particular actuality in its entirety and for seeing its structure clearly; and, third, Being, as well as the ground of Being that is called God. The topic is contained in specific didactic writings and reappears in many others. It is emphasized by Aristotle as "first philosophy" (*proton philosophia*).

This is the most difficult part of his work. It has been ignored by those who were interested in Aristotle's concrete insights into politics, ethics, poetics, psychology, and the natural sciences. Metaphysicians have preferred to ignore these concrete matters and, instead, turned their attention wholly to those fundamental questions that were not simply and unequivocally answered by Aristotle himself. The essence of Aristotelian philosophy can be grasped only as a whole, including the concrete.

It is historically noteworthy that Aristotle never speaks of metaphysics, only of first philosophy. The title of the didactic writings on this subject, *Metaphysics*, originated later, with his school. The name has been interpreted as arising from the coincidence that these books followed those about physics. Today scholars are inclined to acknowledge that the true meaning, "beyond the physical," was intended from the beginning.

2. THE BASIC CONCEPTS

Matter and form; dynamis *and* energeia

The principle by which Aristotle conceived the world contrasted matter and form, but also grasped reality as their inseparable union. His point of departure is graphic illustration, such as the following: Through human art (*techne*) things are formed out of matter and are actualized only in this process. The artisan makes tools out of wood and metals. The sculptor carves the form of the statue out of marble. The builder erects a house out of building materials.

In living beings the appropriately formed shape develops from the seed by assimilating matter in the process of nutrition.

In each of these different instances form is imprinted on matter or permeates it. By means of these illustrations we arrive at the thought of form as such (*eidos, morphe*) and of matter as such (*hyle*). Everything that is—whether body or soul, whether lifeless or living nature or human being, whether numbers or figures or contents of thought—is a whole made up of form and matter. This form-matter relationship is the mother of all that is.

The form-matter relationship has such far-reaching importance that it escapes immediate intuition. But in each particular intuition it can be seen as an instance of the underlying relationship.

This fundamental relationship has another aspect. In the seed of the living entity, the living being is merely possibility (*dynamis*). It is actuality (*energeia*) only when it is grown. The potentiality is not yet the actuality of what has been conceived; yet it is not nothing, but the real possibility of what will develop.

Guided by the development of living things, Aristotle sees the same principle everywhere in the relationship of form and matter. In every instance matter is possibility, and form brings actuality.

Such basic concepts are readily expressed and demonstrated graphically in their points of departure. But these do not present sufficiently what Aristotle means to convey. For him, the points of departure (the human activities of shaping and building, the coming-to-be of organisms) translated themselves into a conceptual scheme that then developed its own inner life. It is the game of refining the differentiation of basic concepts (as ontology) in the application to all that is and by this process is apprehended: the construction of the universe, of the plants and animals, of man and his ethical and political sphere. The coinciding concept-pairs of form-matter and of actuality-possibility become the intellectual means of grasping and assimilating all there is and all that happens.

In this way the depth of their meaning becomes manifest. The graphic point of departure could work for us only because it was already molded by what we derive from it. Primary for us, according to the nature of things, is what comes later, what we first have to find through thinking.

It would be wrong to believe that the concepts we have attained—form-matter, actuality-possibility—are abstractions, overgeneralized and empty concepts that can be used almost arbitrarily because of their ambiguity, for this would be almost the opposite of what Aristotle means. "The natural path . . . leads from that which is clearer and more familiar to us, to that which . . . is clearer and more familiar by nature" (*Physics*, I, 1). That which is clearer by nature is, in its clarity and presence, comprehended in philosophic thought through reason (*nous*). In the leap from immediate intuition, which presents things sensuously to our mind, we arrive at primal intuition, which presents things spiritually to reason. What we at first regard as being clearer to us is by no means clearer as such; it is only the graphic impression of the whole, for example, giving form in human art, or living growth, or coming to be and passing away. The step from what is to us the seemingly greater clarity to the authentic clarity in the origins of all things Aristotle compares with the relationship of word and concept. The word "circle" designates a whole in an indefinite way; the conceptual determination, however, takes the circle apart and makes it individual.

Hence what Aristotle comprehends in form-matter and actuality-possibility is to him not a very general abstraction that carries many meanings, but the concretion of simple and authentically clear primacy. If it is thought in the manner of the analogies with which we began, then these analogies are themselves also the visible presence of what speaks to us through them.

The two limits: pure form and pure matter

All the matter we encounter is already formed, and all that is formed is, in turn, possible matter for something else. Everything that is in the world is in one respect actuality as this form, in another respect it is not yet; it is possibility, that is, matter.

If our thinking progresses to the outermost limits, then we ought to be able to find there pure form without matter and pure matter without form, pure actuality and pure possibility. At the limits there seems to be complete rest, pure actuality that does not have to become, because it already is, and pure possibility that cannot become, since, out of itself, it is nothing but possibility.

Between pure matter and pure form stands all there is as a series of intermediate steps in which the possible as matter and the actual as form are united with each other: this is the world, the world of becoming, of nature. The actuality of our world is motion, the motion from matter toward form and between the two; it is, in the case of every configuration, a whole consisting of both.

Motion (kinesis)

If all worldly being lies between form (actuality) and matter (possibility), then becoming is motion from possibility to actuality. In all worldly being, motion (*kinesis*) is the event in which what as potentiality and disposition is the foundation comes into actuality and existence.

Motion presupposes the mover and the moved. Form does the moving, matter is moved. In their constant motion the things in the world seek and develop their form, which is called their *eidos*, their *logos*, their *morphe*, their entelechy.

Motion is eternal, as are pure form and pure matter, as eternal as the world, without beginning or end. What the world is in actuality, what comes to be and passes away, is in motion between possibility and actuality.

The unmoved mover

But the endlessness of motion in its entirety needs an origin. This origin is pure actuality (*actus purus*) without possibility, pure form. It is itself unmoved but is the ground of motion. It is called the unmoved mover. Out of love for the unmoved mover, the pure spirit, all things, the world begins to move.

The pure spirit, itself nonspatial, borders on space. That which touches it immediately, the outermost heavenly sphere, first starts to move and passes the motion on to the world. For all effect occurs only in the immediacy of touch and not from a distance. The incorporeality of the unmoved mover touches the corporeal.

The causes

In the realm of motion, effects occur in different ways, while still ultimately issuing from pure actuality and pure possibility, from *actus purus* and matter. The causes are structured differently. As causes according to form, they are called final cause, formal cause, conceptual cause, moving cause; as material causes, they are called necessary cause, passive cause, material cause.

The positive meaning of matter

At first matter seems to be that which is only passive, the absolutely nonresisting, the merely possible, that which is ready for form. But how does motion arise? It is not brought about by the form, which, sufficient unto itself, rests in itself, but by matter, which strives after form out of its mere possibility. Like a lover, matter yearns for the form of actuality. The unmoved mover brings forth the world because matter urges toward Him who only is and does not become.

Furthermore, matter has a positive effect on the reality of the world through its resistance. It is not merely unboundedly yielding matter, not only not-yet-being; rather, it has its own power, which eludes formation.

Consequently, the form is not actualized purely, the purpose is not faultlessly carried out. The contingency that disturbs order, the residue of deficiency, whatever turns out badly, all this has its reason in matter, though unrecognizable in the particular instance.

Aristotle considers matter itself to be the source of some vital forms: the difference between masculine and feminine is supposed to have its source in it; animals are imperfect configurations that occur on the way toward the shaping of the human figure, a process that is obstructed by matter.

The universal and the individual entity: the problem of ousia

To conclude our sketch of Aristotle's conceptual schema, we must discuss the most fundamental concept of this sphere.

Confronted with the sea of entities teeming between possibility and actuality, between matter and form, Aristotle's question is: What is that which actually is? He calls it *ousia*, which is *substantia, essentia*, or being. *Ousia* is Aristotle's primal term, and while it provides the possibility for all these translations, none of them is adequate.

What is *ousia*? The individual being or the universal concepts? Aristotle answers: It is the individual being (*tóde ti*) that is called, first and foremost, *ousia*.

Ousia is the individual being as a whole (*symbolon*) composed of matter and form. Hence Aristotle speaks of *ousia* in regard to matter as that which is underlying (*hypokeimenon*), and in regard to form as the actual (*energeia on*). But these viewpoints focus on one thing, which is both.

Whereas the basic concepts have a universal character, every actuality is the actuality of singular beings, of individuals. In the individual beings in the world, each of which is a whole composed of matter and form, matter is the ground of individual existence. It is not the universal that is actual, but the individual being.

But now a great difficulty appears, one that we can comprehend but not really solve.

What do we cognize? Not individual beings but universals. Plato had developed the doctrine of ideas: The universal is the timeless being, while the temporally actual is a nonbeing, which exists only through participation in the universal, that is, the ideas. The ideas are the actual, that which authentically is; matter is that which is not.

While Aristotle agrees that we know only the universal, he maintains that it is not distinct from and other than existents, a being-for-itself;

rather, it is in the things themselves. Ideas are the forms of things, the forces effective in them, the entelechies.

Concepts refer to universals. However, in their fundamental conception universals are not meant as abstractions, but as actuality. Only through this actuality, intuited in reason (*nous*), do these concepts have their meaning. If philosophically considered such thinking is not to be an idle game with words but the presentation of actuality itself, then actuality too is an attribute of the universal and not only of the individual.

Aristotle overcomes this difficulty by differentiating a first *ousia* from a second one. The first *ousia* is the individual being; the second *ousia* is the universal concepts of genera and species. But this differentiation too can be turned around, that is, when Aristotle refers to form as the first *ousia*.

The origin of these reversals and seeming contradictions is clear: On the one hand, form is the ground of the actuality of things; however, taken by itself, as the universal, it is the object of cognition. On the other hand, the universal, taken as form, is the ground of the actuality of things; yet there also is no actuality of individual beings without the ground of matter. Hence the actuality of individual beings is not accounted for by means of the universal alone.

These obvious inconsistencies must have been apparent to a mind as extraordinary as Aristotle's. But for him they were not inconsistencies, because, quite naturally, he discerned the individual beings in the very concepts.

The unity of concept and individual being is evident, surprisingly, in the sole and distinct actuality of pure form, that is, the being of the unmoved mover, the deity. This pure being of form without matter, this pure actuality in the Aristotelian sense, is not, however, the sum or the ordered whole of all universal forms. Rather, it is itself an individual being, the only one of its kind, yet, as individual being, alongside other incorporeal individual beings, the spirits of the spheres and the rational part of man, as well as alongside all the individual beings of the corporeal world.

Whenever we take up the problem of the relationship of the universal to the individual, we realize that it is hardly solved today any more than in the past. The problem surfaces wherever one differentiates between the universal and the individual.

It can be expressed in various ways, depending on the presuppositions of a particular mode of cognition. The mystery aroused by the question simply gathers depth. It is not solved, but more clearly revealed as mystery.

Hence the problem has its own history throughout the ages. It became famous as a central theme in the profound debates over universals waged during the Middle Ages. Do universal concepts have actuality? Or are they merely signs or names which point to actualities by means of abstractions, without ever capturing them, much less *being* them? Those who attributed actuality to concepts were called realists; those who saw only names in them, nominalists. From a nominalist standpoint, to be designated a conceptual realist amounted to an accusation of illusionary thinking.

Aristotle was unaware of these contrarieties, so he did not defend himself against nominalism. Viewed with this later developed position in mind, we would have to call him a conceptual realist. Since by now all of us are, in a manner of speaking, nominalists, we have some difficulty in conjuring up the Aristotelian mind-frame. Aristotle knows the satisfaction derived from conceptions of reasons or principles since he believes that with them he possesses authentic actuality. Hence the comprehension of all things via these basic concepts signifies cognition for him. We, however, would see a cipher in the interplay of thoughts, which arises from the intuitability of things and grows into a picture of what there is. We regard this way of thinking as a specifically philosophical one whose truth cannot be tested through arguments and counterarguments, but, rather, through risking its existential significance, that is, through the power and tendency to mold whoever lives by it. But as cognition of the world we would have to reject Aristotle's entire conceptual structure, for it is not a means of knowledge, but a specific mode of formalization.

3. THE CONCEPT OF GOD

By means of first philosophy Aristotle intends to know what there is as a whole, that is, in the form of universals, and to do so out of its primary grounds. This philosophy has several motifs:

1) It looks for primary reasons and origins (it acts *peri ta prota aitia kai tas archas*); in this way it arrives at matter-form, possibility-actuality, motion, origin of motion, and the unmoved mover. First philosophy as well as physics arrives at the prime mover in the same way. The limit of physics is the origin of motion; it is neither the object of physics nor the explanatory principle of individual motion, but of motion as a whole, of there being motion at all.

2) First philosophy inquires into beings as beings, that is, what Being

is in the multiplicity of all that is called Being. First philosophy encounters Being that is Being itself, the *ousia*—and thus the first unmoved *ousia*.

3) First philosophy encounters the deity in the primary grounds, in Being in its complete actuality. This is the cognition of God. Aristotle calls it theology. This concept, used occasionally by Plato, was intentionally made central in this sense by Aristotle. Since his time this concept has persisted as a creation of philosophy.

Primary grounds, beings as Being or *ousia*, and God are the three coinciding themes of first philosophy; later to come: cosmology, ontology, theology.

Aristotle's concept of God exhibits a certain tension. In his *Physics*, he seems to think of it as the ultimate origin from which all motion proceeds, without, however, being profoundly affected by it; to him it is a purely rational, constructive, and explanatory device.

In his question about Being qua Being, Aristotle ends in *ousia*—in ontological thinking that simply posits Being as the ground of all beings whatsoever.

His physics and ontology can be distinguished from his theology. Formally, they share the same fundamental thought. Yet the content exhibits two totally different aspects. They share, on the one hand, cool, purely theoretical thinking. On the other, we are drawn into the current of Aristotle's thinking, through which the meaning of philosophy and of our existence becomes fulfilled. To think Being is not the same as to think God. Logical assurance, always open to doubt, is not certainty of God.

In his earlier writings, however, and later in his elaboration of the concept of the unmoved mover, Aristotle exhibits deep emotion, awe, and enthusiasm in regard to the concept of God.

By naming first philosophy "theology," by designating it as the thinking about God, Aristotle made it a distinct topic. He himself developed it only in one book (*Metaphysics*, Book 12), which, according to Jaeger, is probably a separate work.[1]

Moods as points of departure

What has everywhere been experienced, believed, and acted on religious grounds was to be raised to the level of cognition, not as psychology or philosophy of religion but as a kind of thinking that is religion in the mode of cognition. But what kind of religion?

[1] Jaeger, *Aristotle*, 221ff.

Aristotle desires to formulate doctrines corresponding to man's pre-
monition of the deity (*De caelo* 2, 284b 3).

He understands the origin of the experience of the mysteries: "Those
who are being initiated are not to learn anything but to experience
something and be put into a certain state . . . once he has become capable
of it"[2]

The concept of God, says Aristotle,[3] originates in two sources—the
experiences of the soul and the contemplation of the stars. Those experiences are premonitions and prophecies in dreams or at the moment
of death. Their basis in moods is demonstrated by a famous passage in
Cicero:

If there were beings who had always lived beneath the earth, in comfortable, well-
lit dwellings, decorated with statues and pictures . . . and who though they had
never come forth above the ground had learned by report and by hearsay of the
existence of certain deities or divine powers, and then if at some time the jaws of
the earth were opened and they were able to escape from their hidden abode and
to come forth into the regions which we inhabit; when they suddenly had sight of
the earth and the seas and the sky, and came to know of the vast clouds and mighty
winds, and beheld the sun and realized not only its size and beauty but also its
potency, in causing day by shedding light over all the sky, and, after night had
darkened the earth, they then saw the whole sky spangled and adorned with stars,
and the changing phases of the moon's light . . . and the risings and settings of all
these heavenly bodies and their courses, fixed and changeless throughout all
eternity—when they saw these things, surely they would think the gods exist, not
only by reason, but by a reason that is transcendent and divine.[4]

The impression of order, of beauty, of abundance, and of the inexhaustible motion in the world awakens immediately the consciousness
of God: this magnificence is God's language.

The proofs of God

What is first experienced immediately in moods is confirmed and developed in thought processes which are called proofs of God. Only after
doubts about the existence of God and the gods enter the mind can there
be thoughts intended to prove their existence explicitly. Following the
Greek enlightenment, Aristotle was the first to do this systematically.
He is the philosopher who initially devised such proofs of God, later to
be reiterated throughout the millennia.

[2] Rose, Fragment 15, trans. from *The Complete Works of Aristotle*.
[3] Rose, Fragment 10.
[4] Cicero, *De natura deorum*, II, XXXVII. Cambridge, MA, Harvard University Press, 1956.

Our world is one of ceaseless motion, of constant coming-to-be and passing away. But it is merely moved. It is, however, surrounded by the world of the stars, which, alongside their self-movement in their regular orbits, keep the motion of the lower world going. The world of the stars is moved and engenders motion. But for these movements to be, there must be something perpetual that causes the moving without itself being moved, namely, the unmoved mover.

The conclusion of this proof proceeds from the fact of motion to the ultimate ground of this motion. In modified form, it proceeds from the merely caused to the ultimate cause.

On a more basic level Aristotle's thought makes use of his concept of matter as potentiality, as distinct from actuality. If we think that beings that are merely possibility might not come to be, then the fact of actual beings implies a necessary Being, pure actuality, which is not possibility. Aristotle does not explicitly explore the thought that there could be nothing at all. In every instance there is possibility, and this is referred to as matter. However, actuality cannot be comprehended out of the merely possible. Something necessary, eternally actualizing has to be presupposed. Thus, according to Aristotle, it is incomprehensible that the universe has emerged out of darkness, according to the teaching of the "theologians," or out of the chaos in which all the things were gathered, according to the teaching of the philosophers of nature. The night or the chaos were never what necessarily actualized or formed the world; it was always the unmoved mover.

A further aspect of proof lies in the basic mood elicited by viewing the heavens. The purposiveness, beauty, and order of the world is a fact. Its originator is inferred from it. This aspect was more broadly developed by the Stoics. The suitability to life of all living things is a fact that becomes ever more astonishing to this day. The discovery of every new unexpected adaptation belongs to the development of biology, just as does the connection of insect life and the pollination of flowers or the instincts of the insect, such as the minutely precise dissection of a leaf by the leaf roller. We could add the beauty of all natural phenomena, the landscape, the forms of life, the seasons, the inimitability of the natural beauty of a meadow in bloom, produced by the random distribution of its flowers, and finally the ordering of things according to measure and number. The Stoics never wearied of intuiting all this, and seeing therein the immanence of God. And by means of the inference of purposiveness they were led to the thought of the author.

Starting with Aristotle, teleological thought is perfected by that of the hierarchy of beings. This hierarchy cannot be incomplete. If the world is the most perfect one, then, in the hierarchy of perfections the highest perfection, God, must also be actual.

Ultimately, one proof of God stood out, based on the unanimity of different peoples: All of them believe in God. Since Aristotle's time such unanimity among peoples has not been considered irrelevant, but, instead, especially convincing. Being human itself testifies, through that which is common to all, to the truth of what is immanent in all men. For an innate concept of God belongs to man qua man and testifies to the existence of God. The actuality of this idea of God must be grounded in something through which it is, and this ground cannot be less than its own content. The idea of God stands at the beginning of the history of mankind; it can come only from God himself.

We have interpreted here the meaning of the Aristotelian proof of God by going beyond his own formulations and drawing on subsequent ones.

Characteristics peculiar to the Aristotelian concept of God

Let us characterize the traits peculiar to the Aristotelian concept of God—a concept wherein the tension between assurance in thought and meaning persists and, for the sake of the fundamental conception, should not be resolved.

a) The aspect of transcendence: This lies in the separateness of the unmoved mover from the world. He is a *khoriston*.

Moreover, the spirit (*nous*) of man does not come to be in the hierarchy of the developing entelechies, but is added from the outside (*thyraden*).

The fact that Aristotle held fast to this transcendence, abandoned by the Stoics, was of historic importance. In this position beyond the world, in this distance from the world, which it yet touched, the transcendent deity could become the place that was later occupied by the corporeal God, at the time when Aristotelian theology had become Christian theology.

The will not to lose transcendence is evident in the statement "God is either mind or something beyond mind."[5]

b) Aristotle's "religious" attitude: Reason posits God as "place." It is thought that arrives at this, and God is something that is thought, the thought corresponding to Aristotle's enthusiastic characterization.

---

[5] Rose, Fragment 49.

Aristotle's God is "distant" and calming for thought. With him there is no cult, no predestination, no intercession by God, no activity of God; there is no prayer directed to him, no love of God for mankind.

But the God who is unhuman and exalted, who calms us from a distance through his existence, can be fulfilled in this form through an original certainty of God, such as that of Spinoza.

God is thought as "place" so that there is no "pantheism," no identification with the all-pervasive soul of nature, the force of nature, the Stoic world-reason. Hence He is suited to be a schema of the intellect that can be filled with the transcendent God—suitable for the great configuration of Christian theology.

c) The "personality" of God: It assumes an impersonal character but does not become mere force.

4. THE INDIVIDUAL SCIENCES: MAN AS POINT OF DEPARTURE

I have given the basic concepts of the Aristotelian vision of Being: all-pervasive nature as motion from potentiality to actuality; the modes of Being and the reference point of all of them in *ousia*; the deity as the unmoved mover who alone is complete actuality and the origin of all motion.

Aristotle's philosophy also contains the entire intuitable reality of the world and all that is in it, including man and his thinking and acting. How does Aristotle see the arrangement of philosophical cognition of these areas, and what place within the whole is assigned to the previously discussed first philosophy? The traditional form of this question concerns the organization of the philosophical disciplines, and of the sciences.

Aristotle's answer is grounded in the way he sees the being of man. Man is the location where thought takes place about everything that is and is thought about. We can call this Aristotle's great but by no means narrow sense of anthropologism. The actuality of man shows us the organs through which he perceives, thinks, produces with his hands, and acts thinkingly. It is in humanity that what there is becomes manifest. What is meant here by "humanity" is not the subjective, which has to be disregarded in order to attain the objective. Rather, it is the unity of the subjective and the objective, the place of the appearance of all Being.

How does Aristotle visualize humanity in this sense?

5. ARISTOTLE'S COSMOS AND NATURAL SCIENCE

The simplicity, comprehensibility, and greatness of the Aristotelian picture of the world by no means prevailed at first. Proper inquiry and increasing understanding remained in flux. But after the disappearance of scientific thinking, as early as the last century before Christ, the Aristotelian worldview attained a dominant position and maintained it for fifteen centuries.

The Contrast to Aristotle's Eternal Cosmos: This is an oddity—since with Biblical religion the true contrast to this Aristotelian worldview acquired actuality.

The Biblical counterview sees the world as transitory. Having been created, it will come to an end. Our lives are set between the creation of the world and its end. Our life, and the world as a whole, are in a state of transition. The eternity of what is now hidden is an actuality preceding and outlasting the world. Authentic Being, and non-Being, is tested in the world, but its pure actuality is attained in eternity.

Aristotle knew about catastrophic events, but they never caused total destruction. Something was always left intact.

The Merits of the Aristotelian Picture of the World: Explications concerning nature are based on notions that make immediately perceived phenomena plausible by the application of thought.

In this process Aristotle evokes ideas and develops trains of thought that open the way to subsequent investigations, even though this was not the original intention.

To a high degree Aristotle's picture is one of a "natural" world. Forced complexities are drawn upon to buttress the naturalness of intuitions that seem to go against nature.

This mode of thinking has the practical outcome of paralyzing investigation. Inquiry is blocked. With a few minor exceptions, Aristotle's thinking is confined to descriptions of what lies ready to view, which then is explicated by interpretation inaccessible to actual verification. This limitation he takes for granted, a given within which he has his being. Its sole purpose: to enable him to encompass, by means of the basic concepts, the whole wealth of what there is and always will be, and make it an object of contemplation.

The Contrast to Modern Knowledge of the World: Has this cosmic picture been devaluated also in its fundamental approach, quite apart from factual errors that have undermined it in the areas of astronomy, physics, and biology? Or does it retain significance as a cipher, valid historically over a long period (though based on the fallacy that it represents the reality of the world itself), so that even today this vision remains meaningful as a way of representing the cosmos?

And does it not endure because of its configuration, if only in the guise of memory? It appears to me that for us the chief value of the Aristotelian world-picture lies in the contrast to the present lack of such a picture. We reach full consciousness of the world within which we live. As a result of our knowledge and our technical prowess, we are always in the presence of something from which, it is true, the Aristotelian immediacy of reality as an absolute has vanished. But that world picture can be granted a detached recognition, as a moment in our experience of the splendor of this world. In this guise the Aristotelian world-picture is exposed as a blissful illusion, an illusion we wish to know and learn about, but which has lost all compelling power.

In the modern understanding, our knowledge cannot be completed; it proceeds in directions of inquiry that have opened up the reality of the cosmos and of all natural things as never before. The last half-century has brought us such tremendous discoveries in physics, chemistry, astronomy, and biology that we are conscious of living in a unique age, one of Promethean creativity.

Hence, for our cognition the world is pulled in several directions, each demanding a different methodology; it is infinitely investigable but is uncompleted and uncompletable.

Moreover, our technological advance has taken a step well beyond Prometheus's lighting of the torch, leading in principle into a different dimension. In the early 1920s, Nernst[6] said: We live on a powder keg —a good thing that man does not find the match to blow it up. This point, it is true, is still far from man's grasp. But that it—a process that would let the limited chain reactions of today suddenly extend to the entire matter of the globe—will be reached no longer belongs to the absolutely impossible. The Earth would glow and our solar system would look like a nova for any other beings alive in the cosmos—just as we observe such novas from time to time in the skies.

Something else has become totally and inescapably certain during the last few years: by means of radioactive substances man can destroy all life on Earth and thus also himself.

We know the unique combination of conditions required for life on Earth to exist. It can be demonstrated how cosmic rays with the capacity to destroy us are warded off by the Earth's protective layer, how the radioactive elements of Earth send out their rays only in amounts that

---

[6] Walther Hermann Nernst (1864–1941), German physicist.

are not life-threatening, and how all other environmental conditions exhibit an astonishing degree of suitability to the demands of living things.

The cosmos is hostile to life. Life is contained in the thin layer on the Earth's surface, between the core that produces fiery catastrophes through volcanic eruptions, and the cosmos, from which we are protected by the earth's shield. Once the precious balance of the physical prerequisites for life, which was created over extremely long periods of time, is destroyed, life will end. We live in a state of instability.

But now man has tried not only to light a fire as did Prometheus, but also to transfer to earth the process by which the almost inexhaustible energy of the sun comes to be. For a few years now we have lived in this situation where our cognition encounters a world that is torn apart and mankind has the incipient capability of destroying life on earth and thus itself. This news is beginning to reach us, yet man cannot grasp it. It does not affect him. He tries to deal with the news by abolishing knowledge.

Gone is the marvelous sense of security pertaining to the two millennia of Aristotle's cosmic view and its later modifications, which did not fundamentally alter human attitudes.

Gone is the outermost sphere of the firmament of fixed stars.

With the two million suns in the Milky Way, we are only a tiny speck of a nebula among hundreds of thousands of stellar nebulas in a cosmos that seems to be expanding due to enormous anorganic quantities of energy.

All this is not cognition, but, rather, speculation grounded in physics. It is a perspective that sometimes arises in the course of research. Such research will go on—until man brings about the event that will end everything for us. This event is likely if man does not change in the depth of his being—a change by virtue of a turnabout taught and demanded by great philosophers since Plato, and demanded by prophets and evangelists, a turnabout that, to be sure, takes place in individual human beings, not in the entirety of being-human.

As long as mankind survives there will be a basic opposition in our perception of the two modes of the cosmos: the cosmos of Aristotle, which needs no turnabout on the part of man, because man is as eternal as the cosmos itself; and the cosmos of our age, which is not concerned about man, and for which even the explosion of the globe would have no more importance than one of the innumerable prominences on the sun's surface, and a change of the terrestrial surface into an inorganic landscape would be utterly meaningless.

But what is life? Where does it come from? How can it come to be? What is man's position in this coherence of all that is alive? Through what means did he come to be?

We do not have the answers, no matter how much we know about things that could perhaps contribute to answers.

There is more in the cosmos than is known or can be known by present-day investigation.

On the one hand, Aristotle's picture of the cosmos has become constricted, full of holes, broken up, and yet, on the other hand, it might be called broad: It keeps open the space for that which we do not know but may not deny for that reason; it leaves open the view on what effected the origin of life and brought human beings into existence, and for what might be called, following Aristotle, the divine as ground of all things, mover and creator of the cosmos, bringing us infinitely closer to the Encompassing.

6. SCIENCE AND PHILOSOPHY

1) Every philosophy is colored, in its thinking, by the conditions, the language, and the ideas prevalent in its time. But every true philosophy enters a timeless presentness in which it manifests its own greatness and its limits.

No one and no age can lay claim to making judgments that are unequivocally derived from the timelessness of suprahistorical truth. But every philosophy moves in that direction and—by virtue of the polarity of its temporal appearance and of its eternal meaning—stands in its existential historicity, which no one can recognize merely from the outside. A philosophy of the past concerns us authentically when it is dealt with in our own philosophizing, either by appropriation or by rejection.

2) We easily make the error of believing that we can cast our glance over all time or any time, as a whole. We then speak of Greek, of Christian, of modern thinking as if each existed as a whole, as if each excluded and included, and therefore was only temporal. We go astray from our own existential historicity into a known, or in principle knowable, history.

What we tend to regard as Greek in Aristotle is by no means Greek in a widely accepted sense. And what, issuing from our mental image of him, we tend to regard as un-Greek is no less Greek than, for instance, Pythagoreanism, which founded a religion and a state, or a tragic sense of life, or science, which, even at that time, owing to its very nature, exhibited the characteristics of modern science.

3) For our understanding of Aristotelian philosophy this last question is of decisive importance: What in it pertains to science and what to philosophy? Are they the same or different, and in what sense can we speak of science and philosophy in Aristotle?

He himself does not draw this distinction. But he differentiates individual sciences, which, to him, are all philosophies, and he differentiates from them "first philosophy," which we call metaphysics.

In view of historical development to the present time, two conclusions have been reached. First: Aristotle is the founder of the sciences in the modern sense. Second: Aristotle is the founder of scientific philosophy. We have to see in what sense these two conclusions, which apply conjointly, are appropriate. Let me anticipate the result: The first conclusion is fallacious if it is meant to refer to what is unique and genuinely great in modern science, whose beginnings Aristotle actually misunderstood. The second conclusion is correct, but in the sense that Aristotle is the founder of *that* philosophy, which ultimately puts an end to authentic philosophizing, even while he still carries it on. However, faced with those two prevailing interpretations, to which I gave such extreme formulations, the unique and enduring value of Aristotelian thinking has to be clearly characterized.

7. SCIENTIFIC INQUIRY AND SYSTEM

Aristotle seems to take hold of all possibilities of cognition. He pays great attention to details and penetrates the most comprehensive horizons. He is rightly considered to be the great systematizer. The question is in what sense we can speak of a system in Aristotle.

Collecting, enumerating, organizing

If "system" means a closed deductive entirety, the opposite of the system consists in collecting and enumerating. Aristotle is the great collector. But enumerations also play an important role; often it appears as though Aristotle had no aim beyond them: for example, in his development of the categories. Having enumerated the four causes, he can say "more or less these," but not "there are no more than these" (*Metaphysics*, 1013b). Aristotle's classifications often retain the form of enumeration as well.

His writings do not represent a system; in this he differs from Hegel and Thomas. If the term "system" is applied to Aristotle's thinking, system would be reduced to a textbook in which information is arranged in various groups and under specific headings, but where the ordering principle is not considered essential or as penetrating fundamental thought.

The fundamental closure of completed total knowledge

Aristotle directs himself toward the totality of the world, including God and man; his thinking is universal as well as comprehensive in content.

His is the architectonic principle which, directed at the whole, would not omit anything. He constantly arranges and develops. His thinking does not reach a final conclusion, yet its fundamental sense is not to exclude anything but to presuppose everything. In Aristotle the nature of closure does not consist in an accomplished construction of the whole, but in the basic schemata of comprehension.

There is something satisfactory in Aristotle's immediate comprehension. All who follow him are included in his schemata of comprehension, which present themselves naturally and immediately, are instantly understandable, and are palpably close at hand.

According to Cicero, he himself had hopes of philosophy's being completed in the foreseeable future.[7]

Investigation of specific problems and system

Aristotle is constantly probing, investigating, and examining. He scrutinizes his predecessors' thoughts on specific subjects. He formulates his questions precisely. He answers questions or leaves them open. This is a constant in his works, alongside the wealth of exposition, description, information devoid of any problem-contexts, and enumeration.

Contrary to an understanding of Aristotle throughout millennia, another interpretation arose:

a) Aristotle did not develop a system; his greatness lies in the development and examination of problems.

b) Even more strongly: He did not aim at a system; the idea was alien to him.

c) Or, put differently: He is the last of the great and still original thinkers; the systems came later. The break in the history of ancient

[7] *Tusculum*, III, 69.

philosophy does not lie between Classicism and Hellenism but between the Original and the Secondary.

Our understanding

Notwithstanding the modes of discursive inquiry, we see in Aristotle a finality of total knowledge functioning as an edifice and the harvest of fundamental knowledge; investigation that is both way and goal; a grasp of the particular derived from the already known whole. He stands in radical contrast to authentic modern scientific research. But for the born disciple there is great satisfaction in Aristotle, as there is for the seeker of tranquillity in knowledge as such, in knowledge as information. By extensive and thorough study of one such as Aristotle, we are at home everywhere, as it were.

Hence what is called for is reading and re-creating the metaphysics as though it were a finished system.

The system *in statu nascendi*: Notwithstanding the magnificent wealth of development, the system fails in its realization, in the unattained unity of principle.

Aristotle's prevailing attitude is still one of examining; it is not dogmatic. He questions, develops possibilities, reports on answers already given, supplies answers himself, but also, at decisive points, allows aporias and perplexities to stand.

Yet the truly strong tendency in his thinking is toward a closed picture of the world, toward the didactic order that has become decisive in the historical aftereffect of his thinking. The process of his thought led to a closed system. The mode of question and answer, proceeding from the mode of actual examination, grows into the didactic form of lucidly articulated finality.

Intellectual work, investigation, gradual unfolding are the modes of his ascertaining what he knows already fundamentally and as a whole. In this process formulations and concepts may change, be modified, even come to contradict each other. Hence, with Aristotle, it signifies to be participating in the movement of thought and not limiting our knowledge to the accomplished schema or system. Aristotle's writings are still "in process," but toward the system—from which goal their impetus derives its meaning—and quite particularly in his *Metaphysics*.

But when trains of thought appear as question, answer, tradition, criticism, aporia, and so on, this is not to be taken as the development of a basic tendency or as goal-directedness.

Comparison of Aristotle with doctrinal systems and with constructive minds

a) *Doctrinal systems* are deliberately intended as bearers of a worldview considered to be the only true one, but standing in confrontation with others that make the same claim.

Specific to a system is that it is refuted only by a later one. The multiplicity of systems is a given.

A universal system—like those of Aristotle and the other creative orderers—wants to incorporate all systems, that is, as moments of the one all-embracing truth: and it does so systematically, so that all others find their "place" in it. It is not eclectic, but recognizes all that is essential as moments. It is characterized by objectivity, calm, nonbelligerence, as well as reciprocal discussion.

b) *Constructive minds:* The question arises whether the constructive minds are to be differentiated from the metaphysicians and systematizers.

Constructs may appear as freely suspended, as hypothesis; or as fanatical intellectual faith; or as architectonic; not as factual comprehension and embracing all Being.

In construction, form as a power makes itself felt. It is not the richness and substance of the world that is made manifest (as, for instance, in Fichte).

The system as closed whole: While systems present a closed whole, they do not take in the world and all Being in their concreteness. Rather, they are instruments of a fundamental knowledge and not attempts at fulfillment. They serve a personal consciousness of Being, and do not represent universal cognition, either in intention or in fact.

The absolutist trait inherent in them is alien to Aristotle.

8. PHILOSOPHY

Two theses were proposed: Aristotle is the founder of modern science, and Aristotle is the founder of scientific philosophy.

The sciences carry on empirical inquiry, mathematics, and logic in the sense of cogent cognition of objects. Philosophy abandons itself when it allows the sciences to take its place.

Philosophy brings forth these sciences or releases them from itself. If, however, philosophy has itself become a science in the process, then it is science in a different form, even if not in a different sense. It becomes science through the methodical form of the progress of thought, through the systematic nature of its intellectual configurations, through concepts concisely defined, through the skill of illumination and impartation in thought, through the artistry of its configured thoughts. This is what came about through Aristotle and ever since has remained a prerequisite.

The consequences are:

1) Philosophical cognition is scientific cognition. There is only one truth. Science is an investigative procedure of the intellect whose results have universal validity; since the sciences and philosophy are the same, they are related to philosophy as parts to a whole or as its material, or like consequences to their basis.

Insofar as science and philosophy were considered to be the same, theology, as cognition of faith, became a science; in this sense Newton called his cognition of nature "natural philosophy," Fichte called his philosophy "doctrine of science," Hegel and Schelling called theirs "science." The intertwining of the meanings of philosophy due to its identification with science has not yet come to an end.

2) A new and lasting objectivity arises. Not only in practice but even in intention, the tendency is toward the impersonal. We want to become absorbed in the matter at hand whose nature it is to be grasped by the mere intellect.

Philosophy becomes "easy" in an existential sense, that is, it becomes mere intellectual labor. Among those succeeding Aristotle, application and effort alone substitute for the seriousness of the thinking being himself.

What is proper in regard to matters of science leads, when transferred to philosophy, to the loss of philosophy.

3) When "scientific philosophy" leads to the separation of science from philosophy (now too become a science), philosophy, by losing its seriousness, falls into thematic sterility, since it has no objects of investigation of its own, in the scientific sense. Its activity takes place in a vacuum. However, it endures by force of the uncomprehended residue of authentic philosophy it continues to contain, providing an ambiguous satisfaction.

Philosophy can gain strength only through the presentness of the sciences, which it wills, whose research it animates, which it experiences as indispensable for itself.

From the very start of science, philosophy has by no means changed ground to become a science in its turn. Without science philosophy would be suspended in a space filled with misleading signals. The rise of the sciences has subjected philosophy to new conditions, under which it might reach for its highest possibilities derived from the eternal origin.

If we speak of philosophy's creative power in terms of the myth-producing imagination or of analogous logical myths, such creations are not voided of their meaning, nor did the sciences preclude creation of effective symbols. These grow from the earnestness of Existenz, and not from science. They have their power through Existenz, and not through scientific cognition. They are not the brainstorms of the researcher, but illuminations of Existenz by a new language.

4) What is called "investigation" or "research" cannot be applied to philosophizing in the same sense as it is to the sciences. Busywork in the interpretation of texts, uncommitted thinking that applies itself in infinite combinations of traditional abstraction and in arbitrary preference for certain categories can no longer be considered philosophizing. Losing philosophy, it has not attained science.

Aristotle's experiential science demands nothing more than description and collection, and, associated with these, interpretations based solely on thinking. This amounts to discursive elaboration, not to scientific investigation. Collecting, describing, reducing to formulas are not the equivalent of scientific inquiry.

The radical difference of scientific research, as represented by diligent thinking operating with an object, consists in evolving a procedure, experimenting, creating combinations of circumstances, calculating measurements in relation to theoretical constructs, interpreting texts in conjunction with ideal-typical constructs—all this in continuous practical operation with the object.

5) The approach of scientific philosophy allows intellectual enterprises to function. Schools in the sense of joining forces and linking traditions; discussions endlessly perpetrated—these keep a movement going in which nothing of real significance is brought about.

While Aristotle's aftereffects lead philosophy onto a ruinous path, he himself stands completely within a philosophizing that, though revealing its fragile nature, still concerns us.

This becomes additionally evident in certain dicta of his on the nature of philosophy.

9. ARISTOTLE'S POWER TO STIMULATE AND TO PARALYZE

Aristotle's compelling power lies in the following:

1) Totality, the truth in the guise of an ordered whole, shown as an existing and attainable goal.

But this goal fell short of being actually attained. In Thomas Aquinas, by contrast, the pursuit of the goal is effected by a recapitulation of Aristotle, by systematization, by conciliation, complementation, and extension of this manifest whole. A system of Being exists, which implied that one had to search for it.

2) Through his aporias Aristotle gives us the impetus to unending discussions; he opens a space for all active minds inclined to argument and discussion.

3) Aristotle displays for us a wealth of concretely perceived phenomena. With him, we practice seeing and formulating; with his help, the ability to perceive the phenomena is aroused.

4) Aristotle has refined the "art of thinking" to such a degree—in the precision of differentiations, figures of thought, and forms of inference; in the order of all kinds and levels of thinking and speaking (logic and rhetoric)—that he is the very source of education.

It is true that in science and philosophy Aristotle has the *power to impel* movements of thought and the shaping of thought sequences, to stimulate questions, the development of the questions, differentiations and aporias, solutions—all of this, however, within the confines of a type of conception that considers only what can be immediately observed.

But his effect on authentic science and authentic philosophy is *paralyzing*.

He promotes all that is didactic, the technique of discussing and imparting exact and structured writings, but essentially only where neither science in the sense of inquiry nor philosophy in its existentially serious sense is at play.

He is, therefore, useful where earnestness is located elsewhere, namely, in faith and in the conservative will to unchanging perpetuity.

10. PLATO AND ARISTOTLE

a) We can speak of a contrast to Plato, and to Aristotle's own youth, only in the sense that Aristotle early understood Plato in the same methodical philosophical form as he did later.

From the outset Aristotle translates everything into doctrines and tenets considered valid in themselves. Without open intent, he removes them from the basic Platonic approach.

Inspired initially by Platonic philosophizing, Aristotle never loses this impetus. But it does not imply Platonic freedom or joy in experimentation, or the prodigality of Plato's spirit. Aristotle's concern is assimilation to what, in principle, is open to everyone.

Aristotle's basic approach is a positive acceptance of life, of the bliss-dispensing religion of the heavens and the heavenly bodies, of contentment with the order of things.

Aristotle rigidified Plato's theory of ideas into a doctrine, analogous to what happened in the Academy after Plato's death. Platonic theory is difficult, and was so for Plato himself; but Aristotle did not reject it on logical grounds. Instead, rejection grew out of the clarification of his own fundamental approach.

The separation of a world above from our world as an expression of unfathomable, passionate, erotic striving; unflinchingly facing depravity; the call for a change of heart; being deeply, unswervingly affected; acceptance of the state of incompleteness in an absolute sense—for Aristotle, all this from the outset falls by the wayside. Nothing of it survives, not even in rudimentary form. Everything is transformed by a radically different basic approach: contentment with the world and eternity. Everything has become cozier, more comfortable, more leveled, more satisfactory. In this mood Platonic thoughts keep their beauty, though stripped of their earnestness: Through objectification they become facts of a case which are refutable; through subjectification they acquire a contemplative contentment, become transposed into images open to embellishment.

The battle against his own Platonic youth consisted in the reshaping of positions, even to the extent of outright opposition. Those earlier positions, however, had been expressions of the same basic approach; they proved inappropriate as Aristotle became more clearly aware of his attitude. At that point not only was the Platonic mind-set transformed into objectified positions, but these positions themselves turned into appropriate expressions for the new attitude toward life or into a fundamental knowledge of world, God, and man, allowing man to arrange himself satisfactorily in this world as it is.

What was it in Platonic thought that Aristotle thus abandoned?

1) The "divine madness," the excessiveness that in Plato called for the utmost—whether in the founding of the state, the "turning around," or the ethos;

2) philosophizing in non-knowledge, supplanted by maximal knowledge;

3) rescue from catastrophes through action appropriate to catastrophes; and eternal discontent with the way things are.

Aristotle has been understood; Plato, virtually never.

b) In differentiating classical philosophy from Hellenistic philosophy, the great systematic philosophies of Plato and Aristotle are habitually assigned to the former. Hellenistic philosophy, no longer original, is considered interesting as part of intellectual history, rather than of philosophy. However, the more profound break may be located between Plato and Aristotle.

Plato thought in the context of political freedom, as a citizen of Athens profoundly affected by the ruin of his native city within a disintegrating world; but in this situation he thought at the limits; his thinking was infinitely open and going beyond those limits. He did not bend to fit into a shell no matter how magnificent the structure. In the movement of thinking, he touched the eternal ground of Being but did not fixate it as something known; in fundamentals his thinking led beyond all objects.

As an alien resident of Athens, a metic, Aristotle's thinking took place in a context of uninvolved observation of political matters that hardly touched him at the core. He established boundaries in a magnificent world-structure, objectified things in his science, at least in intention if not in actuality. He was theoretically interested in everything, including the state and its various forms, which he compiled and categorized. The movement of his thinking, originally a labor of the soul of the widest scope, he ultimately allowed to atrophy into a rational movement of thought devoid of commitment, and repeatable by the application of the intellect only.

HEGEL

Georg Wilhelm Friedrich Hegel was born in Stuttgart on August 27, 1770, the son of a minor government official. He studied theology at Tübingen, with his friends Schelling and Hölderlin, and steeped himself in contemporary and classical literature. A career principally of teaching followed: tutor in Bern, 1793–96, and Frankfurt, 1797–1800; lecturer, then professor, at the University of Jena, 1801–06; editor of a Bamberg newspaper, 1807; rector of a school in Nuremberg, 1808–16; professor at the universities of Heidelberg, 1816–18, and Berlin, 1818–31. He died in Berlin on November 14, 1831.

The presentation of Hegel projected by Jaspers is outlined in the second of the Fragments culled by Hans Saner from Jaspers's notes; it is given here, as "Survey of the Planned Exposition," following part three of this chapter. What follows under the title "The Dialectic" was to have been the first of four topics. It is the only one Jaspers left in a nearly complete state.

THE DIALECTIC

We shall proceed from examples, from a tiny number out of the tremendous mass of Hegel's configurations of thought. Only by participating in the dialectical movements, and not merely speaking about them, can we hope to understand what is happening here.

Without the experience gained from the examples of dialectics, the discussions that follow would be as incomprehensible as a lecture by an art historian about works the listener has never seen and would not be shown. Moreover, the picture shown by the historian of philosophy is not a photocopy of the text itself, but of a reproduction. This reproduction is an art that already interprets as it reproduces.

All direct formulations about dialectics (including those by Hegel himself) become schematizations. As we proceed we shall have to ask whether the one basic principle that recurs in vastly manifold and different variations exists at all. In any case, its appearances constitute a multiplicity of origins that deviate from each other, perhaps in a fundamental way.

I. EXAMPLES OF THE DIALECTIC

A. Sense-certainty

Exposition

Knowledge becomes apparent through my questioning. I ask: What is? The first answer is: Being is what is immediate or that which is in sense-certainty.

However, who asks and who answers? He who himself stands within the appearance of knowledge but who at the same time knows about the appearance of knowledge; that is, the person who philosophizes. He grasps Being by standing within it and grasps it once again by observing this standing-in-it. Let us see how Hegel lets sense-certainty move.

1. *The claim on the part of immediacy to being all of actuality and truth.* Sense-certainty posits the claim to be the richest kind of cognition due to its immediacy. Its wealth has no limit: it stretches away in time and space (extensive infinity); it is not bounded when we take a piece out of this plenitude and by division enter into it (intensive infinity). This kind of cognition appears to be the truest, for it has what is immediate before it in its perfect completeness.

For example, this piece of paper conceived in its infinity: "In the very attempt to pronounce it, it would . . . crumble . . . those who have started to describe it would not be able to finish doing so: they would have to hand it over to others, who would themselves, in the last resort, have to confess to speaking about a thing that has no being" (2, 83; *Phänomenologie*, 73).[1]

Actually, sense-certainty turns out to be the most abstract and poorest truth. For of that which it knows it merely states the following: It is. And the consciousness of this being exists only as the "I" as such. Object and the "I" are only pure "Thises." The "I" is not certain of itself because it moves in diverse thoughts and because it might have undergone de-

---

[1] References giving volume and page are to *Georg Wilhelm Friedrich Hegels Werke*, ed. by P. Marnheinecke *et al.*; those to *Phänomenologie des Geistes* are additionally to the edition of J. Hoffmeister.

velopment; nor is it certain of itself because the object might have shown itself in its rich relationship to itself and in its manifold relation to others. Without such mediation, the truth of sense-certainty is simple immediacy, which is really nothing as yet. Consciousness is only this and nothing beyond it. The singular "I," the pure "this," knows the singular thing, the pure "this."

2. *The "falling-out" of "I" and object.* As soon as we speak of immediacy as "this," more has happened than merely addressing immediacy itself. There has occurred, right away, the first "mediation," in that "I" and object "fell out" of immediacy, a "this" as "I" and a "this" as object.

The philosophical observer sees that pure immediacy has thereby been sublated. For this consciousness in the split of "I" and object is already mediated: I have the certainty through an other, namely, the thing; and the same applies to certainty through an other, namely, through the "I."

With this mediation there begins, in sense-certainty, the movement in which is revealed what it is: first the object, second the "I," third the whole, consisting of "I" and object—all three dissolve in their immediacy.

3. *The dissolution of the object.* Sense-certainty has to be asked: What is the "this"? It is the Now and the Here.

To the question What is the Now? the answer is:

The Now is the night. We write down this truth. If now, this noon, we look again at the truth we have written, it has become stale. The written truth is treated as being, but it turns out to be a nonbeing (2, 75–76; *Phän.*, 67).

The Now is preserved, but as something neither night nor day— a negative as such. Its being something that is permanent and self-preserving is determined by the nonbeing of an other, namely, day and night. A simple thing of this kind, which is, through negation, neither This nor That, a Not-This, we call a *universal.* The universal, therefore, is the truth of sense-certainty. The self-preserving Now is a mediated one and, as such, a universal.

The same applies to the Here as to the Now. Here is the tree. I turn around: here is the house. But the Here itself does not vanish. It abides in the vanishing of house, tree, and so on. Again this shows itself as a mediated simplicity, a universality of the Here (2, 76–77; *Phän.*, 68).

This pure Being, however, the Now and the Here as such, is not what is meant by sense-certainty. What is left over is only the most universal and most abstract, the empty and indifferent Now and Here.

But still left is our opinion, for which the truth of sense-certainty is not the universal. Now the object has become the nonessential. The true essential lies in the object as *my* object, or in the act of meaning. It is because I know of it. Sense-certainty has been driven back into the "I."

4. *The dissolution of the "I."* If everything is now to become truth as *my* seeing and hearing, and the disappearance of the singular Now and Here that we mean is averted by *my* holding on to them, then, to be sure, I see the tree here and now, but another "I" sees the house. Both have the same verification, namely, the immediacy of seeing. The certainty and assurance of both about their knowledge vanishes. What does not vanish, however, is the "I" as a universal, the "I"-as-such. By saying "I," I say all "I"s. Everyone is that which I say: I, this singular I (2, 78; *Phän.*, 69).

When "I" and object have become universal and hence empty, there still remains for us to see the *whole* of sense-certainty as its essence. As an immediacy, sense-certainty holds fast to the whole.

5. *The dissolution of the whole of sense-certainty.* I claim to be pure intuiting. I hold fast to my immediacy. "Since this certainty will no longer come forth to us when we direct our attention to a Now that is night, we will approach it and let the Now that is asserted be pointed out to us. We must let it *be pointed* out to us. . . . We must therefore enter the same point of time or space . . ." (2, 79–80; *Phän.*, 70–71; cf. Mi, ¶105).[2] What happens then?

The Now ceases to be when it is pointed out. The Now and the pointing out of the Now are not something immediate and simple, but a movement that contains various moments. The result, in pointing out the multiplicity of Now, is discovering that Now is a universal.

The Now is already the Now that has been. It is I who maintain that it has been. But it is not that-which-has-been. I sublate the having-been, thus negate the negation of the Now, and in this way return to my first assertion: The Now is.

Hence neither the Now nor the pointing out of the Now are immediately singular, but are a movement with various aspects:

This Now is sublated to the has-been; this sublation is itself sublated in turn and thus returned to the first assertion. "However, this first, thus reflected into itself, is not exactly the same as it was to begin with, viz. something *immediate*; on the contrary, it is *something that is reflected into itself*, or a *simple* entity which, in its otherness, remains what it is: a Now which is an absolute plurality of Nows. And this is the true, the genuine Now. . . . The *pointing-out* of the Now is thus itself the movement which

[2] References to translations by A. V. Miller, in *Phenomenology of Spirit*, are indicated by Mi and the paragraph number. The translators' emendations of Miller are not noted as such.

expresses what the *Now* is in truth; viz. a result . . . the experience . . . that Now is a *universal*" (2, 81; *Phän.*, 71; Mi, ¶107).

The same thing happens with the Here.

6. *The Result.* The dialectic of sense-certainty is the history of its movement or the experience of its meaning. Sense-certainty is itself nothing other than this history.

The philosophical observer lets it speak and lets it point out what it means. He sees the turnaround and vanishing of the meaning of what is said, which does not coincide with what is meant, but arrives at a universal, indeed, at the most abstract.

Reflections

After this summing-up of the dialectical movement of sense-certainty, let us reflect on its meaning, on the continuation of the dialectic beyond it, on the enduring import of sense-certainty in all further appearances.

1. *The Schematization.* Our report could present only an abridgment. Whoever reads Hegel's text experiences the vividness of the dialectic, which eludes any summing-up.

Later on Hegel himself set forth this dialectic in his system, which has become a doctrine (76, 257ff.; *Enc.*, ¶418ff.).[3]

Sentience is *immediate* consciousness; its relation to the object, *unmediated* certainty. As immediate, the object is *singular*. But sentience knows about it only as something that is, a Something. It appears to be the one richest in content but poorest in thoughts.

2. *The Limit.* The *immediacy* of *sense-certainty* constitutes a limit. We look for its beginning but do not reach it, since each experience of sense-certainty that we can express is already mediated, at the least through the split of "I" and object. Exertion is needed to arrive at the limit where there would be nothing except a pure sense-certainty. We approach this limit, do not reach it, and discover that in its place there is the dialectic of sense-certainty, that it is here as movement, not as duration. That with which we would like to begin can never be the real beginning. If we say it is given, we don't know from where, and then this "from where" is pointed out in the system of philosophy in which there is no beginning, only circles.

The clarification of sense-certainty suspends the solidity and absoluteness of a sensuous Being and its certainty. But there remains the

---

[3] References to *Encyclopädie der philosophischen Wissenschaften im Grundrisse* give paragraph number and, where appropriate, Z, for Zusatz, the addendum from notes by Hegel's auditors.

question about the Being that is meant in sense-certainty once everything said about it in universal categories is subtracted. Is it then, at the limits, nothing, or does there remain a Being which is impenetrable, not reached by any universal, absolutely singular, accidental, not subsumable? Is there actually only that which enters into the form of a universal that can be expressed, or is there also, prior to the latter, something that with its core cannot enter into this universal?

3. *What does "sensuous" mean?* Tradition, starting with Plato, calls that "sensuous" (aesthetic) which is a given and a conduct extraneous to the *logos*, a conduct in perpetual flow devoid of durability, the constant flux of merely momentary appearances. It lies between Being and non-Being, namely, Being as genuinely present in endless singularity, unrelatedness, nonattachment, and non-Being as constant disappearing. This content of *aisthesis* evades determination and hence cannot be thought, just as it is itself not thinking.

Hegel has the following to say on what he has in mind regarding "sense-certainty": Sensuous consciousness is not differentiated from later modes of consciousness through the fact that in it alone the object comes to me by way of the senses, but solely through the fact that the object (whether external or internal Being) has no further thought-determination except the one, that is, to be at all and to be an independent other over against me as singular, immediate. By coincidence it occurs just now in consciousness, is a given of which I do not know where it comes from. In this way the immediate or sensuous consciousness could be the form in which knowledge of God is asserted: that He is, that He exists outside us. This form is inappropriate to the content, does not signify anything, claims to possess all in the plenitude of immediacy (7b, 259–60; *Enc.*, ¶418, Z).

4. *What is universal? Language.* Where there is consciousness there is also thought. Sense-certainty exists only at the point where it is thought. And where there is thinking, a universal is being thought. This cannot be thought without language. Thinking is bound to speaking.

The "sensuous 'This' that is meant *cannot be reached* by language, which belongs to consciousness, i.e. to that which is inherently universal." But "what is called the unutterable is nothing else than the untrue, the irrational, what is merely meant" (2, 83; *Phän.*, 73; Mi, ¶110).

Sense-certainty is supposed to say what it means. But it turns out that it cannot do this. It expresses the sensuous, immediate, singular as a universal. But for the sensuous being that is meant, it is not possible ever to be expressed.

It loses the richness it maintained in favor of this universal, which at first is the most empty Being-as-such. In *language* our meaning is refuted right away. Language, however, says Hegel, is the more truthful. Language possesses "the divine nature of directly reversing the meaning of what is said, of making it into something else and thus not letting what is meant *get into words* at all" (2, 84; *Phän.*, 74; Mi, ¶110).

5. *The progress of dialectic beyond sensuous certainty.* In sense-certainty, according to Hegel, natural consciousness finds out through experience what is true in it. But it also forgets, time and again, this experience it has gained, and recommences the movement from the beginning (2, 81–82; *Phän.*, 72–73).

It cannot go on in this manner. The beginning made by speaking impels forward—if experience, instead of merely repeating itself endlessly, goes on to the next level of consciousness. To be sure: "If I speak of a *singular thing*, then I speak of it . . . as something wholly *universal*, for all are one singular thing" (2, 84; *Phän.*, 74).

But sense-certainty does not fall by the wayside as trivial through the refutation of what it has spoken. Rather, refutation is intended to sublate to something higher. That is achieved in Hegel through the transition from "sense-certainty," from immediacy, to "perception." In it, the Here and Now becomes a togetherness of many Heres and Nows; the object emerges as something integrated, as a thing possessing many qualities.

Sense-certainty is taken up into perception—and thus it proceeds on the very long road of the configurations of consciousness, to absolute knowledge.

6. *How sublated sense-certainty returns as an indispensable aspect of truth.* It may appear as if sense-certainty is trivialized through Hegel's dialectic, its impoverishment, emptiness, abstractness exposed in high-spirited formulations. But in fact all that is shown is the abstractness of speaking on the part of the immediate sensuous consciousness: the incapacity of saying what is meant that is contained in the motionless thesis of sense-certainty as the only certain, the richest and actual one.

Hegel does not deny the richness inherent in sense-certainty. But as merely immediate sense-perception this wealth is not present as yet. Rather, it must first work its way out and show itself in the total sequence of knowledge appearing in consciousness, in self-consciousness, in reason, in spirit, in history. Nothing is lost here, and truth in its completion is again present as sense-certainty.

The "incarnation of the divine being" means it enters into sensuous consciousness. In this way it is revealed. The mystery "ceases when the absolute being, as spirit, is the object of consciousness." "The divine

nature is the same as human nature, and it is this unity that is beheld."
"The absolute Being [*Wesen*] which exists as an actual self-consciousness
seems to have come down from its eternal simplicity, but by thus coming
down has, in fact, attained for the first time to its own highest essence
[*Wesen*]. . . . What is called sense-consciousness is . . . this thinking for
which Being is the immediate. Thus the lowest is at the same time the
highest; the revealed which has come forward wholly onto the surface
is precisely therein the most profound. That the supreme being is seen,
heard, etc. as an immediately present self-consciousness, this therefore
is, indeed, the consummation of its concept" (2, 569, 570, 571; *Phän.*, 487,
488, 489; Mi, ¶760).

Once more, at the end of *The Phenomenology of Spirit*, at the point
where absolute knowledge is attained and where the science of philosophy takes place, the return to the beginning of phenomenology in sense-
certainty is reached in the following manner: This science of absolute
knowing (developed later on in Hegel's *Logic* and continued in the
Realphilosophie of nature and history) "contains within itself this necessity
of stepping out of the form of pure concept and it contains the passage
of the notion into consciousness . . . into the certainty of immediacy
. . . or sense-consciousness—the beginning from which we started. This
release of itself from the form of its self is the supreme freedom and
assurance of its self-knowledge" (2, 610; *Phän.*, 520; Mi, ¶806).

This eternal happening which brings about time and space, this
externalizing into this apartness has the following dialectical basis: The
self-knowing Spirit's "knowing knows not only itself but also the negative
of itself, or its limit; to know one's limit is to know how to sacrifice
oneself. This sacrifice is the externalization in which Spirit displays the
process of becoming Spirit in the form of free contingent happening,
intuiting its pure Self as time outside of it, and likewise its Being as
space" (2, 610; *Phän.*, 620; Mi, ¶807).

Thus, Spirit wends its way through nature and history.

7. *On Feuerbach's criticism.* Whoever reads Hegel's sequences of ideas
for the first time finds himself, in most instances, at a loss. What is it
that Hegel wants to prove, what to refute? What is the outcome? Instead
of being given an unequivocal answer, the reader is driven to go on. He
is not allowed to stop, for only in what is to come will truth become
manifest. The result is not the attainment of a specific knowledge-content,
but the whole of the dialectical road traveled, which is now reaching its
completion.

In order to open our senses to this astonishing procedure, a look at objections that have been raised against Hegel is helpful, provided it becomes clear that they obviously miss Hegel's meaning.

Against Hegel's development of sense-certainty, Feuerbach holds that the reality of sense-certainty is not refuted; the universal is not proven to be the real. In greater detail:

For sense-consciousness, all words count only as names. "My brother is called Johann . . . innumerable others are also called Johann . . . does it follow from this that my Johann is not a reality . . . that Johann-ness is a truth?" (II, 212).[4]

For sense-consciousness, language is unreal, a nonentity. For it, words are only signs for reaching its purpose by the shortest road. "Language is irrelevant here. The reality of the sensuous singular being is a truth that, for us, is sealed with our blood" (ibid.).

Sensuous consciousness finds itself owing to the fact that the singular being cannot be expressed or refuted. Precisely in this it finds a refutation of language, but not a refutation of sense-certainty. In this, sensuous consciousness is completely correct. Otherwise "we would let ourselves be palmed off in life with words instead of with things . . . consciousness does not let itself be confused, now as ever it holds fast to the reality of singular things" (II, 213).

To get the better of Hegel's dialectic of sense-certainty is decidedly not easy.

Hegel does not speak of sensuous consciousness but of sense-certainty, which is not able to say what it means.

Hegel does not want to refute sensuous presentness; rather, it runs as an indispensable adjunct through the appearance of the spirit up into its highest configurations.

Hegel, in deeming it "inexpressible," does not intend to refute sense-certainty. For where speaking ceases, refuting also comes to an end. Instead, Hegel sees the unutterable in the entire reality as the accidental, the disparate in which the Idea has freely surrendered itself in order to find itself in it again, now sheltering reality in itself as a moment.

For Hegel, the unutterable as such carries no weight, of course. It has to be elevated into thinking and thus into something capable of expression. Only in this way does it receive the truth of Being in place of the indifference of the endless. This, however, happens in the entire sequence of the appearances of the spirit and in the whole of the philosophy of logical and real Being.

[4] Ludwig Feuerbach, "Zur Kritik der Hegel'schen Philosophie" (1839), in *Sämtliche Werke*, vol. 2. Leipzig, 1846, 185–232.

The ineffability and wealth of the "This" becomes manifest, and thus expressible, only in the whole of Being. This it cannot achieve as mere sense-certainty.

Feuerbach's criticism ascribes positions to Hegel that he does not hold at all. Hegel's dicta, which have their place in the dialectical movement, are taken out of context and fixed in absolute assertions, and as such are "refuted" in an undialectical way. In this process the sense of the Hegelian movement of thought—in which not self-certainty itself but the abstract meaning of sense-certainty is sublated—is being lost: namely, the philosophical energy that firmly holds on to the sensuous even as it brings it into suspension.

If the movement of the dialectic is denied and the experience of participating in dialectical thought missed, the fixating intellect finds a way of using the dialectic, either by shrewd manipulation or by rational refutation. This, however, is not a legitimate way to introduce a meaningful criticism of Hegel and his dialectic, since it does without one's own participation in the dialectic.

What matters to Hegel in his dialectic of sense-certainty is rejection of the assertion that "the reality or being of external things taken as *Thises* or sense-objects has absolute truth for consciousness" (2, 82; *Phän.*, 72; Mi, ¶64). Universal experience teaches us the opposite. Anticipating that the practical sphere will have to be taken into account, Hegel says: Those who assert the truth and certainty of the reality of sense objects "should go back . . . to the most elementary school of wisdom, viz. the ancient Eleusinian Mysteries." They have "still to learn the secret meaning of the eating of bread and the drinking of wine. For he who is initiated into these Mysteries not only comes to doubt the being of sensuous things, but to despair of it; in part he brings about the nothingness of such things himself in his dealings with them, and in part he sees them reduce themselves to nothingness. Even the animals are not shut out from this wisdom but, on the contrary, show themselves to be most profoundly initiated into it; for they do not just stand idly in front of sensuous things as if these possessed intrinsic being, but, despairing of their reality, and completely assured of their nothingness, they fall to without ceremony and eat them up. And all Nature, like the animals, celebrates these open mysteries which teach the truth about sensuous things" (2, 82–83; *Phän.*, 73; Mi, ¶65).

Hegel's playful tone is not directed against sensual actuality but against sense-certainty put forward as absolute truth; that, he says, is not to know what one is talking about and saying the opposite of what one wants to say.

It is not reality that is denied to sensuous things (if they were not real they could not be eaten as food), but absolute actuality. Hegel does not assert that sense-reality is superfluous (for God himself becomes sensuous man), but that an aspect of sense-reality has the character of the absolute (man-become-God dies and has his actuality in time in the form of remembrance).

That Being itself becomes temporal does not signify only the nothingness of the temporal as such but also the authenticity of the temporal. What passes away as finite sensibility in time is sublated in the timelessness of Being where it originated.

As temporal and trivial Being the sensuous becomes an object-image; but in disappearing, it is the manifestation of the eternal.

Comment

On first hearing an example of Hegelian dialectic, the response might well be: Everything seems to be revolving, nowhere can one get a foothold, nowhere is there a conclusion, nowhere a definite standpoint to adhere to. This impression is accurate, but only as a beginning. It represents the vertigo out of which what is at stake here becomes clear: the ordered dialectic that, through its methodically lucid movement, controls the initial vertigo. The confusion is lifted but the movement is preserved. It does not allow a solid, final standpoint, does not yield any ground other than in the whole of the movement itself.

To attempt to practice this dizzying movement brings with it one of the fundamental thought experiences. The true meaning of Hegelian dialectic cannot be acquired in perfunctory appropriation of clever about-faces or in the inflexibility of rapidly absorbed dialectical tricks. But without such a knowledge we remain inwardly unarmed against the dialectics of sophism and unable to grasp fundamental actualities that defy the fixating intellect.

Let me try to give another exposition.

B. The becoming of self-consciousness; mastery and servitude; the further progress of self-consciousness

1. The becoming of self-consciousness

1) *Consciousness* is not yet *self-consciousness*. *Consciousness* directs itself toward the other in the meaning of sense-certainty, in perceiving the

thing, in the intellectual grasp of forces, of appearances, and of the universal.

Out of these configurations of *consciousness*, "for which their truth was a thing, something other than they themselves," proceeds the necessary advancement toward *self-consciousness*. How does this come about? Consciousness comes to the object of the intellect, which in itself is infinity but is not grasped as such by consciousness. Consciousness itself must make its appearance as a new configuration of consciousness insofar as it immediately has the notion of infinity. The notion of infinity becomes its object in distinguishing what is distinguished, or in self-consciousness: "I distinguish myself from myself, and thereby it is in respect to me immediately that what is distinguished is not distinguished" (2, 129; *Phän.*, 111).

Philosophical observation proceeds by way of meaning, perceiving, and understanding to cognition of that "which consciousness knows by knowing itself" (2, 130; *Phän.*, 112). This leads onto a long road.

2) At first Hegel regards *self-consciousness as distinguished from consciousness* through the following elements:

a) The object of *consciousness* is something other than what it is itself: this other is a *lifeless other*. The object of *self-consciousness* is what it is itself: *Life*.

There the object is the singular and universal, the force, the law of events, appearance, the internal—all thought as an Other: I am not involved. *Here* the object is the Other, which is Life, as I am myself; it concerns me; I turn to it as the object of my desire, as an object lacking independence, which I would like to sublate but which lays claim to independence as I do. While consciousness turns into self-consciousness, its object at the same time turns from lifeless Other into Life, and then from the self-less into Self.

b) What has come to be in this manner enters a new process: desire, at first directed toward the Other, devouring and negating it, must negate itself. Self-consciousness experiences the independence of its object. And it now achieves its own satisfaction in another self-consciousness.

The doubling of self-consciousness is the living self-consciousness. The latter reaches its completion as "the unity of itself in its being-other" (2, 139; *Phän.*, 122). Being with itself in the other is its actuality and its truth.

Hegel anticipates this goal before he comprehends the long way to it in its developments, catastrophes, and new foundations. It is the concept of the Spirit, which he already knows by observing the way along which consciousness, the appearance of the Spirit, first has the "experiences of what the spirit is, this absolute substance which, in the complete freedom and independence of its opposite, namely of various self-consciousnesses that are for themselves, constitutes their unity; the I that is We, and the We that is I" (ibid.).

3) *Hegel anticipates the form of this movement before all his representations of concrete movement:*

a) There is for self-consciousness another self-consciousness; it has come outside itself (2, 140; *Phän.*, 123). This has a twofold meaning: it has *lost itself*, for it finds itself as another being; with this it has *sublated the other*, for it does not see the other as a being, but sees itself in the other.

b) "It must sublate its being other" (ibid.). This sublation of the first double meaning is a second double meaning: First, self-consciousness must aim at sublating the *other* independent being in order to become certain of itself as that being; second, it thus aims at sublating *itself*, for this other is itself.

c) The consequence of this ambiguous sublation is an ambiguous return into itself. In the first place it receives its own self back through the sublation; because, by sublating its otherness, it again becomes equal to itself. But, in the second place, it gives the other self-consciousness back again to itself, for it sublates its being in the other and in this way lets the other again go free (2, 141; *Phän.*, 124).

d) Thus all acts of self-consciousness are presented only as acts of the One. But these acts of the One again have a double meaning: They are just as much the acts of the one as those of the other. For the other is equally independent, closed in himself. He has no power over the other if he does not do to himself what he does to him. The movement is that of the self-consciousness of both. Each does himself what he demands of the other. Therefore self-consciousness does what it does only insofar as the other does the same. One-sided action would be useless because what is to happen can come to be only through both (2, 141; *Phän.*, 124).

The same, expressed differently: What prevails for self-consciousness is that it *is* and *is not* other consciousness immediately. Equally, the other is only for itself by sublating itself as that-which-is-for-itself, and is for itself the other only in being-for-itself. Each is the center for the other, through which each mediates and joins with itself. Each is at the same time for itself only through this mediation. "They acknowledge each other as mutually acknowledging each other" (2, 142; *Phän.*, 125).

That means self-consciousness is in and for itself through being for another in and for itself; "it is only as something acknowledged." The

movement of acknowledging comes about only in the ambiguous inter-
twinings and turnarounds, about which Hegel says: "The ambiguity of
what is differentiated lies in the nature of self-consciousness . . . to be
immediately the opposite of the determinateness in which it is placed"
(2, 140; *Phän.*, 123). This, Hegel calls infinity.

e) We must have convinced ourselves, first, that self-consciousness
is not like a thing for self-consciousness; second, that self-consciousness
is not for itself without the other self-consciousness being for itself; third,
that this being for each other, in which each is yet to become for itself,
is not a state at rest, but in movement only.

This Hegelian dialectic of self-consciousness can strike us as strange,
but then as a gripping metaphysical cipher. *What is it that Hegel is talking
about?*

Examined *logically*, the process may appear as a sequence of concepts
that are transposed into their opposite; or, *psychologically*, as an event
between two people who work their way up to mutual acknowledgment
through which at the same time each of them first becomes himself; or,
historically, as the development of a community through the struggle of
individuals with each other and with the whole whereby they arrive at
the realization that the strength of the community is guaranteed by each
individual's becoming himself only insofar as he is equally devoted to
the whole.

This multiplicity of possible interpretations circles around what Hegel means, but without being on target. For certainly each of these three
aspects is correct; each, however, is inadequate at the same time. From
a particular perspective we can understand things more easily because
they appear more graphic and definite. But the intention of the inter-
weaving of perspectives is to give voice to the cipher that in Hegel points
the way to the ground of all that occurs.

This movement, which is so all-encompassing and so sublimely presented, shapes the mystery of the communication of self-being in its
greatest intensification. The movements of stepping apart, of inter-
weaving, of finding each other, are presented clearly, formally, without
illustration. There is no durability to the mere being-together of self-
isolating, coy atoms of being-I, nor is there one entirety of the universal
which eradicates all individuals. Being-for-oneself exists only through
being-for-the-other and vice versa; being-for-oneself does not terminate
when it is won in devotion to the other; rather, one is returned to oneself
by the other, and only then comes to oneself. In the movement there
arise the individual selves as well as the whole. I am not myself if the
other is not himself; I am not free if the other is not free.

The goal "they acknowledge each other as mutually acknowledging each other" is reached only after a long road through the sequence of —as yet not adequate—appearances of self-consciousness. The development, classic in its conciseness and clarity, presented in two pages of text, and carried to extreme abstraction, is to find its fulfillment.

The first step—for us, a further example of concrete dialectics—is taken in the unfolding of the coming-to-be and the movement of mastery and servitude.

2. *Mastery and servitude*

Hegel shows how the process of recognition appears to self-consciousness when, in the struggle for existence, the extremes of mastery and servitude develop into the greatest inequality. Here only the one self-consciousness is recognized, the other only recognizing (cf. Mi, ¶185).

1) *Self-consciousness demands the negation of mere existence.* The I of self-consciousness, in its being-for-itself but confronting all others as the not-I, is not actual as yet. It is something other in its origin than a thing or life. This origin gains actuality only if it does not remain consciousness immersed in the being of life. It must accomplish the movement of absolute abstraction, "of rooting out all immediate being." Self-consciousness can come to itself only when it shows and discovers its superiority to the mere existence of life, and when, in this superiority, it is joined with the other self-consciousness: as long as it is indeed aware of itself but not of the other, "its own self-certainty still has no truth" (2, 142, 143; *Phän.*, 125; Mi, ¶186).

The foundation of self-consciousness is laid in the *encounter of self-consciousness with self-consciousness through life-and-death struggle.* This primal abstraction is shown in the pure negation of the mode of its being as object; it shows self-consciousness as "not being attached to any specific existence, not to the individuality common to existence as such, not attached to life" (2, 143; *Phän.*, 125; Mi, ¶187). Negativity is the underlying sense in the dialectic of becoming oneself: Each seeks the death of the other and thereby stakes his own life. Only thus is freedom won; freedom proves itself only in "that for self-consciousness its essential being is not just being, not the immediate form in which it appears, not its absorption in the expanse of life—but, rather, that there is nothing present in it which could not be regarded as an ephemeral moment. . . . The individual who has not risked his life may well be recognized as a person, but he has not attained to the truth of this recognition as an independent self-consciousness" (2, 143–44; *Phän.*, 126; Mi, ¶187).

2) *Death in battle.* Proving yourself in actual death cancels the possibility of actualizing the self-consciousness that came to be through this proving. "Death certainly shows that each staked his life and scorned it, both for himself and for the other; but that is not so, for those who survived this battle . . . the two do not reciprocally give and receive one another back from each other consciously, but leave each other free indifferently, like things. Their act is an abstract negation, not the negation coming from consciousness which *sublates* in such a way as to *preserve* and *maintain* what is sublated, and consequently survives its own sublation" (2, 144; *Phän.*, 127; Mi, ¶188–89). In this experience, self-consciousness learns that life is as essential to it as pure self-consciousness. Death in battle can be neither goal nor completion. Proving yourself is unavoidable, scorn of death a condition of authentic self-consciousness.

3) *Two configurations of proving oneself.* The first result is two opposing configurations of consciousness. The first wants to stay alive at all costs; he submits; but he becomes, as he deserves, nonindependent consciousness, becomes servant; the substance of his life is there for another. The second risked his life, and becomes, as he deserves, independent consciousness, becomes master; the dependent other is at his service.

The condition thus reached is the following: The servant is kept on a chain, in fear of death, from which he cannot break free in his struggle. The master, who proved in struggle that he is contemptuous of life, insofar as being "is to him a negative" (2, 146; *Phän.*, 128), is the power over the other.

This power is evident in that the servant works for the master while the master consumes what has been gained through this work. If we call that which is being worked on the "thing," then the *servant* stands in immediate relation to this thing; he too has a negative attitude toward it and sublates it; but it remains, at the same time, independent for him, because through his negating he does not get done with it to the point of destroying it, but merely works on it. The *master*, on the other hand, has a mediate relationship to the thing through the servant who works on it, but an immediate one only through the sheer negation of the thing, or the enjoyment of it. What desire failed to achieve, due to the independence of the thing, the master succeeds in doing, because the servant is interposed between him and the thing. Thus the master takes to himself only the dependent aspect of the thing and has the pure enjoyment of it. The aspect of independence, however, he leaves to his servant who works on it (cf. Mi, ¶190).

This, however, as little as any other, is not a quiescent state, a state that endures unchanged and represents the end. Instead, the master as well as the servant now experiences a new movement—in fact, the very reverse.

4) *The master.* Only the master has the unrestricted consciousness of his being-for-himself. The servant acknowledges him, but he does not acknowledge the servant. There has come about a one-sided and unequal recognition. Lacking here is the recognition that what the master does to the other he also does to himself, and that what the servant does to himself he should also do to the other (cf. Mi, ¶191).

In achieving his mastery, the master has, in fact, gained something quite different from an independent consciousness. Because he alone is independent, is for himself, and only through recognition by his non-independent servant, he finds himself the empty point whose independence has lost the movement that he sees only in the actions of the servant. The master can fight, risk his life, and subjugate others but does not come to himself by doing so, since, being alone and without concerted movement with other independent individuals, he becomes empty himself. He cannot make use of being master once the struggle and the risk to life have ceased.

The master finds himself at a dead end.

Influenced by Hegel's thought, Hebbel had Holofernes say: "Sometimes, surrounded by all these imbeciles, I feel as though I were the only one existing. . . . Oh, for an enemy, a single one, who would dare to defy me! . . . Everything I respect I must destroy. . . . What a wretched place the world appears to me. I think I was born to destroy it . . . let him come, my challenger, he who will overthrow me. I long for him! It is tedious to have nothing to honor save oneself."[5] Frederick the Great is said to have exclaimed: "I am tired of ruling over slaves."

5) *The servant.* The servant posits his own consciousness as unessential, first, in working on things whose obstinacy confronts him, and by fashioning them through his work to become something objective; second, in his dependence on another existence, the master, whom he obeys as the free self-consciousness he recognizes. Unable to achieve mastery over Being and to arrive at the absolute negation of his existence in death, the servant now does to himself, in the existence preserved in him, what the master does to him.

But this is indeed an analogue to trial by death. For he who became a servant has experienced death. "For this consciousness has experienced fear not for this or that, or at odd moments, but for his whole being;

---

[5] Friedrich Hebbel (1813–1863), German dramatist; references are to *Judith*, Acts 1 and 5.

since it has felt the fear of death, the absolute master. In that experience
it has been quite unmanned, has trembled in every fiber of its being,
and everything solid and stable has been quaking" (2, 148; *Phän.*, 129;
Mi, ¶194).

Such an experience has transformed his essence; but only such an
experience is able to do that. "If it has not experienced absolute fear but
only some lesser dread, the negative being has remained for it something
external, its substance has not been infected by it through and through."
If it had not been that way and remained that way, then "the entire
contents of its natural consciousness had not been jeopardized," then
"determinate being in principle still belongs to it," then, having "a mind
of one's own" is obstinacy,[6] a freedom still enmeshed in servitude (2,
150; *Phän.*, 131; Mi, ¶196).

As though he had died, the servant eradicates his existence in servitude, obedience, labor. But herein freedom is accrued for him and not
for the master. For the nature of self-consciousness is absolute negativity.
It has actualized itself as creative, negatively in death and in the empty
self-consciousness of the master, and positively only in the servant. This
self-consciousness fulfills itself actually in service instead of dissolving
totally into nonactuality. "Through his service he sublates his attachment
to natural existence in every aspect; and gets rid of it by work." By
serving he achieves what he wanted to avert by refusing death: he sublates
his dependence on natural existence. This occurs through labor and
servitude (2, 143; *Phän.*, 130; Mi, ¶194).

Work: Through work the servant comes "to himself." "The negative
relation to the object becomes its form and something permanent. Work
is arrested transitoriness, or: it educates" (2, 143; *Phän.*, 130; Mi, ¶195).
The object gains independence and so does the worker (even if at first
merely "in itself," not "for itself"). Working consciousness arrives "at
the intuition of independent being as itself" (2, 149; *Phän.*, 130). Through
being made external to him the result of his work does not become
something other than the worker. "It is precisely in his work that he
acquires a mind of his own" which is no longer obstinacy (ibid.). He
brings forth a world ranging from agriculture to the creation of churches
and palaces, which are enjoyed by others. But this is a world in which
he recognizes himself, in which he is free with himself, and is in himself
free in the other, and in what has been produced, whereas the consumer
approaches the meaning—if he understands it at all—only at a distance
and passively. Whereas the master enjoys and, in his desire and its

---

[6] Hegel's play on words: a mind of one's own = *eigener Sinn*; obstinacy = *Eigensinn*.

satisfaction, achieves nothing permanent, and moreover misses his potentiality; work is "desire held in check" (2, 148; *Phän.*, 130). It creates form in resistant matter and thus shapes the shaper at the same time. It creates enduring forms, as opposed to mere fleetingness in the existence of the master.

This is not the place to consider Hegel's later conception of work or his concerns regarding the complete transformation of labor brought about by machines.

Servitude: In the beginning labor develops not in freedom but in servitude. Without the fear of death and the obedience engendered by it, it would not have started. "Without the discipline of service and obedience, fear remains at the formal stage and does not extend to the conscious reality of existence." It is in servitude, however, that formative activity takes place, without which "fear remains inward and mute" (2, 149; *Phän.*, 131; Mi, ¶196).

Summary: True, in his disregard for his own life the *master* achieves dominion, but gains for himself nothing but empty independence. In holding fast to life the *servant*, to be sure, becomes subservient, but owing to his labor he acquires self-consciousness and ultimately an independence that is not empty but is a world fulfilled.

Not the master, but the servant continues the movement of the spirit. The former is bogged down undialectically, fruitlessly; the latter finds himself in a progressing dialectic. Hegel expresses this as follows: "The truth of independent consciousness is . . . the servile consciousness" (2, 147; *Phän.*, 129; Mi, ¶193).

Servitude will, "in its accomplishment, really turn into the opposite of what it immediately is; as a consciousness forced back into itself it will . . . be transformed into a truly independent consciousness" (ibid.).

Then true freedom comes into being, "the identify of one with the other." I am "truly free only when the other is free also and is acknowledged by me to be free" (7b, 276; *Enc.*, ¶431, Z).

6) In his *later system* (*Enc.*, ¶423–37), Hegel repeated the dialectic of master and servant at the place proper to it. Comparison of the presentations shows, on the one hand, the schematization in which the convoluted dialectic of the *Phenomenology* becomes more easily comprehensible, and, on the other hand, graphic additions and amplifications that, by their concretization, also help us to reach an easier understanding of the subject.

Historical references: The life-and-death struggle for recognition takes place solely in the state of nature where men live only as "singular" individuals. It is absent from bourgeois society and the state because recognition is already present there. In the state the individual obeys the laws. "In the state the citizen receives his honor through the office he holds, through the trade he practices and through his other work-related activity. Through this his honor has a substantial, universal, objective content no longer dependent on empty subjectivity; this is still lacking in the state of nature." "The struggle for recognition and the subordination to a master is the phenomenon from which arose man's communal life, which is how states started to be" (7b, 278, 279–80; *Enc.*, ¶432, Z, 433).

Pedagogical import of servitude: The servant "works off, in serving his master, his individual will and his self-will, sublates the inner immediacy of desire and, in this divestment and his fear of his master, takes a first step toward wisdom—the transition to universal self-consciousness" (7b, 281; *Enc.*, ¶435).

And in its general application: "Without having experienced the discipline that breaks self-will, nobody becomes free, rational, and capable of commanding. Hence, in order to become free—to become capable of ruling oneself—all peoples have had to pass first through the strict discipline of subjugation to a master" (7b, 282; *Enc.*, ¶435, Z).

Appraisal of the servant: "Those who remain servants do not suffer any absolute injustice; for whoever lacks the courage to risk his life for the sake of gaining his freedom—he deserves to be a servant." But to the extent that the servant does in fact raise himself above the selfish individuality of his natural will, he stands, "as far as his value is concerned, on a higher plane than the master who is caught in his own egotism . . . and who is recognized by an unfree consciousness in a formal manner. The subjugation of the egotism of the servant constitutes the beginning of the true freedom of man" (7b, 281–82; *Enc.*, ¶435, Z).

Universal self-consciousness: Out of the struggle evolved the division into the extremes of master and servant; out of the development of the servant universal self-consciousness will evolve, which is the knowledge of myself in the other self.

This universal self-consciousness "is the form of the knowledge of the substance of all essential spirituality—of family, fatherland, state, as well as of all virtues, of love, friendship, valor, honor, renown" (7b, 283–84; *Enc.*, ¶436).

7) If, in *assuring ourselves of the truth of this dialectic*—through visualization based on inner actions and vivid events—we ask about the origin of the evidence, the question becomes more specific: Is it a matter of movements in the self-consciousness of the individual? of the meaning of work for liberation in the creation of a world? of the fear of death

in the origin of human transformation? of the inevitability of the discipline of obedience for freedom to come into being? of historical processes, the development of society, which become conceivable in this way?

Obviously Hegel touched on all these. That he allowed for their interplay can be confusing: Time and again, the object seems to have changed (without our noticing how this came about); we try to differentiate in order to test the truth of what is differentiated, to grasp it in its methodical meaning, and end up in an almost endless process. But the interplay can conversely act like a revelation of the depth: Our glance is arrested by the underlying process in the origin of Being in motion, the different aspects of which lie logically in categories, historically in events, sociologically in structures, psychologically and pedagogically in motivations, existentially in turning points; in penetrating all these we arrive by way of speculation at insight into that which authentically is.

The first, selective, probing, appropriating, or rejecting, procedure is open in each instance to every rational being. The second, the absolutely philosophic insight, originates in different promptings. Whether I go along here or whether I battle a cipher of Being that for me is clearly fallacious but seductive can be discussed only in a criticism of Hegel as a whole.

3. Self-consciousness in the wake of the appearances of spirit

The dialectic of self-consciousness, anticipated as a whole and then shown in its first step (master and servant), now proceeds in the wake of the appearance of spirit. Where is it completed?

The anticipation of the goal of the movement—" 'I' that is 'We,' and 'We' that is 'I,' " or "They recognize each other as mutually recognizing one another"—allows us to pose the question regarding the meaning of these words; wanting to be recognized is not understood satisfactorily if it is understood as the will to self-assertion, which, if taken by itself, would mean the loss of substance (2, 139, 142; *Phän.*, 125; Mi, ¶177, 184).

The substance is contained in what I am and in what the community is into which I was born and in which I come to myself. As Hegel says: "The substance must become subject," mere Being must turn into the movement of coming-to-oneself. I am substance not by virtue of simply being such as I am, but, rather, by virtue of my foundation, which—finding it—I posit for myself. I take myself over in my being-such, but this being-such, as something taken over, in the movement of its coming-to-itself, is no longer the same. I become what I am by being I myself in being-other, by being with myself in the other. The words "I," "we," "recognize," "mutual" point toward communication that reaches into the ultimate depth of the I and of the We through which they have first become what they are, by means of radical changes and turnarounds, in which nothing is lost through the new creation, and in which the subject becomes by not giving up the substance but by bringing it to itself.

The great problem of communication as ground and condition of authentic being-human is a famous one. The question is whether Hegel—after he has sketched out the becoming of oneself in its whole scope, although in the extreme abstraction of pure conceptuality—fills this scope in his philosophy.

1) *Hegel's basic attitude as a whole.* Hegel leads to the "experience of what spirit is, this absolute substance which, in the complete freedom and independence of its opposite, i.e., of various self-consciousnesses that are for themselves, constitutes its unity; I that is the We, and We that is the I." Only in self-consciousness, in the notion of spirit, can consciousness find "its turning point, where it leaves behind the colorful illusion of the sensuous here-and-now and the nightlike void of the supersensible beyond and steps out into the spiritual daylight of the present" (2, 139–40; *Phän.*, 122; Mi, ¶177).

The pathos of these anticipatory sentences at the beginning of the depiction of self-consciousness expresses Hegel's basic certainty, his knowledge of Being, the actuality of his life:

a) Presentness is eternal present, the "now."

b) It is only that which is manifest and thus is also present to the senses; but it is not simply present as *the* sense-certainty that has been lost in judging the immediate.

c) The empty Beyond, an absolute transcendence, splits self-consciousness, deceives and defrauds it. The sensuous, however, in its mere immediacy, is itself nothing as yet. Rather, spiritual daylight, that is, the fulfilled present, the eternal presence of the Divinity is, alone, the actuality of my being in my world: It completes itself at all times as the actuality of Being in the world.

But this whole becomes present only in the entirety of the circle of appearances of the Spirit, of which each one is a necessary and irreplaceable link. This whole is in eternal movement, which, as the temporal movement of the Spirit, possesses the moment of its appearance.

This movement must pass through philosophizing without allowing a gap, in order to take firm hold of the whole, to live in this whole, to absorb each moment, avoiding being drawn into any particular moment as though it were the absolute one.

Sense-certainty is the beginning to which the circle returns in the end, having, on the way, already experienced in increasing fulfillment a return to this certainty. In the same way self-consciousness is for self-consciousness in mutuality the point of departure whose immediacy is the mutual struggle, then in the relation of mastery and servitude, then in the new dialectics of being-master and being-servant only to enter farther into the movement at the end of which stands the reconciliation in the spiritual daylight of the eternal present.

2) *The completion of recognizing each other as mutually recognizing each other.*

a) On the way to the complete unity of self-being in the multiplicity of selves lies the "life of a people." This is the "universal substance." "Reason is present here as the fluid universal substance . . . which in the same way bursts apart into many wholly independent beings just as light bursts apart into stars as countless self-luminous points" (2, 265; *Phän.*, 232; Mi, ¶350). The individuals are conscious of being these single independent beings through the sacrifice of their singularity and because this universal substance is their soul and essence.

b) Between two singular individuals the movement completes itself in forgiveness and reconciliation.

First of all Hegel describes the moral consciousness of the other. The one who judges, who sets himself up in this inactuality and conceit of knowing-better, places himself above the deeds he discredits and wants the "words without deeds to be taken for a superior actuality." Hegel calls this "insidious" and hypocritical because it "passes off such judging not as another way of being wicked but as the right consciousness of the action" (2, 502; *Phän.*, 430; cf. Mi, ¶666).

Thus the one who acts recognizes him who passes judgment as his equal. "Perceiving this identity and giving expression to it, he confesses this to the other, and expects likewise that the other—having in fact put himself on the same level—will also respond in words in which he will express his identity with him, and expects that this mutual recognition will now exist in fact" (2, 503; *Phän.*, 430; Mi, ¶666).

"But the confession of the wicked: This is the way I am, is not followed by a reciprocal similar confession." Quite the contrary; the judgment "rejects this community of nature and is the hard heart. . . ." It remains for itself and rejects any community with the other. It refuses "the emergence of its own inner being into the outer existence of speech" and contraposes the "wicked with the beauty of his own soul"; it counters "the confession of the penitent with his own stiff-necked . . . character, mutely keeping himself to himself and refusing to throw himself away for someone else." This is the "extreme form of revolt of the Spirit certain of itself." It refuses to initiate communication with the one who made the confession, who, in his admission, renounced separate consciousness. It reveals itself as a consciousness forsaken by the spirit, for it does not recognize "that spirit, in the absolute certainty of itself, is master over every deed and actuality and can cast them off and make them as if they had never happened" (2, 503–04; *Phän.*, 430–31; Mi, ¶667).

The scene has been reversed. The judgmental and separated "beautiful soul" has become Being devoid of spirit as well as devoid of actuality in the immediacy of this firmly held antithesis. It ends "unhinged to the point of madness in its unreconciled immediacy and wastes itself in yearning consumption" (2, 505; *Phän.*, 432; Mi, ¶668).[7]

The path leads in another direction: The "breaking of the hard heart" is the same movement that was expressed by the one who "made confession." The consciousness confesses: "The wounds of the spirit heal without leaving scars; the deed is not imperishable but is taken back by the Spirit into itself." The one who confesses "exhibits the power of the Spirit over his actual existence," as the breaking of the hard heart shows "the power of Spirit over the specific concept of itself" (2, 505; *Phän.*, 432; Mi, ¶668–69).

The result is forgiveness. The one who judges renounces his unactual nature by equating it with that other which was a real action: "The word of conciliation is the objectively existing Spirit which beholds the pure knowledge of itself qua universal essence in its opposite" (2, 506; *Phän.*, 433; Mi, ¶670).

Here Hegel's language rises to the comprehension of intuition. "It is the actual I, the universal knowledge of itself in its absolute opposite, in the knowledge that remains in-itself, and which, on account of the purity of its separated being-in-itself, is itself completely universal. The reconciling Yea, in which the two I's let go of their antithetical existence, is the existence of the I which has expanded into a duality wherein it remains identical with itself, and in its complete externalization and opposite, possesses the certainty of itself; it is God manifested among those who know themselves in the form of pure knowledge" (2, 507–08; *Phän.*, 434; Mi, ¶671).

   c) Religion and, finally, absolute knowing, complete, as actual con-

---

[7] Hegel's play on words is lost in translation: *Schwindsucht*, the German word for the disease "consumption," can mean the strong desire to waste away.

sciousness of the whole, the reconciliation of all opposites, now on a supratemporal plane, carried away, as it were: Communication is no longer a process occurring between men, but is the revolving duration of the eternal.

3) Here we sense the *critical limit* in Hegelian completion. Can the supratemporal be completed in time? The alternative seems to be whether movement in time can, within time itself, cease in the absolute, which is the unity of all opposites, one in all, circle of circles (in the "ethical order" of the state, in the absolute thinking of religion, art, philosophy); or whether, within time, everything remains open, where, to be sure, there are exalted moments and unwavering loyalty, where eternity and temporality are indispensable, yet where thought does not attain universality but must always move anew, and finds itself face to face with limit situations and with foundering in existence.

Hegel's dialectical thinking would incorporate the second into the first, the latter being the Encompassing. However, existential truth breaks through this Encompassing and holds fast to temporality as the only existential possibility, that is, to the never-completed task of communication.

At this point the wondrous "reconciliation" may become actual as purely and simply historic. Beyond all "getting along together," all "talking things over," all forgiveness, it remains mute. For, having been expressed, it is transformed into a possession we can express and refer to. But by thus becoming temporal-supratemporal actuality, it is contaminated and spoiled. Speech does not hinder or uphold it, nor does it aim at completing itself in silence, as though in this form it could become truth and true possession.

But reconciliation strives, instead, toward realization in the palpable phenomena of temporal reality. In Hegel it leads to consummation in absolute knowledge and not into the uncharted depths of the authentic movement of Existenz in time. It sublates existential communication into speculative intuition of absolute knowledge. He fails to see the ineluctable movement toward turning, as Existenz in time, to the other Existenz, in sustained communication, and beyond it toward a mutually shared experience of unspoken transcendence which cannot find its consummation in time. Speculative contemplation takes the place of communication.

C. Being; Nothing; Becoming

Another example: the beginning of Hegelian logic.

For Hegel, logic is the movement of thinking in the "heavens of absolute knowledge,"[8] in the "thoughts of God before creation,"[9] is His timelessly eternal thinking. This logic proceeds through all thought-determinations (categories) which align themselves dialectically in a mighty whole and close into a circle. It is the most comprehensive doctrine of categories, perhaps unsurpassed to this day. But in its progress it lays claim to being in a truer and purer sense what earlier was called metaphysics and ontology.

a) The first is _Being_. What is Being? It is the indeterminate (for it has shed all determinations—this is its purity); hence it has no dissimilarity, toward the inside or the outside; it is equal only to itself and not yet unequal as measured against the other. It is the immediate that has come to be without mediation (3, 77).

There is nothing to intuit in Being; it is sheerly pure, empty intuition itself. Neither does it contain any substance for thinking; it is only this empty thinking.

It turns out that Being, the indeterminate immediate, is empty. It is, in fact, Nothing (3, 78).

b) What is pure _Nothing_? It is "equality with itself, complete emptiness, lack of determinacy and content; lack of differentiation in itself" (ibid.). Insofar as we speak of intuiting and thinking, there _is_ nothing in our intuiting and thinking, which is empty intuiting and thinking.

When we consider what cannot be said about Being, it turns out that the same is said about both Being and Nothing. Hence pure Being and pure Nothing are identical.

Hegel uses a parable:

Being is imagined as pure light, as the clarity of unclouded vision; Nothing is imagined as pure night. But in absolute clarity we see as much or as little as in absolute darkness. The one as well as the other is pure seeing, the seeing of Nothing. Pure light and pure darkness are identical emptinesses (3, 92).

c) It would seem that we reach the conclusion right from the start. If Being and Nothing are identical, we have reached a dead end. This

---

[8] Jaspers probably noted this reference from memory. He is most likely referring to Hegel's _Lectures on the Philosophy of Religion_, 12, 434: "Logic is God in the ether of pure thought" —Hans Saner.

[9] In _Logic_, Introduction, 3, 36, Hegel characterizes logic as "representation of God . . . as He is in His eternal essence prior to the creation of nature and of a finite spirit" —Hans Saner.

is the situation for determinative reason, for which Being as well as Nothing qua total indeterminateness are and remain the same.

But we can go on in the eternity of absolute thinking, which becomes manifest in the speculative thinking of dialectics. This thinking tells us: Neither Being nor Nothing nor their being identical is the truth. In the progression the truth is, rather, "that Being does not turn into Nothing or Nothing into Being, but that one has turned into the other" (3, 79).

What does this having-turned-into mean? Being and Nothing are just as absolutely differentiated as they are absolutely undivided. Each vanishes immediately into its opposite. This movement of immediate disappearance of the one into the other and of the other into the one is *Becoming*: a movement in which Being and Nothing are differentiated, but by a difference that has dissolved just as immediately. The "Being . . . that remains with itself in Nothing is Becoming" (6, 176; *Enc.*, ¶88).

What is, and what is the meaning, of this first triad of Being, Nothing, Becoming? Is it a play on words? Is it a figure composed of interconnected meanings? Is it a way of expressing the mystery of Becoming by thinking it as Becoming prior to all time, without time? Is it the most abstract origin that cannot be transcended and the enduring structure of all that is? Is it that it cannot be thought at all with the intellect alone, or is it, using the intellect as means, a speculative intuition that is simultaneously present or absent? Whether this triad seems plausible or absurd, if we want to try to understand Hegel's meaning, we have to discuss this quickly finished triad, which at first appears so simple.

To be sure, this triad, which cannot be thought rationally but is speculatively so exciting, can be thought only as an act that is intuitive in its extreme abstractness. But we can try to follow this thought—a paradigm of Hegelian logical-metaphysical speculation—to the point where it attains this importance. It is merely the beginning, but it contains the primal metaphysical intuition, which resurfaces in all understanding of things eternal and infinite as well as temporal and finite. It shows an incalculable wealth of fulfillment through which its very poverty proves the scope of its receptiveness.

I.

Becoming overarches the triad, or is its center and encompassing meaning. Becoming is the first concrete, coalesced thought, against which Being and Nothing are empty abstractions.

"If we speak about the concept of Being, it can consist only in being

Becoming; for as Being it is empty Nothing, but as the latter it is empty Being" (6, 176; *Enc.*, ¶88). Becoming is the first concrete, and hence the first genuine, determination of thought.

About Being and Nothing all Hegel says is what either is not. In both cases his statements are the same. Becoming, however, is expressed positively as the turning and having-turned on the part of Being and Nothing into the movement of the one disappearing in the other.

This does not mean that the Nothing is merely nothing. When I think Nothing, I have already thought it as Being. It exists through my expressing it. The Nothing that is meant to be only nothing, receives an existence in thinking, imagining, or speaking (3, 139).

2.

In Becoming, Hegel thinks a "concrete identity." Identity as unity of equals is an abstract identity (A = A). Identity as unity of different beings—inseparability—is concrete identity. Thinking abstract identity is an act of the intellect, which fixates and does not progress. Thinking concrete identity is genuine speculative thinking to which what is manifests itself. Because Being and Nothing are the same concrete identity "they are no longer Being and Nothing. . . . The unity remains . . . as their foundation, out of which they no longer emerge as the abstract meaning of Being and Nothing" (3, 111).

3.

The statement *"Being and Nothing are the same"* expresses the identity of these two determinations—which are not yet supposed to be determinations—both of which it also contains as differentiated. Hence "in itself it contradicts itself and dissolves." It is a statement that "contains the movement of disappearing through itself"; there happens to it that "which is supposed to constitute its true content, namely, *Becoming*" (3, 88–89).

The statement "Being and Nothing are the same" appears to be such a paradoxical statement to the imagination or to the intellect that it might not be recognized as seriously meant. But in Hegel it possesses an all-dominating seriousness.

To be sure, the statement is indeed "one of the most difficult that thinking demands of itself" (6, 171; *Enc.*, ¶88). Being and Nothing are opposition in its full immediacy; as yet no determination containing the relation of the one to the other is being thought in it. Yet in it I think, in an abstractness lacking determination, of what in all of philosophizing recurs in specific definite forms: There is "nowhere in heaven or earth anything . . . that does not contain both, Being and Nothing." All further logical determinations are "examples of this unity" (3, 81, 82).

4.

The proposition *Being and Nothing are "to all intents and purposes different"* is just as correct as its opposite (6, 172; *Enc.*, ¶88; cf. 3, 89–90). Becoming would not be Becoming, but static identity, if only the being-the-same of Being and Nothing were valid. Only the fact that the unity of Being and Nothing maintains absolute differentiation in itself constitutes its concrete concept.

The differentiation of Being and Nothing is, as such, devoid of relation. Hence to express the difference as Being and not-Being would be inappropriate: the relation to Being would be introduced through the word "not-Being." The Nothing is "the negation devoid of relation—something one . . . could express also through the mere: *Not*" (3, 79).

5.

Since Being and Nothing lack all determination, that is, remain within immediacy, difference is also not as yet determined. It is *the inexpressible, the merely meant*. Both Being and Nothing are "the same ground-lessness." Being is "not a particular, definite thought, but, rather, the still wholly indeterminate thought that precisely for this reason cannot be differentiated" (6, 171; *Enc.*, ¶87, Z).

It is impossible to indicate a difference between Being and Nothing, for in order to do so we would need a determinateness. Both, however, are the sheerly indeterminate. "If Being and Nothing had any determinateness at all by means of which they would differ, they would be . . . determinate Being and determinate Nothing, and not pure Being and pure Nothing. . . . Hence the difference between them is completely empty; each of the two is the indeterminate in the same way"; they are "empty thought-things" (3, 91, 82).

The first thought is that of Becoming, in which Being and Nothing are thought, whereas they cannot really be thought each for itself. In Becoming, Being and Nothing have "their consistence." They are differentiated in their Becoming. They consist only in an other, in a third, in Becoming. Their consistency is only their being in one (3, 82).

6.

The question is asked: How does the static unity of being-the-same of Being and Nothing turn into the *moving unity of Becoming?*

Hegel answers: Within the sequential presentation of the text, Being and Nothing are discussed first, followed by Becoming. But in truth Becoming is first (3, 93; 6, 175–76; *Enc.*, ¶88, Z). Comprehension proceeds from Becoming. Becoming does not become, but is the beginning from which we think back to that which—in an act of meaning-reference to the unthinkable—is isolated, devoid of relation, as Being and Nothing, only to be sublated at once. Becoming is the first concrete concept (all true concepts are concrete concepts) following what is merely meant.

It is always this way in Hegel's dialectics of becoming-manifest: The result is in fact the beginning. Bringing-itself-forth is not a result that follows cogently from beginnings merely expressed. Hence the circle is the correct picture for this thought-process, which does not know a real beginning aside from itself as a whole, but which is the movement that illuminates itself.

7.

We repeat once more this thought-experience: Being and Nothing are everywhere bound to each other—one does not exist without the other—in each instance in a definite and particular configuration. Only here at the beginning do we find the thought that wants to advance beyond all determinateness into the abyss and there wants to grasp Being and Nothing, but discovers that it falls into the void and is not really a thought but a meaning: the absolutely differentiated shows itself to be the same, that is, Being as Nothing and Nothing as Being.

Out of this experience grows the first thought, which returns from the abyss, from the vertigo of mere meaning, which no longer rested on any ground; it thinks Becoming, and thinks it from the start as the unity of the difference of Being and Nothing.

The fundamental experience of thinking carried out in this specu-lation can proceed in the opposite direction: I think Nothing when I ask: Why is there anything at all and not nothing? That there is Nothing may seem to be the natural state of things. That there is Being—this is the miracle.

Hence I arrive—out of my attempt at thinking Nothing—at a rec-ognition of the miracle: Being is. It is the standing-still of thinking before

Being, prior to all determination, a holding of one's breath, as it were: Being is. The first thought necessary is the thought of Being. The possibility of not-Being can be thought only as the second thought, for it refers to Being whose not-Being it is.

But Being qua Being cannot be grasped in this form. After all, what is this Being? Thought only as Being, without any determination, in pure immediacy, it is as Nothing. It is that which is not derivative, cannot be transcended but, when more closely grasped, *is*, to be sure, but like nothing that we encounter as Being.

Once I have at the origin experienced the belonging-together of Being and Nothing, I can think Being as the unity of Being and Nothing, that is, as Becoming. The contrariety in my experience of the origin now constitutes everything that is and is encountered as Being.

8.

It is said: This whole method of thinking and what it expresses *cannot be comprehended* (6, 173; *Enc.*, ¶88). Comprehension demands representation, an object-image with which thinking, as it is practiced, is familiar. Hegel gives us two answers.

To begin with: In asserting that the representation of the unity of Being and Nothing is impossible, you really imply that everyone has an infinity of representations of this unity. The very assertion that you do not have them can only mean a lack of recognition of the relevant concept in any one of these representations. Thus, says Hegel, everyone has a representation of Becoming: In analyzing it, you have to see that the determination of Being, as well as that of Nothing, is contained in it. Another example is the representation of the beginning: A thing that is not as yet at its beginning is not its nothingness but already contains its Being.

Further: The "manner of philosophical knowledge" is, "to be sure, different . . . from the manner of knowing habitual in everyday life, as well as from the one prevalent in other sciences" (6, 173–74; *Enc.*, ¶88). The inability to comprehend this shows one's being unaccustomed to persevere in abstract thoughts without any sensuous admixture, or to grasp speculative statements. (In this context, you should consider: psychologically, it is perhaps impossible to do without concomitant phenomena of sensuous representations, though they have no bearing on the matter at hand; a thinking-as-seeing, a categorial intuition of what itself cannot be represented, has to be tried by everyone. Whoever con-

siders himself unable to do so has no right to deny that something of
this nature exists; he may not be aware of it as he himself carries it out.)
In maintaining about a concept that it eludes your faculty of imagination
merely signifies the wish for a familiar representation. It seems as though
without a familiar mode of representation the ground under one's feet
were lost. What is demanded, however, is not to think beyond the concept
itself (6, 7; *Enc.*, ¶3).

9.

The beginning of logic is considered the beginning in absolute knowledge
that represents itself. But as far as man thinking in time is concerned,
this beginning has to be reached, because it is immediate only in the
timelessness of the eternal movement of thought; for the thinking person
it is mediated in temporality. He needs preparation, guidance to lead
him to the beginning. In Hegelian philosophy this road differs from that
of the mystics with their spiritual exercises and stages of meditation, of
initiations into esoteric doctrines or, as nowadays, of the indoctrination
of a fundamental position, such as a Marxist or psychoanalytical one.
Rather, it is itself a thinking that provides "the ladder" for the seeker
through the "phenomenology of spirit" (2, 21; *Phän.*, 18). In thinking,
he can stride there through the levels of consciousness, of self-consciousness, of a spirit manifesting itself in the configuration of a world. He
then sublates and preserves them all and arrives at absolute knowledge
in which only now logic begins with the first triad of Being, Nothing,
and Becoming. What in logic begins immediately as such is reached by
us through mediation.

10.

A second way to arrive at the beginning of logic is *abstraction*: in thinking
I advance to the limit where thinking is with itself, where it becomes
pure thinking without object, the thinking of thinking.

a) I, the "I think," is "the universal in and for itself. . . . All other
men have this in common with me, to be 'I.' . . . But 'I,' in the abstract
as such, is the mere act of self-relation, in which we make abstraction
from all representation and feeling, from every state of mind. . . . To
this extent 'I' is the Existence of a wholly *abstract* universality, of abstract
freedom" (6, 37; *Enc.*, ¶20; cf. W. §20).

"It is by the free act of thought that it occupies a point of view in which it is for its own self, and thus gives itself an object of its own production" (6, 25; *Enc.*, ¶17; W, §17).[10]

But that means that the "I" as such has vanished in Being itself. The process of production is the rule of the matter itself in pure thought, which, as thought, simply has the form of the "I think."

The road of this experience leads to the limits where no special thought is carried out any longer and no object is thought, and where Being and the thinking of Being in the self-being of the "I" are the same; where I, having stood at the edge of the abyss, am indeterminately certain of Being in all its possibility; where, out of the stillness of coming to a standstill, I am, after all abstraction, again I, thinking I, and hear myself, as it were, by experiencing the dialectic of the movement of thought through carrying it out.

b) The beginning is the "decision *to want to think purely*, achieved through the freedom that abstracts from everything and takes hold of its pure abstraction, that is, the simplicity of thought." Reaching the beginning demands "total absence of *presupposition*," total skepticism must precede everything so that now *pure thought* can be accomplished and develop its certitude (6, 146; *Enc.*, ¶78; W, §78).

Hence the beginning of philosophy is "a beginning only in relation to the person who proposes to philosophize." The beginning has no relation "to the science (of philosophy) as such" (6, 26; *Enc.*, ¶17). Being has no beginning, nor does the thinking which is this Being itself. The thoughtful action of the individual human being has a beginning, as does its presentation in a work.

c) What is achieved for us through the mediation of abstraction is the immediate, that which is not mediated by anything.

"The indeterminate, as we have it here, is the immediate, not the mediated indeterminate, not the sublation of all determinateness, but the immediacy of indeterminateness preceding all determinateness, indeterminateness at the very first" (6, 166; *Enc.*, ¶86, Z, 1). It cannot be felt or perceived by sense or pictured in imagination: it is pure thought.

d) We free ourselves from all that is determinate, submerge ourselves in the abyss of the indeterminate of Being, which is Nothing.

If I want to grasp it determinately as Being, it is already in existence; it comes to be and passes away. Then Being and Nothing cease "to be abstractions by receiving a determinate content ... only existence contains the real difference between Being and Nothing, namely a Something and Other" (3, 85).

---

[10] References preceded by W are to *Hegel's Logic*, trans. by William Wallace, emended as needed.

If I want to grasp it determinately as Nothing, then I think by means of a determinate Nothing the determinate Being whose Nothing it is.

What is Being? Neither the solid Being nor Nothing, but, rather, Becoming.

e) The path of abstraction, taken in order to arrive at the immediacy of the beginning, can be transformed into an easy and cheap act: I could abstract from everything; then nothing would be left. The Nothing would be attained as the beginning, and thus the end would be reached at the same time.

Hegel counters this: If "we presupposed that abstraction from *everything*, which after all is everything of what there is, then . . . the result of the abstraction from all that is, is . . . first of all abstract Being, Being as such." "And then it would seem that in the end it is also possible to abstract from this pure Being, and Being were to be relegated to all that from which one has already abstracted; what then remains would be Nothing" (3, 101).

This act is something completely different from the transformation of Being into Nothing, which is not a further abstraction but the movement at the origin. However, we would expect that the person who, by reasoning in like manner, enters upon this path of a superficial game of abstracting would continue due to his "ability to abstract," that is, to abstract further from Nothing ("just as," says Hegel, "even the creation of the world is an abstraction from Nothing"), but "then there remains not Nothing—for one abstracts precisely from this—rather, one has arrived once more, in this manner, at Being" (3, 101).

f) The Being of the beginning must be comprehended in its universality as being devoid of content or weight:

It can be reduced to the meaning of the copula in sentences: Everything that I state is expressed in sentences through the subject and the predicate which are being connected by the copula "is." There is the void, the universal of the indeterminate Being in all statements, nonbinding and insignificant.

Or it is binding as the germ of everything, as the totality in which what develops has its origin. This form as origin, the Being of all there is, signifies that from the very beginning everything is One: the unity of the logical in the development of all categories and, grounded in it, the unity of all Being, the One.

g) This total abstraction has an *existential meaning* for Hegel. "The directing from particular finite Being back to Being-as-such in its abstract universality must be considered as the very first theoretical as well as practical requirement." Man ought to raise himself "in his way of thinking to this abstract universality in which finite things become matters of indifference, in which it makes no difference to him whether or not they exist, whether he is or is not, that is, is or is not in finite life" (3, 86–87). "Indeed, philosophy is precisely what frees man from endless finite goals and intentions" (6, 172; *Enc.*, ¶88).

11. Frequently raised objections to the dialectic of Being, Nothing, and Becoming

a) "Pure thinking" is not possible. Actually, Hegel at every step uses an intuition that did not arise from pure thinking but is brought about. Thus Becoming is brought about only with the aid of the intuition of time and does not arise out of Being and Nothing through pure thinking. Hegel says: "The statements 'that everything that is carries the germ of its passing in its birth, and that, on the other hand, death is the entrance into new life,' basically express the same union of Being and Nothing" as Becoming. "But these expressions have a substratum on which the transition takes place; in time Being and Nothing are kept apart, are represented as alternating in it, but are not thought in their abstraction and hence not in such a way that they are the same in and for themselves" (3, 80).

Hegel anticipated Trendelenburg's objection. Trendelenburg denies that Hegel's demands can be carried out in thinking.[11] On the level of the rationalistic intellect and of the psychological descriptions of the representations that always accompany our thinking, we can merely determine the impossibility. The question remains, however, whether, for Hegel, something else is happening which is not at all affected by such objections and which we have to try to experience ourselves. Trendelenburg's criticism is astute but without substance, blind to the language of dialectical speculation, incapable of intuition in thinking itself. He is right in challenging Hegel's claim of cogent proof and solid cognitions in challenging the "science" of Hegel and the Hegelians. He intends to base himself on science, to which Hegel denies the character of philosophy, since science is the knowledge of finite things; he sets little store by it and at best makes use of its results, after first interpreting them. But in fact Trendelenburg does not base himself on this ground either; he bases himself on the old rationalistic mode of argumentation, by means of which no cogent knowledge is gained that possesses objec-

---

[11] See nineteenth-century German philosopher Friedrich Adolf Trendelenburg's *Logische Untersuchungen*, 3rd ed., Leipzig, S. Hirzel, 1870, 36–129, and *Geschichte der Kategorienlehre*, Berlin, 1846, 355ff.

tively relevant character, just as it cannot be gained through Hegel's pure thinking. Thus, in deriving all categories from "movement," clear-minded Trendelenburg himself unwittingly carries out a speculation devoid of content. He was widely acclaimed among the pseudoscientific academic philosophers of the nineteenth century whose thinking had lost real seriousness. No genuine philosopher, that is, one who knows the mode of his particular knowledge, came forth to oppose him.

b) It is said that when Hegel speaks of Being, Nothing, Becoming, he uses—in the very first sentences—categories that are presupposed but not derived. This objection to the claim of a development without presuppositions states something obvious. Without this, speaking would be impossible for Hegel, as for everyone. What is met with only later as categories begins functioning from the very beginning of the presentation.

Naturally Hegel knows this too. Hence he asks only that all categories be clarified and determined in their proper places; he does not demand the impossible, however, that is, to dispense with them altogether when-ever thinking is focused on that which is prior to these categories.

c) The modern Thomist Alfons Lehmen argues in an undialectical, rationalistic manner against Hegel's dictum that indeterminate Being is the same as Nothing: if they were the same, then their opposites would also have to be the same. However, the opposite of absolute Nothing is all Being; that of indeterminate Being, determinate Being. Hence being-Nothing and indeterminate Being are different in their essence. It is false to assert that two things coincide because they are identical in one characteristic (indeterminacy).[12]

This can be countered as follows: A Hegelian dictum is here removed from the dialectical movement, isolated, and "refuted" according to the rules of formal logic. These rules apply where we speak of a determinate or indeterminate Something. This kind of refutation can be arrived at very simply by juxtaposing Hegel's immediately following statement, that Being and Nothing are absolutely different, with the preceding one. That there is contradiction is obvious, but precisely this contradiction is at the heart of dialectical thought. The contradiction cannot be solved by rejecting it on a formal, logical basis and declaring Hegel's proposition to be nonsense. The truth that is thought here can be experienced, if at all, only by plunging into the contradiction and trying out what the movement displays.

d) In his struggle against Hegel, Feuerbach too aimed at destroying

[12] Cf. Alfons Lehmen's *Lehrbuch der Philosophie auf aristotelisch-scholastischer Grundlage*; I: *Logik*, 358; 4th ed. Freiburg-im-Breisgau, Herder, 1917.

the beginning of Logic in Being, Nothing, and Becoming. His thesis is: Being exists in actuality, but Nothing, not-Being, exists only in the imagination and in reflection. "Nothing is that which is . . . devoid of thought and reason. Nothing cannot be thought at all, for thinking is determining . . . and therefore would cease to be Nothing" (II, 223).[13]

All of Hegel's propositions about Nothing are, according to Feuerbach, in fact already determinations (simple self-identity, and so on).

"Thinking cannot go beyond beings since it cannot go beyond itself, because reason only means positing Being, because only this or that being but not Being . . . can be thought as having become" (II, 224).

"The thinking of Nothing is self-contradictory thinking. He who thinks Nothing just does not think . . . hence it can be thought only by being made into Something. Thus at the same moment when it is thought, it is not thought, for I always think the opposite of Nothing" (ibid.).

"Nothing is the limit of reason . . . which reason posits for itself" (II, 226).

"Nothing is just Nothing, — hence also Nothing for thinking; Nothing further can be said about it; for Nothing refutes itself. Only imagination turns Nothing into a substantive." "Admitting that it occurs . . . in our thought, does it therefore belong in our logic? Even ghosts occur in our thought" (II, 229, 227). Feuerbach's critique lives in and by Hegelian thought. There is hardly anything in it that has not been said by Hegel himself. But all Hegel's statements are changed in their meaning; they cease to be links in a dialectical movement that advances into the ground of Being and allows whatever may issue from it; rather, they become a game under Hegel's direction but as such denatured, merely a clever game of constant self-sublation, its stake not speculative understanding but the banality of finite existence and being-there, of an intellect which grasps only finitudes. Nothing remains of Hegelian speculative experience except that its dicta are used for defiant banality. It is from this remaining trace, reflected in the emptying and twisting show, that the superficial vitality and the illusion of spirit in this childish game arise.

Such objections make us see more clearly what Hegel means and what he does, but also about what perhaps he remains in the dark, carried away by the conviction that in universal dialectic he is bringing to mind absolute knowledge. We shall now try to explain what this dialectic is.

[13] Ludwig Feuerbach, "Zur Kritik der Hegel'schen Philosophie" (1839), in *Sämtliche Werke*, ed. by W. Bolin and F. Jodl, II, 185–232. Stuttgart, Frommann, 1903–.

II. ANALYSIS OF THE DIALECTIC

Introduction

We want to bring to awareness, in a methodical manner, what is done in dialectical thinking. This procedure of analyzing dialectics is not itself dialectical.

Hegel would reject this procedure. Not being itself dialectical, it cannot understand the dialectic. It amounts to prattle from the outside that fails to reach the heart of the matter. In other words, it is reflection that is arbitrary, multifarious, unproductive, and endless. Dialectic can be grasped only with dialectic through dialectic. We have to move within it—only then do we move within truth. Standing outside it, we stand also outside truth. But Hegel himself carries out reflections, not only in order to reject false ones but also to further the understanding of the meaning of dialectic. Insofar as Hegel would like to persuade us (at times even by wielding his authority) to entrust ourselves to the course of the dialectic as he presents it, we may confront him with the Hegelian dictum: Everyone has the right to demand that what is true be present to himself. On the other hand, insofar as Hegel engages in reflection whereby he indicates from the outside what he does in his thinking, one may be able to follow him and proceed on this road.

We must ask whether we might be able to carry the dialectical movements out ourselves and to analyze them on the basis of our own dialectical experience. Through intuition gained by carrying out the movements, and with the aid of the intellect we would then regard what we ourselves are acquainted with and examine its claim of having arrived at authentic truth—beyond intuition and beyond intellect.

What has precedence? Is it the dialectic, which purports to embrace and include everything and to grasp the truth completely? Or a mode of thinking that renounces such absoluteness, that uses every way of convincing oneself, of thinking for oneself, of evidence, of making critical distinctions—a criticism that inexorably transcends all that is thinkingly done and said, and is able to question each claimed absolute since it is something occurring merely in the world of thought? Do we perhaps want to regard and judge the higher position from the lower? Or bring experience of a higher plane to our consciousness on our lower level? Or, with the limited nature of our intellect, grasp what outstrips the intellect? Not at all. Instead, we want to avoid taking the experience of thinking on the plane of speculation for absolute knowledge.

Methodical awareness consists of sovereignty in thinking, keeping it open, exposing it to ever new pitfalls and new assurances, which alone guarantees the mastery of my thoughts and keeps me from being enslaved by a form of thinking, an absolute asserted in thinking, a mode of the movement of thought.

Here we reach a crossroads of thinking where through an existential decision a choice is made in the light of insight into philosophical logic.

By relinquishing historic Existenz in which the individual assures himself, we choose the objective and at the same time absolute road of a dialectic that soon exerts its tyranny by means of specific and divergent schematizations. Or, in a decision originating in non-universal Existenz, dialectical experiences that can actually be carried out are affirmed and brought to the open world of thought in which Existenz becomes possible, and are joined to all other thought-experiences, which in their totality do not shape themselves into a whole, a system.

Thinking that imparts itself in a universally comprehensible manner moves within the dichotomy of subject and object, that is, thinking refers to objects jointly. This does not call into question the thinking that— reaching beyond the subject-object dichotomy—aims at moving in the unity of thought and being; but it can always be challenged when, expressed in the form of communicable knowledge, it makes absolute claims because of this form. Such thinking—the specifically philosophical attempt to assure ourselves speculatively on the mystical foundation (the *unio* of thought and Being) of the deepest truth attainable to us and to secure communicability for it—is credible only in the operation of thought whose articulation it is, or through its translation into practical life, where what it is and its actual meaning first become manifest.

The great choice is not that between utterable opinions and modes of thinking, but in this: The unconditional nature of Existenz (the actuality of man knowing himself as given to himself as gift through transcendence and existing in relation to transcendence) cannot be attained by way of meditative, contemplative thinking, but only in existential decision and its repetition. However, what happens in meditative thinking and also in dialectical thinking is not, as in scientific cognition, unchallengeable by the universal validity of its material content. Rather, it is binding through the Existenz that lives in it, finds its meaning there, and testifies to it through both thinking and doing.

The basic attitude is: Having operated within all methods and lived within them in thinking awareness, we face them again from the sovereignty of our possible Existenz. Existenz will not allow subjugation to a specific form of thinking, to identification with a specific form of thinking. It refuses to tolerate imprisonment in thinking that pretends to be absolute. It throws off the net of objectivities pretending to have transcended the subject-object dichotomy. This sovereignty of Existenz is not arbitrary, since it yields to every manner of evidence. But it sees that none commands the character of absolute knowledge. Out of this sovereignty every manner of testing is put into action. This sovereignty teaches us to set limits and to set free. It opposes the self-certainty of knowing-it-all, the arrogance of believing that we exist in the state of truth, the delusions of possessing truth.

Our criticism of dialectics is twofold. First, we have to make an analysis of the dialectical methods with regard to their truth content, and be willing to appropriate them. We have to pursue each particular dialectic to the origin of its evidence experienced in carrying it out, to try to test the dialectic from below, as it were, in its particular configurations, and not to judge it first from above, in its entirety. Thus we gain the means of recognizing the difference between what is plausible and what is absurd. We can appropriate the truths without losing ourselves in the current of the repugnant, obscure, and dictatorial.

Second, our critique is aimed at the untruth in the *universalization and absolutization of the dialectic*. It is an aspect grounded on the untruth of the Hegelian system, which, paradoxically, still appeals to us as irreplaceable in its greatness, through an abundance of truth.

A. The answer to the question: what is?

If I ask, What is Being? I want to know what it is. Hegel supplies the answer. Being has opened itself to him completely in thinking the truth, but has done so in a manner alien to everyday thinking. The true can be grasped almost nowhere, or everywhere. Nowhere, because it is in no thing, in no object, in nothing determinately known; everywhere, because it is in motion. The true does not lie in a statement, in which it would be firmly embedded. The true is the whole, in which the movement completes itself.

1) Wherever I take hold, that which I know as Being turns out to be something it is not. It is—not authentically, not absolutely—but in a vanishing configuration.

That which authentically is, is not in the sense of a thing. It is not a fixed, self-enclosed object. These objects are merely in transition. They come on the scene and melt away, they are here and are sublated in the movement of truth, which preserves in itself everything it traverses, thus steadily becoming richer.

2) Being is knowing and being-known. What would that be which is known by no one and cannot be known? It would be as nothing. If

we try to think it, then, ineluctably, it immediately becomes something that is thought, something that exists for a subject who thinks it or can think it. It is a Being-in-itself, which only is by becoming an object for a subject. Whatever is in itself is this at the same time for an other.

A Being which knows nothing of itself and about which no one can know is unthinkable.

3) Hence the point of departure of all assurance is something that is not merely a thing. Instead:

Being is that which refers to itself, as in self-consciousness. I know myself, am one and double, the knower and the known (expressed in a subjectifying manner).

Being is that which from the start either has an other outside itself or divides itself in itself. Whatever I think is one and other, differentiated from the other and at the same time related to it (expressed in an objectifying way).

4) Hence, if I want to know, I must move in my thinking, objectively from the one to the other, subjectively from me as the knower to me as the known. The two are not inflexible relations but merely forms in which the movement is continued. The movement always needs a fixed point; yet every fixed point is left behind.

Truth consists in moving on. I am driven out of rigidities, whether of opinions or of things. Nothing, it turns out, is solid. Something overturns them, from the outside or the inside. In the dialectic they overturn themselves, they change. The firm opinion goes into a tailspin as it no longer understands itself.

5) Where does the movement go? It either continues into endlessness or it returns into itself. There it loses its ground, here it completes itself. There it is endless, here it is unending. Hegel calls it unending because it has no limit, that is, it is closed in a circle. The unending, not endless movement knows itself and has an overall view of itself. In this way it is at home in the whole, in Being itself.

Expressed in an objectifying way, this means the whole is a circle of circles. The dialectical circlings enclosed each other until the one all-embracing circle is reached and all knowledge is enclosed in the system of the whole.

Expressed in a subjectifying way, it means Being is reached when, in knowing, I know the other as I myself, when I am with myself in the other. Consciousness is no longer in opposition to what it knows, is no longer alienated. It has sublated its subject-object dichotomy and has reached unity.

No matter whether expressed in an objectifying or a subjectifying manner, I move—or what is thought moves—in circles whose unremitting motion, as a whole, is complete stillness (the old mystical simile). "The true is thus the Bacchanalian revel in which no member is not drunk; yet because each member fades away as it passes out, the revel is just as much transparent and simple stillness" (2, 36–37; *Phän.*, 31; Mi, ¶47).

B. The dialectic universalized and absolutized

In his understanding, Hegel achieves this completeness because the dialectical movement is the only all-embracing movement of Being that is present everywhere, recurring in the greatest and the whole as in the smallest, repeating itself in infinite reflections of its basic logical forms through everything that is.

We, who want to understand Hegel, visualize the dialectic as we carry out concretely each particular one. In this way we come to understand this universalization into a single all-penetrating dialectic as the formalization into an abstract movement of thought in which one time this, another time that dialectic, differing in origin, reverberates, a difference, however, that becomes insignificant in pure abstraction.

In Hegel this is quite different. For him, the one dialectic in the ground of all Being is such a manifest actuality and so much the actuality of all Being that he apprehends and comprehends, that is, gathers the particular dialectic from that ground and into the one whole. This is what makes Hegel, as one studies him, so impressive: his implicit faith in the all-comprehending dialectical discourse, his consciousness of standing within truth itself, his ever-renewed profound emotion before a manifestation that retains no mystery. Here language becomes a totally conciliatory, blissful meditative intuition of that which is, of the Deity, of absolute Spirit, of Reason, of the Concept (or whatever words we choose from among the many which in Hegel intend the same thing they bring before the eyes, or, rather, into the thought of absolute knowledge in a variety of forms).

Requisite for the understanding of Hegel is at least the attempt to reach this basic intuition; the inability to make it one's own is the basis for criticism of Hegel.

What are the fundamental characteristics of the one universal dialectic?

1) *The dialectical movement* of all that is *proceeds from the matter itself.* It is the "concept's own life" (2, 41; *Phän.*, 35) and is not caused by an external impulse.

In the movement of our philosophical thinking, the movement of being-thinking is reiterated. It is not we who carry out our reflections in essential cognition; instead, concepts "examine themselves" (6, 87; *Enc.*, ¶41, Z, 1).

Dialectic, therefore, is the same whether in the operation of our thinking, in the objective prerequisites of what is thinkable, or in the real action itself.

What I think takes place not only in me as "rethinking," but also in thinking as such; in concepts as pure concepts in logic (which therefore is at the same time "metaphysics" in Hegel's sense, God's thinking prior to creation), thus in nature as the being-asunder in space and time, thus in the process of the spirit. This spirit is to be understood as the real happenings in man, from his inner life to the objective spirit of history throughout the ages, up to absolute spirit, which in its eternity comprises all time and all actuality, and which is transparently manifest in the absolute knowledge of philosophy, according to the mode of its presentness, in the intuition of art and the representation of religion.

In philosophizing dialectically I am only an observer; as I see all-inclusively what happens everywhere I allow my contingent subjectivity to vanish. There is nothing that is not dialectical. And there is no comprehending that does not rethink this dialectic.

Dialectic is the form that breaks open everything and brings it to light. It is the contemplative knowledge of philosophy, but what is known is the active movement of Being itself in all its spheres.

2) *The movement of the dialectic* occurs through a single factor, the *negativity* that lies at the bottom of things.

Negativity (being-other, contrast, contradiction—differentiating, opposing, thinking the contradiction)—this infinite power of the intellect —is the goad that drives us on. Negating creates movement.

What is negativity? Let us bring to mind its multiple meaning.

a) If I think Something, I must right away think the Other. Something is only if there is the Other. In fact, for the understanding, that which it searches for at every moment does not exist at all. There is no Being which, standing still, as it were, is this and only this and everything. Through its determinacy it has excluded the Other. This Other, however, brings itself into play. Hence no matter what I think according to my understanding (that is, fixed and self-same), I am by the nature of the thing driven onward to the Other. No matter what I would like to turn into something fixed and final: As such it slips out of my grasp as I am carried to the Other.

b) I am only in confronting the Other: the thing, the alien self, myself. Being is in division. The basic attribute of Being in existence is that it is split. I am only when objects are for me, and objects are only when I am a subject as such.

Where I take hold of truth I must take hold of the whole, the other and myself, and both in the movement in which they separate and find each other.

However, the understanding specifically makes what it takes hold of into objects. Then the insoluble ontological question arises as to how the object gets to the subject. But things are a mode of Being which cannot be thought only in itself but only together with the one for whom they are things. Being is not something enduring, but something that is moved through splitting; it is divided and at the same time "Being in itself," "Being for the other," "Being in and for itself."

c) Being-other, confronting each other in division, and also contradiction, opposition, mutually repelling forces, polarity, mere difference —all these Hegel subsumes under the all-embracing concept of negativity.

d) The real objection to Hegel's dialectic usually concerns the way in which he accepts contradiction. He explicitly comes out against the principle "that contradiction cannot be thought; as a matter of fact . . . the thinking of contradiction is the essential aspect of the concept. Formal thought too thinks it in actuality but looks away from it immediately" (5, 342).

e) In Hegel's dialectic negativity has not only a negating meaning but also one that propels the new Yes. The negative sublates what has been grasped by it, but in a threefold sense: It destroys it; it preserves it; it raises it to a higher plane. That which preserves and drives upward is "what is most important in rational cognition"; "to preserve in the result the positive in its negative, the content of the presupposition" (5, 340).

The negative is false as the merely negative, "which does not catch sight of the positive in itself" (2, 47; *Phän.*, 40). Thus the absolute freedom of the French Revolution is the point of departure for the terror in which the negation becomes "the meaningless death, the pure terror of the negative which harbors nothing positive, nothing fulfilling" (2, 449; *Phän.*, 386).

3) *Immediacy and mediation:* Being is immediate; I am immediate in my murky torpor, am not actuality but possibility. Only negation awakens, by creating movement.

Examples: According to Hegel's dialectic of master and servant I am actual for myself as self-being only when I have risked my life and have experienced and assimilated total upheaval. For only then do I possess myself (a possession that eludes me if all I have is fear, a fairly easy escape followed by forgetting). Or: a friendship is not handed to me like a gift. Authentic friendship is the fruit of struggle with the inherent risk of a break, a break overcome only in loving struggle.

In abstract form: Negativity is the wellspring of authentic Being, which is nowhere immediately, and becomes positive only as the negation of negation, as the overcoming of negativity in positivity. This is true for Being in every sense, for thinking, for the unfolding of Existenz.

Immediacy is sublated through negativity and through this mediation is raised to a new, higher immediacy to which the same happens in turn. In Hegel the immediate is everywhere; it is as manifold as negativity. It is not yet actual, not yet true, because it is still in progress. Hence it is subjected to the dialectical process in order to come to itself. But in that which has thus come to be there is a new immediacy.

The beginning, the immediate only, seems to be clear, but it turns out that this is really not so, that it is not yet what it will become. The immediate does not endure, but is the origin that develops through negativity.

The immediate cannot maintain itself. The dialectic comes upon it, from outside or from inside.

Hence Hegel sees the actuality in all Being as "the seriousness, the suffering, the patience, and the labor of the negative" (2, 15; *Phän.*, 13); he sees everywhere the being-other, the alienation—and the overcoming of this alienation. The life of the spirit "wins its truth only when in utter dismemberment it finds itself; it is this power only by looking the negative in the eye, by abiding with it. This abiding is the magical power that converts it into Being" (2, 26; *Phän.*, 22; Mi, ¶32).

4) *The thinking of the understanding*, by fixating and thus separating and negating, is the aspect of the dialectic itself that is indispensable to gaining the determinacy and clarity in which the strides, steps, and turns of the dialectic are to be executed.

Thus Hegel does not reject rational thinking in favor of a dialectical reason that would not need it. (In general, Hegel's thinking cannot be determined so easily by an alternative, for, according to the meaning of the dialectic, every alternative is taken up into the whole of this philosophy.) The understanding is the determinative and thus the negating aspect; hence, to be sure, it is overcome through the negation of its negation, but is at the same time also preserved. Therefore Hegel speaks of the "strength and labor of the understanding as the most wondrous and greatest or rather the absolute power." It is "the tremendous power

of the negative . . . the energy of thought" (2, 25, 26; *Phän.*, 22). "Death
. . . is of all things the most dreadful and to hold fast to what is dead
requires the greatest strength. Lacking strength, beauty hates the understanding for asking from her what she cannot do. But the life of the
Spirit is not the life that shrinks from death and keeps itself untouched
by devastation but rather the life that endures it and maintains itself in
it" (2, 26; *Phän.*, 22; Mi, ¶32).

The activity of the understanding is compared here to the devastation
of death. The inner action of Existenz influences the spiritual activity
of observing dialectically, lends it weight but also allows it to become
ambiguous. In any case, what is decisive for Hegel's philosophy is the
following: It is not mysticism, not edifying talk, not whispering, sug-
gesting, limiting, but, rather, what he calls "the exertion of the concept"
(2, 46; *Phän.*, 39). The understanding serves dialectical speculation as a
means in every one of its movements. No dialectic without understanding! Yet the dialectic cannot be comprehended by means of the understanding that serves it. It is "mysticism for the understanding" (6, 59;
Enc., ¶82, Z).

5) *What* the *understanding contrasts* (negative dialectically) *is linked
together by reason* (positive dialectically). The static concept of the understanding, which is used in every proposition, is taken up into the
concept of reason only in the sequence of propositions, where it manifests
itself in its wholeness.

Being is torn apart just as much by negativity as bound into oneness
and wholeness. The struggle of *separation is followed by reconciliation* in
wholeness. Negativity drives forward the movement, which in the end
is completed in the reconciliation of all opposites.

At bottom and as a whole, Being is separation and return to itself.
Negativity is the suffering of existence, and this suffering is the foun-
tainhead of actualized Being.

Hegel knows no limit in the development of sufferings through all
their configurations up to the "speculative Good Friday." "God . . . is
dead" (1, 157). This proposition denotes the most extreme negativity,
which immediately turns around dialectically into "God is risen." Each
suffering seemingly fated to end in despair soon finds its way to return:
it was merely the dialectical negative movement. Reconciliation is the
encircling bond of the whole. Thus, in studying Hegel's philosophy,
which penetrates into all abysses and seems to risk the ultimate, the
reader remains unperturbed; in the end everything is in order, secure
and positive.

In other words, the dialectic is not carried into infinity. Just as each

individual dialectic is determined by the whole that precedes it and is
its goal, so the entire, massive, almost incalculable dialectic of these
particular dialectic wholenesses is in turn bound or forced into the One
that is no longer subject to the dialectic but embraces all dialectic, in
which it unfolds and reveals itself.

The progress of the dialectic is *not linear, but circular*. The whole is
a circle of circles of circles. . . .

6) *The schematism of dialectical operations:* Since the dialectic becomes
a method by means of the movement of understanding—a method that,
however, goes beyond the understanding it makes use of—it finds itself
in an ambiguous situation: It can succeed only if it proceeds freely and
creatively in every instance. But as a method it is used as a plan to
discover and as a means to invent, in the same way an operational formula
is used.

Seemingly it then becomes easy to follow the instructions for the
philosophical thought process, as, perhaps: posit, posit the opposite, seek
the synthesis for thesis and antithesis. Or: consider the whole, dismember
it into opposites out of whose movement the originally regarded whole
then presents itself as composed, determined, as movement within itself.

Hegel turns against such schematization of the dialectic, against such
formalism of method.

a) As early as his preface to *Phenomenology*, Hegel rejects the procedure of "triplicity" as being "shallow mischief" (2, 38–39; *Phän.*, 33;
also *Logic*, 5, 344). For it makes use of the schema for an "external
ordering" and applies it "without a concept or immanent determination."
That is easily done. But what is important is to allow the dialectic to
proceed anew in each instance out of the matter itself, freely to stick to
the matter itself in our thinking, to have it present in ourselves, and to
be illuminated by it. Such fulfilled thinking is not an applicable method
or a technique to be replicated. It requires at every moment guidance
from the absolute.

For this reason Hegel rejects the term "construction" for dialectical
drafts that Schelling had used (5, 344). To him, they do not appear as
operational constructs, but as the reflections of pure observation. Construction would be contrivance. Absolute method is a matter of discovery,
conducted in pure dedication, by way of the exertion of the concept.

Without intuition into the true presence of a particular idea of the
whole, all that can be achieved is external ordering in the manner of
triadic tables, without there being any intrinsic insight. Rosenkranz[14]

[14] Karl Rosenkranz (1805–1879) was a German Hegelian philosopher who interpreted Hegel in
a somewhat liberal, semi-Kantian manner.

spoke of "innocent triads," which are empty. A dialectic that runs on wheels, as it were, and rides over everything without actually looking at it, reaches nothing and brings no insight.

b) Connected to the schematism is the tendency to turn the dialectic itself into an object knowable through the understanding. The thrust in that direction is implicit in the wording, which, through the use of "is," lays claim to "Being." Truth "is just as much immediacy as mediation; but propositional forms such as: the third is immediacy and mediation; or: it is their unity, are not capable of grasping it, since it is not a third at rest but is precisely this unity that is a movement and activity that mediates itself with itself" (5, 345).

c) Hegel does not even maintain absolutely the schema of triplicity. Here the number carries no weight. "Instead of the triplicity the abstract form can be taken as a quadruplicity" (5, 344). Then the road proceeds from a wholeness that is divided into an opposition; the return to the whole takes place by way of this opposition. It is the road from the undeveloped germ to a totality articulated within itself. Quadruplicity arises when the negative or the difference is counted as a duality.

The reader of Hegel still needs a knowledge of the schematisms. Only in this way does he recognize them, does he avoid falling under their spell, and sticks to asking in each instance about the concrete matter. By applying the schema he has not as yet taken hold of the matter, but reaches it only via discovering the content of each wholeness, which explicates itself to him dialectically in a unique way. Only the openness in the original life of the original allows the operation to succeed— otherwise it is a mere mechanism of the circular motion of thinking.

Insofar as they are supposed to be variations of the same thing as the dialectical turns that obliterate particularity, the multivocal triads confuse. They can cast a spell provided they bring about a consciousness of this sameness residing in the core of everything. Let me enumerate a few comprehensive triads according to their groupings:

Thesis, antithesis, synthesis—position, negation, negation of negation.

Immediacy (in itself), mediation (for itself), new immediacy (in and for itself).

Position, contradiction (opposition), concrete unity of opposites— abstract, reflected, concrete—Being, reflection, totality.

Abstracting understanding, reflecting understanding, speculative reason.

Substance, subject, substance-become-subject—objectivity, subjectivity, the absolute—the object, the subject-object-dichotomy, the identity of subject and object—object, subject, object-subject—to the outside, to the inside (reflection), identity of the outer and the inner.

Universality, particularity, individuality—concrete objectivity, individuality, penetration of concrete objectivity and individuality (the matter itself).

Unconsciousness, consciousness, self-consciousness—sensibility, understanding, reason.

Reason (in itself), nature (being-other), spirit (being-in-and-for-itself).

Dogmatism, skepticism, dialectic—metaphysics, critical philosophy, speculative philosophy.

C. Thinking and cognizing in Hegel

Through all great philosophy there runs the question regarding the thinking that unlocks the truth, allows it to show itself and to become manifest. Such thinking is not the everyday thinking of the understanding, which grasps, ad infinitum, things as static and which, in practical life, has specific goals in the world. For this reason a doctrine of a ladder of levels in our way of thinking runs, in variations, through the history of philosophy.

In Hegel the highest level of thinking—which preserves, at the same time, all the lower ones in itself but out of which it cannot be comprehended itself—is the dialectic as the absolute method or absolute knowing.

1. The ladder of the "Phenomenology"

Absolute knowing in absolute method does not come about merely on its own.

Consciousness thinks something, its object. But the object contradicts consciousness and itself. The experience of not being-in-agreement-with-oneself drives the movement of consciousness forward into the dichotomy of consciousness and object (of subject and object) until it reaches the point where subject and object coincide, and thought and Being, no longer contradicting each other, are the same. Here thinking is with itself in pure transparency without any separation of subject and object.

True to his intention, Hegel carried out the movement through all configurations of consciousness in his *Phenomenology of Spirit* and thus made available the "ladder" on which we are to climb up to absolute knowing, that is, in passing through the stages of consciousness and of history, the configurations of the conditions of the particular individuals and the configurations of a world.

One example of the compelling origin of the meaning of dialectical insight is the course of consciousness.

a) Consciousness seems to be firm and identical to itself when it grasps its object as static and considers such knowledge to be the truth. However, consciousness must be tested against its object, for what is meant in the object as being-in-itself is, as it refers to knowledge, being-for-it. "Thus in what consciousness affirms from within itself as *being-in-itself* or the true, we have the standard which consciousness itself set up by which to measure what it knows" (2, 68; *Phän.*, 57–58; Mi, ¶84). However, consciousness has this experience through an inner contradiction, because what it meant turns itself around, and something happens to it that it does not as yet comprehend. Consciousness is transformed.

b) Hegel allows the appearance of knowledge to express itself or to conduct itself or to act, and then he observes that no appearance of knowledge is to be adhered to as the absolute one. Hence we must differentiate in his texts where he lets the standpoint of the appearance of knowledge speak, which in each instance considers itself to be final; and where the philosopher—who already knows the whole of the movement of appearing knowledge—allows this knowledge of the movement to come into play.

The differentiation of what consciousness does in knowledge of appearance and of how the observing philosopher understands it poses a twofold task for the philosopher: at first to be receptive, refraining from changing anything in the way it presents itself, keeping comprehension separate from reception for the time being, and then to follow up by observing what happens in this appearing knowledge, observing its actual movement and basing comprehension on it. Such comprehension completes itself only in the total movement of appearing knowledge and ultimately proceeds from appearing knowledge to absolute knowledge.

In observing the appearance of consciousness, we allow the examination to take place as a process within itself (in the dialectical explication) and "all that is left for us is simply to look on." Thus it turns out that consciousness must "alter its knowledge," but in fact in altering the knowledge the object itself also changes for knowledge. The object, as well as the criterion, undergoes change, and so does consciousness. This course traveled by consciousness—a course meant to be followed in thought by Hegel in *Phenomenology of Spirit*—he calls "experience of consciousness." The new object shows itself to have come about "through a reversal of consciousness itself." The philosophical "science" of the succession of experiences through which consciousness passes is not known to the consciousness that we are observing. The coming-to-be of each new object in the succession of the configurations of consciousness happens "behind the back of consciousness, as it were." The coming-to-be of the new object presents itself to consciousness "without its knowing how this happens." And, further: for consciousness "what has thus come to be exists only as an object, for us it appears at the same time as movement and a process of becoming" (2, 69, 72, 71; *Phän.*, 58, 60; Mi, ¶85, 87).

In each of its configurations consciousness is true as a moment of the whole but false as self-contradictory. Therefore it is driven onward, unstoppable, through all configurations, until it finds rest in absolute knowledge in which all semblance is cast off and "appearance becomes identical with essence" (2, 72; *Phän.*, 60). The progression of consciousness, brought to completion, "comprises nothing less than . . . the entire realm of the truth of spirit" (2, 72; *Phän.*, 60; Mi, ¶87).

c) The dialectic in the progression of consciousness is not at all of one kind, but of almost indeterminably different kinds. In the examples cited above we saw the movement of consciousness taking place: in sense-certainty as the progress of meaning and saying what it is, in the movement of master and servant as the progression of self-consciousness. Further, it takes place in Stoicism as experience gathered in the mode of being sustained by the truth by which I attain satisfaction and tranquillity, but which then leads to the sublation of this tranquillity; and so on.

Hegel sees the process of spirit appearing in consciousness in the individual person, in communal consciousness, in the configuration of a world.

d) Hegel gained his grand insight from transformation, reversal, and the progression of consciousness, counter to the opinion that all consciousness is the same.

However, for him this change is not an open, indeterminable, multiply divergent process, but a single one which the philosopher now views clearly in its completeness, up to its consummation in the moving unchangeableness of true knowledge. The movement of appearing knowledge completes itself up to the point where there is no more contradiction, no more difference between knowledge and truth. This completion does not come about by finally reaching a distinct, separate step, which consummates itself as the only now true one. Rather, all the steps, without exception, are perceived and held fast as moments of the whole. The truth of knowledge rests in the circle that is formed by all the steps of appearing knowledge.

Self-consummation and self-dissolution of knowledge take place at every level; the philosopher who has reached a clear overview of the whole brings to mind the event of emerging knowledge. To be sure, each and every configuration regards itself as true, yet has to experience that its thinking is turned around; it then either abides within itself or is driven beyond. But only the philosopher knows the meaning through which, and the goal toward which, and the road on which this takes place.

e) Everywhere consciousness intends the truth, but reality does not coincide with it. So it keeps on going, destroying and reappearing anew. Only in completion do consciousness, truth, and actuality coincide. But on the road to this completion the following applies: "Actuality is in league with truth against consciousness."

Consciousness believes itself to grasp truth in the phenomenality of thought and so to encounter actuality. But what it experiences is discrepancy.

There it can erupt, as it were, into skepticism and nihilism. But these, together with their lapse into hopelessness, ultimately are only moments of the one whole, true, and actual, and are the critical turning points of radical negativity, which bring about what is new in consciousness, a newness of which actuality itself makes sure.

When Hegel, in a lecture at Jena, demonstrated the course of knowledge in its appearance and dwelt repeatedly upon the reversals, thus arriving at nihilistic turnings, a student jumped up, after an hour of this, and exclaimed: "Now everything is destroyed." Not at all: To be sure, Hegel presented the negative with devastating consistency; but he did so with the tranquillity that had been present from the start, based on the knowledge of the whole truth, a knowledge that had never ceased.

f) Each instance of coming-to-be of the new object in a consciousness transformed by it happens by means of a leap. All the conditions are present under which the birth of the new can take place. The leap itself brings about a new manifestness, or a resolve; in a crisis this leads to an act out of the depth of our ground. The negative does not necessarily bring about the new position for our understanding by violence; instead, by understanding the conditions and possibilities, the new is like a gift (as, by willing suicide, you may come to yourself with a new will to live; or, in the despair brought about by the loss of faith and the collapse of all objects of faith, a new faith may come into being).

It is said about this leap (a term Hegel avoids, since it would deny the necessity of progression) that it takes place "behind the back" of consciousness. An entirely different meaning of "behind the back" is operative in Hegel and is nothing short of decisive for the progression of the whole, which, without this other meaning, would elude insight in the following way: The circumstance that novelty arises, as if by magic, according to the "necessity of the concept"; for example, the reality released by the *logos* follows the world of the *logos*; the organic follows the inorganic; India follows China, and so on. This is not comprehensible through an inward movement that is experienced; neither is it a matter of the incomprehensibility of a leap that may be regarded as possible under understood conditions; rather, it is totally incomprehensible.

Whereas the movements occurring in consciousness through its experience with itself are comprehensible to us, this mode of happening "behind the back" strikes us as surprising, artificial, forced (grounded metaphysically) if it is meant to arise out of the necessity of logical concepts. On the other hand, we are able to comprehend a situational matrix arising from consciousness but behind its back, that is, through the unanticipated consequences of its actions and of its conduct in the world, or, put another way, when conditions of life are changed through what consciousness brings forth and consciousness itself changes in an unforeseeable way.

2. *The unification of subject and object*

The fundamental difficulty in understanding Hegel is to grasp this thinking of absolute method in absolute knowledge. Let us recall some theses that carry the entire Hegelian philosophy:

First: Subject and object have become one in absolute knowledge.

After all, we always think as consciousness directed toward the particular intended object. And Hegel does not deny this: Absolute knowledge is not attained by our abandoning this clarity of consciousness of the understanding in order to move toward something beyond; instead, it occurs in this medium through the movement that—while remaining in this medium—transcends it in the direction of the absolute, which is subject and object in one and in constant motion. This movement is the "absolute method," the "movement of the concept."

Second: The movement of the absolute method is that of the matter itself, in which subject and object coincide.

The method is the concept that knows itself, and that has, as its object, "the absolute, the subjective as well as the objective" (5, 330).

The "concept that knows itself subjectively" is, at the same time, the objective "substantiality of things." For representation and reflection the concepts appear as the other; in truth they are, in their movement, the matter itself. For reflection, the method is universal and applicable to everything. In its idea and actuality it is the particular method of each matter itself." The concept corresponds to its reality "as an existence which it, the concept, itself is" (ibid.)

The method of the movement of the concept can be called the form in which all content lies. This form is "the soul of all objectivity"; "all otherwise determined content" has its actuality "only in the form" (5, 329).

Third: The infinite power of the method.

The movement of the concept, the method, is "the unrestrictedly universal, inner and outer mode" of "absolute activity," which has the "simple infinite power against which no object could put up any resistance." The method is "therefore the highest power, or, rather, the only and absolute power of reason—not only, but also—its highest and only impulse to find and to recognize itself through itself in everything" (5, 330–31).

3. Character of the absolute method

In speculative philosophizing, we are, in the execution of the absolute method, with the absolute itself. Hence Hegel calls the thinking of logic "divine service." All of philosophy is the thinking of the reflection of God's primal thoughts and their activity in nature and spirit. "Everything else is error, murkiness, opinion, striving, arbitrariness and transitoriness; the absolute idea alone is Being, imperishable life, truth that knows itself, and is all of truth" (5, 328).

Therefore Hegel says that "everything must begin with the absolute, just as all progress is merely its representation insofar as what is in-itself is the concept" (5, 334).

4. Resistance to mathematics

The absolute method cannot be attained, substantiated, or understood from any lower one. Only from the absolute standpoint do relative methods, methods of cognition of the finite, reveal themselves in their meaning. Hegel senses only one science as threatening to philosophy. Starting with Pythagoras and Plato, *mathematics* occupies a position of superiority, in itself as well as in being a gateway to philosophy. Hegel opposes this view with something approaching hate and bitterness in his remarks:

"The essential point of view is that it is altogether a matter of a new concept of scientific treatment. Philosophy, insofar as it is purported to be a science, cannot . . . for this purpose borrow its method from a subordinate science such as mathematics; neither can it leave it at categorical assurances of inner intuition" (3, 6–7).

It cannot be said that Hegel was ignorant of mathematics. As is shown by his detailed exposition of mathematical problems, his knowledge is by no means negligible. But number as such "is the pure thought of one's own renunciation of thought," "the abstract thought of superficiality itself"; thinking finds itself here "in the violent activity of moving within thoughtlessness" (3, 246).

The numerical unit is "the totally inactive, lifeless and indifferent determinateness in which all movement and relation is extinguished, and which has broken off the bridge leading to living existence" (2, 215; *Phän.*, 189).

5. What is meant by proof

Hegel's proving goes by way of the dialectical development. Proving "in philosophy means the same as showing how the object—through and out of itself—turns itself into that which it is" (6, 161; *Enc.*, ¶83, Z).

a) Proof in the finite sciences and in mathematics "falls outside the statement that is supposed to be the truth" (15, 402). In mathematics "the mode of cognition remains external to its subject matter" (2, 33; *Phän.*, 28; Mi, ¶48). So it is too in the kind of philosophy that appropriates this manner of proving and states its theses on such grounds. "To be sure, it is proved and one has to be convinced, but the subject matter is still uncomprehended. There is a rigid necessity of proof which lacks the aspect of self-consciousness" (as does the inadequate method of Spinoza) (15, 402).

Hegel therefore complains: ". . . once the dialectic has been separated from proof, the concept of philosophic demonstration has been lost" (2, 52; *Phän.*, 44; Mi, ¶65).

b) The true proof to which Hegel lays claim for his cognition is the one out of the wholeness, within which each insight follows through the movement of the matter itself. Hence the truth cannot be contained in any thesis. The "thesis, in the form of a judgment, is not suited for . . . expressing speculative truths." Truth is "only as a Becoming" (3, 89, 193).

"The true is the whole. But the whole is the essence consummating itself through nothing other than its development. Of the absolute it must be said that it is essentially a result, that only in the end is it what it truly is; that precisely in this consists its nature of being actual, or subject, or becoming itself" (2, 16; *Phän.*, 14; cf. Mi, ¶20).

c) The proof lies in coherence, in necessary coherence. In philosophy this coherence is, first of all, not an external but an internal one, and, second, one that is completed and proved only in the absolute whole.

Speculative thinking is not scientific inquiry; it is not experimental getting-to-the-bottom-of-things, not methodical approach to dealing with worldly things. Rather, it means surrendering to the matter into whose innermost depth we enter.

Whatever is discovered, whatever is intuited in light of the matter, whatever becomes clear as meaning, in terse formulation—none of these, nothing is valid for Hegel in isolation, out of its separate self, as a clever aphorism; only in its coherence is it valid for him, and the latter only in the completion of the whole. What Hegel calls "science" is thinking the coherence systematically.

On this point two things need to be said:

First: The claim that something is true only at its place within a totality and can be understood solely in this context reveals insight. It expresses that which, counter to the dissipation of current opinions and sudden inspirations, points to the ground without which everything turns into mere prattle.

Second: This coherence is not open-ended and to be sought unto infinity, as it is in the Kantian idea, while effectively providing guidance to movement and exercising control over random meanings. Rather, the coherence is completely present in the system. Hence everything that happens in it is "proved" through the preceding dialectical movement, and for the purpose of conclusive proof requires the presentness of the whole system, which, self-encircled, has neither beginning nor end.

Thus it says at the end of *Logic*: "It is too late to ask for proof that the idea is the truth; the proof of that is contained in the whole exposition and development of thought up to this point. The idea is the result of this course of dialectic. . . . It is . . . its own result and, being so, is no less immediate than mediated" (6, 387; *Enc.*, ¶213, Z; W, §213).

d) The proofs for the existence of God are a special example of philosophical demonstration. In the way Hegel shows them to be true, they have the significance "that they should contain the ascent of man's spirit to God, and express, for thought, how the ascent is an ascent of thinking, moreover to the realm of thought." This ascent is "essentially founded on the nature of our spirit and is necessary to it. It is this necessity that we are confronting in this ascent, and the characterization of that very necessity is nothing other than what we ordinarily call proof." The ascent is not "provable from outside; it proves itself out of itself . . . it is necessary for itself; we merely need to observe its own process" (12, 300–01).

"The method of proof employed in finite cognition displays altogether the perverse position of requiring some objective ground for God's being, which would make it appear as mediated by something else. This mode of proof . . . is embarrassed by the difficulty of passing from the finite to the infinite" (6, 73–74; *Enc.*, ¶36).

6. *Resistance to reflections*

In the true dialectic, what goes on is the progression of the matter itself. This progression should not be interfered with. Hence the demand "to let go of specific opinions and presuppositions and to let the matter prevail in itself."

But when it proceeds in this manner, Hegel himself often inserted reflections about it. Such reflections can serve "to facilitate the overview and thereby the understanding." The disadvantage is "to look like un-justified assertions, reasons and bases for what follows. Hence one should not take them to be more than what they are meant to be, and should differentiate them from that which is a moment in the progression of the matter itself" (3, 114).

But we are to resist reflections arising out of finite understanding devoid of any intuition of the whole that dialectical movement comprises in regard to the theses it incorporates. These are inexhaustible. Their endlessness would have to be countered by an endless refutation, which, however, by means of the repeated attempts to raise reflection, would have no other result than progressing from mere understanding to di-alectical reason.

Totally to be rejected is the demand—inherent in the understanding's reflection—for conformity to its conceptual mode. This conceptuality "belongs . . . to the bad manners of reflection, which looks for concep-tualization but simultaneously presupposes its static categories, thus knowing itself forearmed against the answer to what it looks for." In this way, for example, reflection provides the "presupposition of the absolute separation of Being from Nothing." Becoming, then, turns into something incomprehensible for reflection, since it has been superseded by this presupposition. But then again this Becoming, and "this contradiction which one posits oneself and whose solution one makes impossible, is called the incomprehensible" (3, 96, 107).

The understanding, which is always the indispensable means for the dialectic movement, cannot itself comprehend the dialectic. Hence Hegel calls it "mysticism for the understanding."

7. Attempt to understand the dialectic through differentiating between two logics

Logic examines the forms of thinkability as empty forms that are the conditions for the correctness of all cognition but are not the basis of the content of cognition.

Another logic sees, in the forms of thinking, the content itself and the truth of Being.

Lask called the first logic the *analytic* logic, because it allows concepts to emerge, according to their content, out of their abstraction from experience; the second logic he called *emanatistic*, because it lets the content of cognition flow forth, as it were, from the concept.[15]

For analytic logic the concept having the widest perimeter is the emptiest; it is the concept of a universal. For emanatistic logic the concept with the widest perimeter is, to be sure, at first devoid of content, but it shelters the entire fullness of content that emerges from the concept through its self-movement; the concept is not the concept of a universal but the concept of totality present at the beginning as a germ and at the end in its complete development.

At first glance this differentiation seems apt. Hegel states it time and again: By abstracting, "the finite cognition according to the understanding" produces that universal which leaves out the concrete, which it later again takes up just as externally. "The absolute method, on the other hand, does not behave in the manner of external reflection but extricates the determinate from its object, since it is itself the object's immanent principle and soul." For Hegel, the universal is "not merely something abstract but . . . the concrete totality" (5, 335, 334).

Because of this alternative, the matter seems clear for a moment. It appears that we can choose which logic to consider the true one, and accordingly we have to reject the other. We can show this difference historically in the permutations of the medieval opposition of nominalism (concepts are mere names, produced by our thinking, an order of valid relations all its own) and realism (concepts are themselves actualities).

---

[15] Emil Lask, *Fichtes Idealismus und die Geschichte*. Tübingen, Leipzig, J. C. B. Mohr, 1902, 28ff.

Formal logic can be contraposed to metaphysical logic and, finally, Kantian logic to Hegelian logic. But the simple differentiation, and especially the subsequent simple rejection of the one or the other, is inappropriate.

a) It runs counter to Hegel's intention. For Hegel incorporates the logic that is contraposed to his into his own as its moment. While acknowledging the demolishing opposition as justified, he exposes it as inadequate, as a step that becomes false when it presumes to be the ultimate one.

b) The plenitude of meaning-relations without which Hegel's work would not be so astoundingly impressive might be subordinated to a logic belonging within the logical clarifications but not justified in claiming absolute authority.

c) The very positing of the alternative presupposes a single absolute logic. Hegel's absolutism is opposed by another absolutism, a position that, in its deepest ground, seems to manifest a likemindedness with Hegel. We can choose between two logics, but in such a manner that one is false. The choice is the fundamental act that is shifted into the realm of theoretical knowledge; criticism is taking here the wrong turn.

It would be just as mistaken to give both logics equal status, granting either one absolute validity, depending on the situation, and to consider logic as a series of possibilities from which we choose according to circumstance.

8. *Hegel on the dialectic and what he actually does*

Hegel's own statements on the dialectic in his writings, though sparse, are of great importance.

He is a "hands-on" philosopher, explaining what he does only in passing or in context, at the appropriate place.

He does not promise what he does not also carry out.

He does not indulge in whispers, secretive hints, or portentous presentiments, in the style of the Romantics; nowhere does he present his cause as mysterious. He sets down, builds up, is involved, and guides his reader to participate; he rules out what is vague as well as merely questioning. He knows within an absolute knowledge and comprehends this knowledge in its wholeness. Everything has become manifest. Nothing could resist the "courage of truth" (*Enc.*, Preface to 2nd ed.).

This stance is admirable, to be sure. Hegel's "exertion of the concept," his dialectical-constructive apprehension and appropriation of an immeasurable plenitude of concrete material knowledge, his capacity for absorption, and his power of mastering this knowledge are unique.

But though the vagueness of Romantic intimations repels us as weakness, as lack of clarity in the Existenz of the thinking person, as indulging in fanciful utterances that have actually nothing to say, though they might sense the extraordinary which ought to be said, Hegel equally repels us with his imperious assertion of knowledge in its all-encompassing totality, knowledge achieved by the practical labor of thoroughgoing construction that brings meaning to appearance—a knowledge, however, that is flawed in its deepest ground. Whispering Romantics reach for too little; Hegel's dictatorship, for too much.

Perhaps there is a relationship between the two. The one tends toward the other: fanciful conjecturing prepares for the claim of setting a universal standard; hypnotized fixation on the incomprehensible mystery tends toward submission to the dictator; the cheap assertion of authority of the one reflects the compelling power laboriously built up by the other.

D. The actual multiplicity of the dialectic

We have discussed two possibilities: *Either* the dialectic is seen as the one universal method—in which case it seems to leave an indeterminate universal arrived at by empty abstractions; to get lost in a tangle of assertions of the unity of logical interrelations, comprehensible spiritual meanings, and the real course of events, and to collapse in absurdities. *Or* the dialectic is retained in the multiplicity of its concrete meaning, and analyzed according to the specific modes of its evidence, its content, its movement.

In this second instance the further question arises as to the reason all this is to be called dialectic, what it all has in common. And, further, what in this commonality (which resides in the movement through contrariety and contradiction) are the radical differences, and whether there is a difference within the dialectic that bursts the system open, namely, the difference between a conciliatory conclusive dialectic and one that remains or breaks open and leads, without conciliation, to the limits of irreconcilable contradiction.

Perhaps Hegel did not comprehend what he was actually doing by bringing the dialectic into the one form of universal method and absolute knowledge, that is, when, instead of looking at particular concrete dialectics, he looks at that which, according to his understanding, happens in all dialectics. While Hegel often works out a specific dialectic, in other instances he presents us only with dialectical phraseology instead of concrete illuminations, and allows the great transitions of the whole to become obscured and lost in pictorial images and parables.

Strangely enough, we do not as yet have a systematic analysis of the modes of the dialectic or their clear differentiation; nor do we have an elaboration of the range of each particular meaning, and of their diverse importance for the methodical cognition of actuality.

Such an analysis would exhibit the particular originality of each meaning of dialectic in the movement of consciousness, in the comprehension of biological actuality, in historical movements, in logical-categorial relations. While all these phenomena confront us with a dialectic, its universality precludes it from being as "explicative" as concretely illuminating dialectic would be.

If it is to remain explicative, however, it must be only as explication of the entirety of the absolute idea; and here we ask whether the idea can be carried out; we ask about its intuitability and presentness. For example, our understanding of the coexistence of things in the created world rests on the idea of being-other, with which the logical idea is fully compatible. Each kind of thing is one moment of the wholeness of reality; the inorganic, life; the soul, spirit. These moments do not produce each other; they succeed each other in thought. Hegel, however, lets them bring each other forth dialectically in this order. Because the logical idea realizes itself, all of its moments must also be present in reality. Experience appears to confirm what must become dialectically real.

Without evidence or necessity Hegel has the things that are here "leap forth." Hence the infinite multiplicity of accidental individuals. Just how odd this fundamental idea is becomes evident when this "leaping forth" is called an "eruption." Hegel juxtaposes the eruptions of skin ailments with the eruption of stars in the heavens and the pointlike marine phosphorescence (7a, 460ff.; *Enc.*, ¶341, Z). All of them are moments of the course of the idea that surrenders itself to the accidentality of being-other without losing itself in it. For this reason all such eruptions are, as arbitrary multiplicities, assuredly factual but also indifferent.

In order to think along with Hegel's dialectic we need the most acute intellect combined with sensual, psychic, and spiritual intuitions—all within human reach. But, additional to this the illumination of another intuition is required, which represents the cipher of Hegelian philosophy: that of the absolute being of the dialectic in the ground of all things. This intuition is not easy to reach; it can occasionally be discovered as movingly present in Hegel, though not in every Hegelian, for it is easily lost in formalism, in the tricks of antithetical games, in the mere imitation of Hegel's formulations. Hegel's cipher appears to be unique: personally his, and not honestly repeatable by imitation.

III. CHARACTERIZATION AND CRITIQUE
OF HEGELIAN DIALECTIC

1. Once more: the positive aspect

Prior to our critical remarks let us look once more at the viewpoint of this astounding philosophy:

The center and surrounding circle of Hegelian philosophy is the dialectic as concretely carried out by him and comprehended in its entirety. To achieve understanding of it, we attempt time and again to leap into it, as it were, to share Hegel's experience via the figures of thought that are in motion, to vibrate along with him in and toward the One itself, to attain the plenitude of the absolute that Hegel believed he had grasped and recognized anew in all things, in logic, in the world, in nature, in man and his history, and in the actuality of the philosophy that, by understanding everything and the whole, understands itself.

We go on accompanying him in the circular movements, whose operations nowhere permit us to come to a halt; for only in the completion of the movement, not at its end but, rather, through it as such, when it returns within itself in its infinite circle of circles, is the tranquillity achieved in which the answer to all questions is given.

Hence there is no answer if we demand that it be in the form of an intelligible unequivocal statement.

Hence in following Hegel we find ourselves in ever new circular movements, whose whirling may confuse us, until we grasp, by way of trial, the configuration of thought that keeps recurring within them and in this way the great order pervading the whole.

If we understand him on his terms, we arrive at a whole that, in the magnitude of its rich development and the inexhaustible, constantly expanding plenitude, as well as in the detail of the individual content of thought, always speaks the same language, out of the absolute of the ground of all Being. All things reflect in each other the same plenitude, which, however, becomes manifest only as individual being through the completion of the mirroring in the infinite movement.

2. Mystification? But a grand achievement

Did Hegel, with his dialectical method as absolute, place impossible expectations on human thinking? And did he himself fall prey to an illusion? Do we deal here with a mystification, on a grand scale and unintended as such, to be sure, and seductive in its sweep?

Are we faced here with the astounding situation that this thinking, being "with the matter itself," indeed claiming to be "the matter itself," knows this matter in its wholeness as the absolute, as God, and itself thinks God's thoughts, God's thoughts before creation (in logic), after creation as operative in the process (in the philosophical "real sciences" of philosophy of nature and philosophy of spirit)?

The grandeur of the actual achievement, the attractiveness of so many intuitions of actualities, the acuity of Hegel's powers of thought, in all of which a most serious contemplation of the deity can be felt, do not readily allow us to reject this philosophy because of its disconcerting inferences and postulates. But for the same reason they must not demand that we surrender to them. The power of Hegel's achievement demands our effort to immerse ourselves in it. Only then can we experience that which becomes apparent to us in such an effort. The study of this philosophy, which, as a configuration of thought, belongs to the few in the history of philosophy which are most comprehensive, remains imperative. It reveals itself surprisingly rewarding by insights as well as by eliciting opposing powers of which without Hegel we would hardly be fully aware.

Hegel's dialectic may repel as grandiloquent nonsense, but only if it is regarded one-sidedly in its fallacious inferences and applications. It keeps its attractiveness as profound insight only if its significance is critically considered, analyzed, and resolved. To undertake this successfully requires a position that is not overpowered by the dialectic itself, but still can make use of all its true elements. Where do we find such a position?

It cannot be a matter of a determinate "standpoint" or of the rationality of finite intelligence. Rather, thinking has to be guided by Existenz at one with reason.

3. Characterization of the universality of the method

When dialectic, as universal method, has become a method, then it is —with its universal form of negativity, movement, wholeness, circle— itself an abstraction.

In distinction from the many origin-structures, it is no longer comprehensible in the sense of a content unless this abstraction becomes the cipher of faith that looks into the dialectical movement of the absolute itself.

No convincing reason is given by Hegel why, given the infinite variety, the dialectic is always the same. In trying to express this sameness, we are stuck with a formal schematism which as such is not an evident content but gains evidentiality only through the particular fulfillment of each specific dialectic. The evidence for this does not always exhibit everywhere the same character that is comprehensible from the universal schema; on the contrary, the universal schema originates in the specific dialectic.

4. Critique of the "absolute method"

The critique of the dialectic can be directed radically only against the "absolute method."

a) The comparison between the reality of what is understood through dialectic and the dialectical meaning-structure shows what in reality does not fit the understood meaning. The same reality can also be grasped through a different dialectical meaning-structure. This means that each dialectical meaning-structure is a construct arrived at by an understanding that arises from the nature of intelligibility. The type of construct can be applied to reality. Insofar as reality conforms to construct, it has been comprehended in a specific aspect but not as a whole.

The wholenesses of the absolute dialectical method are intended as real substances. The wholenesses of the dialectical meaning-structures are sketches of constructive evidence which are useful as tools for grasping reality and recognizable as reality in the sense of an individually limited line of effectiveness.

b) Each dialectic is to be questioned as to the evidence specific to it. If this is lacking, we recognize it to be a formal and superficial toying with concepts.

c) The meaning of dialectic resides in its specificity in each case. Universal or absolute dialectic is an abstraction from formal analogies. The critical appropriation of the dialectic takes place in concrete specificity and not in the totality.

5. Critical breakthrough by means of the method

When Hegel's dialectic seeks its completion in the absolute knowledge of the absolute method, the following radical objection may be raised against it: The dialectical method must itself break in upon every total structure of the dialectic, must sublate it and drive the dialectic further. Hegel's method must also close in on his system as a whole. It has to be applied to the work itself. After all, man's thinking and cognizing do not come to an end with Hegel. The dialectic of history drives on and beyond him.

The first reply to the foregoing is: In principle Hegel's dialectic is all-encompassing. The dialectic must overwhelm each particular dialectic but it has no power over the completed total dialectic. Any dialectic opposing Hegel's would be absorbed in his totality and restricted from letting this totality become again a moment of something more comprehensive. From this angle we are justified in saying that Hegel anticipated the Marxist dialectic of the labor process, located in a few paragraphs of his *Philosophy of Right*—in the dialectic of bourgeois society. In the same way we are justified in saying that Kierkegaard's concept of Existenz is anticipated in a few passages of Hegel's *Aesthetics*—in the Romantic Spirit. Admittedly, in neither instance has the meaning of Marx or Kierkegaard been captured, much less developed. But seen from the Hegelian perspective, its anticipated incorporation might be claimed by means of seemingly identical concepts. Hegel's breadth is extraordinary and is of a sort that, if one remains within it, can be broadened even further.

But if the dialectic as a whole cannot be overcome by dialectic, it can still be penetrated by something that itself is undialectical (or is something that forces itself upon us in a dialectic that leaves things open and does not arrive at synthesis, at reconciliation): first, by true scientific knowledge and research, going forward into infinity; second, by existential decision in historicity; third, by the "place" of being-human as an indeterminable place within the indeterminable whole. Man has no overview of the whole; rather, by going forward into incalculable distances, he penetrates it. He does not know what he himself truly is but goes forward in his decision to his unforeseeable, incalculable actualization.

6. The presupposition: faith in the whole and in the method

Hegelian dialectic presupposes the "whole" through which the movement takes place and is guided, the circle that, as the circle of circles, closes on itself as it reconciles all. And faith too is presupposed, which, being unified and all-penetrating, sees the absolute in this dialectic.

The actual design can be improved, completed, corrected in its details, following Hegel's own incessant labor. Hegel's faithful successors occasionally attempted to facilitate reflection in accordance with their personal intentions, but measured against Hegel, their endeavors appear as arbitrariness and whim, derived in part from undialectical intellectual motives.

That faith is presupposed is easily noted in discussions concerned with interpretation of Hegel. No general reflection about dialectic as such can arrive at a convincing result, whether affirming or rejecting. The movement always takes place within a reflection detached from the matter at hand. However, it is only continuing examination of the concrete dialectic that can lead to experience of each specific evidence, and, conversely, can expose the mere toying with formal dialectical conceptuality. In proceeding along this path, it becomes noticeable that those Hegel interpreters who take the dialectic equally seriously everywhere will arrive only at a boring—because uncritical—replication. For Hegel believers this is their training, which to them is not boring since its constant repetition of an act of faith is to them satisfying in itself.

Only he who is predisposed by his readiness to believe and susceptible to indoctrination can agree to uncritical surrender, maintaining that only someone able and willing truly to accept the dialectic can understand it at all. Concomitant with this alleged insight is that nothing exists outside the all-embracing dialectic. Anyone who thinks in terms of opposition is, on the contrary, within it at a place already understood as bound to be overcome. Refusing to become part of it amounts to lack of clarity in thinking, to being arrested in a subordinate position, to being lifeless instead of going forward in living movement. Every opponent is considered overcome once his own particular necessity is recognized. The opponent becomes himself a proof of the truth of dialectical faith. This faith is an enormous snake devouring everything: Standing up to it is not an encounter; whatever does this becomes, instead, prey that is destroyed and assimilated by it. This "refutation" (which occurs analogously in Marxism and in psychoanalysis) leaves us with a choice: to identify with our own "position" as it is characterized in the dialectic and thus blend it into the living dialectical flow, or to allow ourselves to be declared dead, to be excluded, and, if the matter becomes involved with political power, to be destined for annihilation.

7. The limit of Hegelian dialectic

Comprehensive as Hegel's dialectic may be, it is nonetheless a specific dialectic, because circle and reconciliation are the ultimate for its absolute method.

Hegel excludes the dialectic that leads to the limit of seemingly irreconcilable opposition, a dialectic that opens up, that confronts us with irresolvables, antinomies, the irreconcilable either/or.

It excludes the dialectical forms of speculation that touch the unthinkable in paradoxes and want to make the unutterable utterable.

8. History of the dialectic

Hegel sees his dialectic in its historical derivation and summarizes it. Heraclitus is the most ancient philosopher of dialectical insight; Plato is the originator of dialectic as method. Dialectic has always been misunderstood by popular philosophy and common sense. The Eleatics used it to deny the truth of the world and of motion, since that which contains contradiction must be illusion. Educated skepticism has always made use of dialectic. Thus dialectic has had a negative result throughout history, and is even called the "logic of illusion" by Kant. The *coincidentia oppositorum* of Nicholas of Cusa, and the mystical speculation and the broad current of genuine philosophy are all for Hegel a single testimony to the eternal truth. Hegel is conscious of being the first to develop dialectics to its full extent, in its comprehensive and positive import, making use of all preceding achievements, especially those of Kant, Fichte, and Schelling. In Hegel the all-penetrating method becomes not only the one actively effective everywhere, but also the one that orders everything in a system, in which respect Proclus is the precursor.

Hegel praises Kant as the one who revived dialectics because of this infinite achievement and at the same time opposes him in regard to the way in which he took it up. It is important for us to contrast the two.

For Kant's dialectical synthesis, the idea is the regulative principle of progressing into the infinite, into the open world. For Hegel's dialectic, the process of the concept is itself the substance of Being, the eternal, internally moving permanence. For Kant there exists the wholly other, in the form of the turmoil of the emotions and in the forms of diversity and chance. For Hegel the other is merely the other of the concept, which he posits as a moment of itself released by itself. Kant knows cognition through experience and comprehends its possibility. Hegel knows and understands the cognition of the absolute. For Kant there are limit-concepts, the encounter with mystery, the incomprehensibility of freedom. For Hegel there is no limit to cognition, no darkness, no mystery; everything is comprehensible and comprehended.

The origin of the content of Hegel's dialectic is religious in nature. The notion of "reconciliation," to which he held fast with unwavering certainty and which in the end brings a comforting conclusion to the most extreme ruptures, is of Christian origin.

The motor of dialectical penetration in Hegel is the understanding ofmeaning. All other modes of cognition (for example, causal explanation) are taken up from the aspect of their meaningfulness. Hegel carries out what Nietzsche was to explicate forcefully: Cognition is interpretation, and total cognition of Being is the interpretation of interpretations. Nietzsche refers to philology. Reading a text is a great art. To carry out this art when faced with the text of what is, is philosophy. Knowing and being-known are here understanding and being-understood. Because in philology and theology the process of understanding texts is called hermeneutics, we can speak of hermeneutic philosophy. In this respect Hegel is the master of a philosophy regarded as the hermeneutics of what is.

FRAGMENTS

1. The systematic spirit

From early on, the systematic spirit predominated in Hegel in a variety of meanings:

1) In his boyhood he acquired well-organized knowledge. There was nothing that did not interest him. He started his copious collections of excerpts. Throughout his life he preserved a capacity for sustained work which enabled him to master any subject.

The thoroughness that brought him close to whatever his subject never dissipated in diversity. He always aimed at the essence of the matter, the principle, the particular characteristic. He took the detail as guide to the general or representative of the fundamental—which, in turn, he pursued down to the detail.

Hegel's thinking, moreover, was always underpinned by closeness to life and by intuition. We find him early in his life passionately following and interpreting national political events. He took note of everything the world offered in matter and content. All through his life he was a diligent reader of newspapers, an eager traveler, an interested observer of all realities he encountered. A world-system demands the repleteness of the world.

2) He sought the whole of all Being at the foundation. From the very beginning he was in the thrall of a metaphysical attitude—we might point to his fundamental religious experience and see him in relationship to the religious, Christian, specifically Swabian Protestant theological tradition.

3) He aimed to discover the interrelatedness of all things, the method

by which the uniting, permeating, moving force that holds everything together in one ground and goal can be recognized and grasped in our cognition. If we set aside specific concepts, contents, and thought-operations and concentrate on the pervasive mood, the basic attitude as a whole, in other words, on his will to system, we may say that Hegel's thinking, from beginning to end, stands as a singular great whole.

This becomes all the more clearly palpable if we observe the considerable developments, changes, and transformations of Hegelian positions. All are overshadowed by the whole of the unity; they are themselves understandable, in their astounding manner, out of this whole, which makes such changes possible, indeed demands them, and takes all of them back into itself.

2. Survey of the planned presentation

Hegel's system is the richest in content as well as the most consistent in the history of philosophy.

The systematic basic thought, or the systematically creative basic movement, or the organ through which all things are seen is the dialectical method. However, Hegel is convinced that dialectic is not just a method of our thinking, but is also the movement of Being itself; it is that through which everything is out of the ground of things. Dialectics does not think in relation to an other, an object; rather, it considers what, as thinking, is the nature of God and all that is created.

Here for the first time dialectics is conjointly the creative principle of operation, the principle of objective cognition that reappears everywhere in the individual object, the systematic principle of order, and the principle of Being.

Hegel took over in particular the contents of tradition and of his age, then at a point of spiritual culmination, putting to use his tremendous intellectual capacity. Even the basic formula of dialectics (thesis-antithesis-synthesis) comes from Fichte, and Schelling was the first one to apply it in a systematic, objective way. Nonetheless, Hegel's work as a whole and in its organization of the particular has the originality that gives his system its birthright and magnificent character. Hegel had no systematic precursor, such as Thomas had in Aristotle.

In order to understand Hegel we have to understand dialectics; it is the *first* subject of this presentation.

Second, we shall discuss some basic Hegelian concepts, the manner in which they have been shaped by dialectics and have arisen in the dialectical movement; for example, freedom, spirit, time, the concept of the concept.

Third, we shall consider the entire system in a brief overview of the structure of the whole and its simple outlines. To give a succinct account of the tremendous system with its almost immeasurable richness of historical, political, religious, aesthetic, biological, logical intuitions would be impossible, and even absurd. No matter where we start the reading of Hegel's work, it promises intellectual exhilaration, which, to be sure, can be furthered by our discussions of fundamentals but for which there is no substitute in the form of abstracts.

Fourth, we shall try to understand what Hegel's conception of philosophy is and what philosophy means to him.

3. Hegel's fundamental concepts

Hegel's fundamental concepts are so closely interconnected that they lose their meaning apart from the whole, and each becomes a mirror of the whole.

The rich development of differentiations and dialectical movements gives the impression of a single thought that cannot be expressed in one sentence. It is modified, appears in simple and complicated, abstract and concrete, intuitable and speculative configurations. It takes in the world and all that is in it, needs it for its self-assurance, but is in its totality conscious of itself as the final truth in its completeness and certainty.

Such concepts, envisaged in their apparent separateness, singled out and aligned in juxtaposition in an undialectical manner, and perceived as repetitive and yet always as of astonishing novelty, can be enumerated as follows:

Spirit. Freedom. Idea. Truth. Subject-Object relation. Finitude and Infinity.

And, further: Reason. Providence. World spirit. National spirit. Principle. Development. Ultimate purpose. *Bildung*.

4. Characterization and critique of Hegel's thinking on time

Such criticism would have to differentiate between the possible notions of time, something readily done nowadays.

The specific nature of Hegel's thinking on time as a transcending cogitation, in which time is a vehicle and a cipher of authentic Being, would thereby be clarified. Time would have to be understood as itself, and criticism would have to assume the standpoint of metaphysics, from which alone it has any meaning.

Criticism comes into play:

1) metaphysically in the whole of the philosophic attitude—perhaps by absolutizing time against Hegel—

2) within Hegel's meaning:

a) where the transcending meaning is abandoned or misused in favor of temporal manipulations, plans, evaluations—

b) where transcending self-consciousness no longer allows the temporal to be illuminated by that which obliterates all time, but, rather, goes on to determinate interpretations as universally valid contents of knowledge—

c) where, by disregarding the dimension of the meaning of time, we no longer penetrate the depths before which such differences become mere semblance and relativities and are irrelevant, but where confusion arises because of the immanent applications of the transcending thoughts.

5. Critical study of Hegel

Hegel's precision in formulation; the necessity of concentrating attention on every word; the staying power of organized thought; the power of intuition: persuasive as tremendous spiritual power and work.

But always also: the blurring of limits; the dialectic operative not just in the conscious method but also in the ambiguity of words; the fuzziness: a powerfulness that makes us feel as though in a web, to be unraveled in constant effort if what we seriously want is not merely uncommitted understanding but cognition of the truth.

Unique greatness in the work (perhaps the only thoroughly formulated and closed system—not accomplished by anyone else—of which all his works form part) alongside the absurdity found in the principles. True insights are thus almost constantly vitiated by something destructive that obfuscates, deludes, perplexes.

An easy way out is simply to play the game after some practice. By turning off our critical acumen, by allowing the questioning rapier to become dulled, we may, interpreting ad infinitum, delight in abandoning ourselves to this all-knowing, this absolute knowledge, whether interpreting it metaphysically in its entirety or not.

Hegel carries out, in effect, an understanding unique in the history of philosophy and open on all sides. But the strange thing is: This openness is lost in the conciliatory conclusion. And, further: Hegel's understanding kills what is understood. Interesting as are his philosophic-historical interpretations, he cuts the heart out of the great thinkers and presents their towering figures as configurations of thought bereft of life in the dialectic movement. His grand design of the history of philosophy— noted as the first philosophical history of philosophy and as an interpretation of the entire history and of a spirit that links everything to a necessary development of historical thinking—deprives his followers of the chance to arrive at an original understanding of great philosophy out of itself by penetrating the infinity of its essence.

6. *Confusion of dialectical reconciliation with dialogical communication*

a) Total dialectical reconciliation in the circle of circles and authentic will to communication are mutually exclusive (unless reconciliation remains a cipher that cannot find its fulfillment in actuality).

The grandiosity of uniting everything with everything in the one, unique, dialectically all-embracing, cognizable and now cognized truth is, recognized in its essence, violation, and no less so when the compass and the breadth of contents in their inexhaustible richness tend to deceive us.

The universal principle of dialectics actually sublates discussion in favor of all-inclusive integration.

b) 1) Objections to the rupture of communication:

against: the conventionally accepted practice of breaking off brusquely, leaving the room, slamming the door—

against: "you should not have said that" (instead of: good thing you said that—now we can talk and mutually see what is true, and what is not true in the matter)—

against: the method of alleging insult and refusing to talk in protest (a hollow notion of honor in social relations), whereas everything depends on:

(a) clarifying the content of the "insult";

(b) refusing to play the insulted, though not the use of juridical method by which to attain complete clarification of factual assertions—

against: everything that renders verbal exchange and conciliation impossible or hampers frank, lucid opposition; against lack of clarity, muteness that sublates everything by stealth, whereas you, as overt opponent, come close to becoming a friend, in the spirit of openness—

against: the claim that any human being is perfect, and you may judge and measure the other against an ideal, whereas this is permissible only in respect to yourself.

2) This will to communication—particularly where the opposites are extreme—repudiates, in the end, the all-embracing objective reconciliation in the circle of circles.

Considered in this sense, Hegel's philosophy of dialectic, in all its admirable greatness, is reduced to assertions that cannot be fulfilled without self-delusion.

Such reconciliation in philosophical thought trivializes and opens the door to practices such as obstructive silence; protestations of insult; outright defamation in accusations of shallowness, superficiality, moralism, abstractness, buttressed by notions such as pure coincidence, lack of actuality, incapacity of doing justice to the concept, and accusations of rebelliousness, of constituting a threat to the state.

It repudiates what is not in accord with it, by way of totally breaking off communication, leaving no chance for the excluded, spurned one, reminiscent of Christian eternal punishment in hell (a cipher that contains truth provided that no one and no institution dares to anticipate, to think, or to express God's judgment of a person) and leading to the exclusion of races, classes, the opposition of political parties.

7. The three possible meanings of the relativizing that effects abeyance

Hegel demands: Movement, no stopping! Everything turns out to be in flux. Truth is everywhere, provided there is superseding. Nothing exists absolutely. I am open to everything, I let nothing take hold of me.

Whoever agrees with this is gripped by the method. It does not lag behind the skeptical and nihilistic movements reappearing throughout the history of philosophy. Hegel seems to absorb all of these. This is not the struggle between contending positions; it is not criticism that puts in doubt in order to attain to the unassailable. Rather, it is a matter of radicalizing criticism, of procedures that are contradictory and use contradictions for the purpose of resolution—establishing a universal method of totally dissolving everything solid. It is no longer criticism as polemics in spiritual battle, but is the thinking that sweeps us along into the movement, with no foothold whatever. The magic of eradication penetrates the consciousness of greatest freedom.

However, this formally consistent procedure has a totally deviating meaning in the radicality itself.

In the first place, it is possible, in the sense of the philosophical attitudes actually termed skepticism and nihilism, to attain via this procedure the despairing of everything and thus the total tranquillity of the Nothing.

Second, it is possible to attain in this universal movement—which dissolves everything determinate—precisely the reverse, that is, Being, whole and fulfilled, the truth and actuality itself. This is what Hegel means and wants. The true is at no place, no standpoint, on neither side of alternatives, in nothing enduring; instead, it rests in the entirety of movement itself. For the latter not only eradicates, but also, in sublating, it preserves what it has eradicated. What is untrue by itself becomes true as moment. According to Hegel, to sublate has the following threefold meaning: to negate, to preserve, to raise to a higher level. The ground of the movement is the plenitude of Being that unfolds in this movement. It does not trickle away into endlessness, does not come to Nothing, but completes itself in wholeness. The means of the movement is negation, is contradiction, is pain and death, is untruth and evil. But within the wholeness there is constant reconciliation. The movement is not an arbitrary one, but is necessary and must be understood as such. All that is terrible, destructive, divisive turns out to be the road to the tranquillity of truth and actuality. The experience of soaring is itself a moment of bringing this tranquillity into the present.

Third, it is, however, possible that the movement is the medium in which historic Existenz finds its unknowable tranquillity. In the liberation from the cogent and coercive capacities of objective positions and statements and established truths, Existenz—not through casting them off, but through mastering them—attains self-certainty based in its unique historicity and its results: its irrevocable decisions and actualizations. For Existenz, objective visions of reconciliation such as Hegel's are seen as possible ciphers among other ciphers which may unpredictably bring their language to bear in existential situations.

8. Characterization and critique of Hegel's philosophy

My exposition of Hegel's philosophy constituted the attempt to understand, while preserving the tension noticeable in it. Something is awry. Hegel's philosophy stands as something uniquely magnificent, but magnificence is not yet truth. We encounter a wealth of truth, but even when much is true, the whole is not necessarily true.

If I now attempt a critical characterization that both wards off and appropriates, a few words need to be said on the meaning of such a critique.

A critique such as Schopenhauer's is meaningless: he merely scolded. Equally meaningless is that of liberalism: it separated out reactionary and conservative consequences, considering them in isolation as Hegel's philosophy. Meaningless are the strictures of the positivist nineteenth century, which thought to have demolished the entire philosophy by pointing out empirical errors.

Critique presupposes having-been-there. You must have changed yourself into Hegel, and watched in what sense it is possible at all to criticize: not pass judgment by means of logical argument and empirical data, but by attaining the awareness of a different unconditional attitude of soul, which is authentically yourself and, believing in its authenticity, finds that it does not understand itself in Hegel.

However, the presupposition of critique is penetration into what for the intellect is mystical. We do not practice yoga in order to arrive at the truth. But what we must do is analogous, namely, attain a transformation of consciousness that goes beyond objective understanding. Out of this transformation we arrive, be it in agreement or in opposition, at the truth which we ourselves are and with which we can therefore live.

It is obvious that Hegel's philosophy (or any other philosophy) does not represent inquiry in the sense of empirical or objective examination. Based on its presuppositions, philosophy does something different: Hegel calls it "translation into the concept" or "elevation into the concept."

Is this the playful construction of an idle intelligence? Such is the judgment passed by the positivist camp in the nineteenth century.

Or is it the expression of Being attempting to express what truly, absolutely "is"? Under this aspect, Hegel's philosophy is the reading of the cipher-script of existence, and an expression of that which is understood, knowledge about Being.

Philosophy cannot possibly be knowledge comparable to that of the natural sciences; the world is their domain; philosophy remains empty-handed. Philosophy is possible only via the sciences and grounded in the sciences, as the thinking illumination of your own being as absolute consciousness. Philosophy, if it is philosophy, creates results that are not permanently valid, but, rather, a stance of consciousness that is the stance of the soul. Its thoughts are the space of an absolute consciousness.

(Hence, to be sure, the history of philosophy needs the history of the sciences and the history of images of the world, but it is itself the history of truth as the effected freedom of the absolute consciousness on the part of unique Existents.)

But such knowledge becomes untrue when it is retranslated into the intellect to become something that you now can possess as objectively valid. Philosophy is neither rational knowledge nor rapturous emotionality. It is thinking self-illumination in communication with other philosophizing human beings; it is not cogent, nor can it be proven as objectively valid, but it is true and binding in your life. Hegel calls it speculation, a word that has become an invective but is precisely the one that he who philosophizes has to live with.

9. Hegel's historical position

Why did Hegel not become the Thomas Aquinas of Protestantism?

1) Because there is no all-embracing Protestant church; instead, there is the multiplicity of those who struggle against each other, set themselves off from one another—the ground for the all-uniting system is missing.

2) Because he does not seem to understand what is specifically Biblical and Christian in the conception of transcendence, namely, that God's revelation is the incomprehensible irruption into natural history, which cannot be resolved into universal thought. Hence the accusations of pantheism leveled against him.

3) Because the lifelong training of the mind, the life of constant contemplation does not hold sway in the Protestant world.

Question: whether Hegel's system—richer, intellectually more demanding and profound than Aristotle and Thomas—might someday play a role, as Aristotle did for Thomas, in a way of faith that is new, transcending, completing, and uniting masses of human beings. We cannot divine this way in its content and its reality. Then it would not be the Hegelian system itself anymore, but its completion and reworking by means of new impulses and horizons. It would furnish the intellectual tools, as Aristotle had done.

10. Hegel's steps, and circles, and circle of circles compared with my modes of the Encompassing

1) Hegel "deduces" by means of dialectic; I discover through bringing to awareness the fundamental differences in what I find myself to be and wherein I find myself.

2) Hegel's "moments" belong exclusively to the Encompassing of the spirit;

they deny Existenz and transcendence—

they do not clearly differentiate knowledge as consciousness-as-such (sciences)—

they trivialize existence by reducing it to the accidental—

they do not allow "reason" to come into its own, but substitute for it the closed circle of spiritual creation.

3) Our impulses are analogous but not identical: the will to appropriation in communication, inclusive of all of tradition—the tendency toward the widest scope—in Hegel, however, closing up at the end; in my case, opening up.

4) In Hegel a tremendous volume of intellectual creativity, a huge opus; in my case, weakness, "confinement" within the factual, a scant opus—and yet I believe I see truth unknown to Hegel, and continue to believe, after all the critique of Hegel, once more and by original thought to have seen through his untruth as a whole. Yet how paradoxical, how out of proportion such a claim appears, coupled as it is with such a discrepancy in intellectual achievement!

11. Guidelines for critique of Hegel

A critique of Hegel means: self-understanding versus self-understanding: positing a whole against another whole. But with the premise that both are true, true for each in his respective historic situation. The opponent, for me, represents neither absolute untruth nor truth. For us, Hegel is the magnificent, unique, irreplaceable adversary. By understanding him completely we gain self-understanding: Two people who philosophize can never be objectively identical. But we who are not creative feed off the Greats, who lead us by the hand. Thus Kant, Kierkegaard, Max Weber may appear utterly disparate to us, yet in confrontation with Hegel they appear a unified front.

But up to now, all of them exist as isolated monads, as it were. We are only at the beginning of a discussion that would also signify the appropriation of origins, following an extended period in which doctrines were only being paraphrased. The "adaptive reworking," as Hegel calls it, has not come to an end; such a task can itself be authentic philosophy. Whoever has perceived the grandeur of Hegel and Kant will not expect another philosopher of such stature in the present or the immediate future. Just as in antiquity no new Plato or Aristotle appeared, though a Plotinus was possible, we may conceive as possibility a life of the mind of our own, growing from authentic criticism.

12. May Hegel be granted a place at the side of the two ancient great orderers?[16]

1) Among the three great creators of systems in the West, Hegel is still so close to us in time that we cannot know whether we can place him legitimately alongside the two others. His historical impact, which, to be sure, has grown up to our day, must yet prove itself in the long term.

Above all, he is close to us in his world and his humanity. We know more about his life, and his development is much better documented, than are those of the other two.

2) Also, the principle of his system is an entirely new one, much more difficult to comprehend than that of the other two. Whereas Aristotle and Aquinas address our intellect and are comparatively more accessible to our understanding, there is something in Hegel's thinking that may strike us as odd, as nonsense. To penetrate to his meaning, a different kind of effort is required. We are never sure of having truly understood him. He himself called his thinking "mysticism for the understanding."

And yet this difficulty can suddenly vanish. Then it is as though we had learned a trick and now everything for the understanding falls into place in a grandiose unanimity of method.

3) On the other hand, he is richest in tangible substance. It is possible (even if, in Hegel's sense, it is a misunderstanding) to keep to the wealth of interesting contents and concrete intuitions, to forget about dialectic method, and to appropriate his genuine insights into history.

4) Hegel can be seen as a figure at the conclusion of an era, but one who conceals dynamite within the method, a figure of the Western spirit as it comes to a "conclusion" in "Verstehen" [comprehension]. In that respect Hegel is a "hermeneutic philosopher."

[16] Aristotle and Aquinas.

BIBLIOGRAPHY

This Bibliography lists the main primary sources used by Jaspers in his exposition of the individual thinkers. In some cases several editions in different languages were drawn upon to explicate the same thinker. Also included under primary sources are standard English editions used in translating the text; they are identified in the text. Included under Secondary Works are some consulted or referred to by Jaspers.

Xenophanes

SOURCES

Capelle, Wilhelm: *Die Vorsokratiker: die Fragmente und Quellenberichte.* Leipzig, Kröner, 1935.

Diels, Hermann: *Die Fragmente der Vorsokratiker.* Ed. with additions by W. Kranz. 3 vols. 6th ed., Berlin, Wiedmannsche Verlagsbuchhandlung, 1956–59.

Freeman, Kathleen: *Ancilla to the Pre-Socratic Philosophers: A Complete Translation of the Fragments in Diels, Fragmente der Vorsokratiker.* Cambridge, MA, Harvard University Press, 1971.

SECONDARY WORKS:

Bowra, C. M.: *Early Greek Elegists.* Cambridge, MA, Harvard University Press, 1938.

Freeman, Kathleen: *The Pre-Socratic Philosophers: A Companion to Diels, Fragmente der Vorsokratiker.* 3rd ed., Oxford, Blackwell, 1953.

Grünwald, Michael: *Die Anfänge der abendländischen Philosophie, Fragmente und Lehrberichte.* Zurich, Artemis, 1949.

Jaeger, Werner: *The Theology of the Early Greek Philosophers.* Trans. by E. S. Robinson. New York, Oxford University Press, 1947.

Democritus

SOURCES

Diels, Hermann: see under Xenophanes.

Freeman, Kathleen: see under Xenophanes.

SECONDARY WORKS:

Barnes, Jonathan: *The Pre-Socratic Philosophers.* London and Boston, Routledge & Kegan Paul, 1979.

Guthrie, William: *A History of Greek Philosophy.* Cambridge, Cambridge University Press, 1962.

Snell, Bruno: *The Discovery of the Mind: The Greek Origins of European Thought.* Trans. by T. G. Rosenmayer. Oxford, Blackwell, 1953.

Empedocles

SOURCES

Diels, Hermann: see under Xenophanes.
O'Brien, Denis. *Empedocles' Cosmic Cycle: A Reconstruction from the Fragments and Secondary Sources.* London and New York, Cambridge University Press, 1969.
Wright, M. R., ed.: *Empedocles: The Extant Fragments.* New Haven, Yale University Press, 1981.

SECONDARY WORKS:

Barnes, Jonathan: see under Democritus.
Kranz, Walther: *Empedokles. Antike Gestalt und romantische Neuschöpfung.* Zurich, Artemis, 1949.

Bruno

SOURCES

Giordano Bruno: *Gesammelte philosophische Werke.* Ed. by L. Kuhlenbeck. 6 vols. Jena, E. Diederichs, 1904–.
The Ashwednesday Supper. Trans. with an Introduction by S. Jaki. The Hague, Mouton, 1975.
The Expulsion of the Triumphant Beast. Trans. and ed. by A. Imerti. Brunswick, NJ, Rutgers University Press, 1964.
The Heroic Frenzies. Trans. and introduction by P. M. Memmo. Chapel Hill, University of North Carolina Press, 1964.

SECONDARY WORKS:

Cassirer, Ernst: *Individual and Cosmos in Renaissance Philosophy.* New York, Barnes & Noble, 1963.
Michel, Paul-Henri: *The Cosmology of Giordano Bruno.* Paris, Hermann, 1973.
Singer, Dorothea: *Giordano Bruno: His Life and Thought.* New York, Schumm, 1950.
Yates, Frances: *Giordano Bruno and the Hermetic Tradition.* Chicago, University of Chicago Press, 1969; repr., 1979.

Epicurus

SOURCES

Bailey, Cyril, ed.: *Epicurus: The Extant Remains.* Oxford, Clarendon Press, 1926; New York, Limited Editions Club, 1947.
Diogenes Laertius: *De vitis . . .* , Book 10.
Gigon, Olaf Alfred: *Epikur. Von der Uberwindung der Furcht.* Zurich, 1949.
Mühll, P. von der: *Epicuri epistolae tres et ratae sententiae.* Leipzig, Teubner, 1922.
Nestle, Wilhelm: *Die Nachsokratiker.* Jena, E. Diederichs, 1923.
Strodach, George, ed.: *The Philosophy of Epicurus.* Evanston, IL, Northwestern University Press, 1963.
Usener, Hermann, ed.: *Epicurea.* Leipzig, B. G. Teubner, 1887.

SECONDARY WORKS:

Asmis, Elizabeth: *Epicurus' Scientific Method.* Ithaca, NY, Cornell University Press, 1984.

Bailey, C.: *The Greek Atomists and Epicurus.* Oxford, Clarendon Press, 1928.
Jones, Howard: *The Epicurean Tradition.* London and New York, Routledge, 1989.
Mitsis, Phillip: *Epicurus' Ethical Theory.* Ithaca, NY, Cornell University Press, 1989.
Rist, John M.: *Epicurus: An Introduction.* Cambridge, Cambridge University Press, 1972.

Boehme

SOURCES
Jakob Böhme's sämmtliche Werke in sieben Bänden. Ed. by K. W. Schiebler. Leipzig, Barth, 1831–47; 2nd ed., 1860.
Jakob Boehme: *Sämtliche Werke.* Leipzig, Barth, 1922.
The Works of Jacob Boehme. Glasgow, D. Bryce and Son, 1886.
Concerning the Three Principles of the Divine Essence. Trans. by John Sparrow. London, John Watkins, 1910.
The Confessions of Jacob Boehme. Comp. and ed. by W. B. Palmer. London, Methuen, 1920.

SECONDARY WORKS:
Benz, Ernst: *Der Vollkommene Mensch nach Jakob Böhme.* Stuttgart, W. Kohlhammer, 1937.
Elert, Werner: *Die voluntaristische Mystik Jakob Böhmes. Eine psychologische Studie.* Berlin, Trowitzsch & Sohn, 1913.
Hegel: *Sämtliche Werke:* see under Hegel.
Koyré, Alexandre: *La philosophie de Jacob Boehme.* Paris, J. Vrin, 1929.
Martensen, Hans Lassen: *Jakob Böhme, Theosophische Studien.* Leipzig, J. Lehmann, 1882.
Richter, Liselotte: *Jakob Böhme. Mystische Schau.* Hamburg, Hofmann und Campe, 1943.
Stoudt, John: *Jakob Boehme: His Life and Thought.* New York, Seabury Press, 1957; repr., 1968.
Walsh, David: *The Mysticism of Innerworldly Fulfillment: A Study of Jakob Boehme.* Gainesville, University Presses of Florida, 1983.

Schelling

SOURCES
Schelling, Friedrich Wilhelm Joseph von: *Sämtliche Werke.* Ed. by K. F. A. Schelling. Stuttgart and Augsburg, Cotta, 1856–61.
Werke. Ed. by M. Schröter. Munich, Beck & Oldenbourg, 1927–56.
The Ages of the World. Trans. and introduction by F. Bolman. New York, Columbia University Press, 1942.
Bruno, or, On the Natural and Divine Principles of Things. Ed., trans., and introduction by Michael Vater. Albany, State University of New York Press, 1984.
Ideas for a Philosophy of Nature. Trans. by E. Harris and P. Smith. New York, Cambridge University Press, 1988.
The Philosophy of Art. Ed., trans., and introduction by D. W. Stott. Minneapolis, University of Minnesota Press, 1989.
Schelling: Of Human Freedom. Trans. by James Gutman. Chicago, Open Court, 1936.
System of Transcendental Idealism. Trans. by Peter Heath. Charlottesville, University Press of Virginia, 1978.

The Unconditional in Human Knowledge. Trans. by F. Marti. Lewisburg, PA, Bucknell University Press, 1980.

SECONDARY WORKS:
Benz, E.: *Schelling. Werden und Wirkung seines Denkens*. Zurich and Stuttgart, Rhein-Verlag, 1955.
Brown, Robert: *The Later Philosophy of Schelling*. Lewisburg, PA, Bucknell University Press, 1974.
Esposito, Joseph: *Schelling's Idealism and Philosophy of Nature*. Lewisburg, PA, Bucknell University Press, 1977.
Hayner, Paul: *Reason and Existence: Schelling's Philosophy of History*. Leiden, E. J. Brill, 1967.
Jaspers, Karl: *Schelling: Grösse und Verhängnis*. Munich, R. Piper, 1929. Also in Hans Saner, ed., *Karl Jaspers: Aneignung und Polemik*. Munich, R. Piper, 1968.
Marx, Werner: *The Philosophy of FWJ Schelling: History, System, Freedom*. Trans. by T. Nenon. Bloomington, University of Indiana Press, 1984.

Leibniz

SOURCES
Opera philosophica. Ed. by J. E. Erdmann. Berlin, G. Eichler, 1839–40.
Die philosophische Schriften von G. W. Leibniz. Ed. by C. J. Gerhardt. 7 vols. Berlin, Weidmann, 1875–90.
Sämtliche Schriften und Briefe. Ed. by P. Ritter and E. Hochstetter. Darmstadt, Reisel, 1923.
Discourse on Metaphysics. Ed. by R. Martin and S. Brown. New York, St. Martin's, 1988.
Logical Papers. Ed. by G. Parkinson. Oxford, Clarendon Press, 1966.
New Essays on Human Understanding. Ed. by P. Remnant and J. Bennett. New York, Cambridge University Press, 1981.
Philosophical Papers and Letters. Ed. by L. Loemker. Chicago, University of Chicago Press, 1956.
Philosophical Writings. Ed. and trans. by Mary Norris. New York, Dutton, 1951.
The Political Writings of Leibniz. Ed. by P. Riley. Cambridge, Cambridge University Press, 1972.
Theodicy: Essays. LaSalle, IL, Open Court, 1985.

SECONDARY WORKS:
Aiton, E. J.: *Leibniz: A Biography*. Boston, A. Hilger, 1985.
Broad, C. D.: *Leibniz: An Introduction*. Cambridge, Cambridge University Press, 1975.
Brown, Stuart: *Leibniz*. Minneapolis, University of Minnesota Press, 1984.
Frankfurt, Harry: *Leibniz: A Collection of Critical Essays*. Notre Dame, IN, Notre Dame University Press, 1976.
Kabitz, Willy: *Die Philosophie des jungen Leibniz. Untersuchungen zur Entwicklungsgeschichte seines Systems*. Heidelberg, C. Winter, 1909.
Rescher, Nicholas: *Leibniz: An Introduction to His Philosophy*. Totawa, NJ, Rowman and Littlefield, 1979.
Wilson, Catherine: *Leibniz' Metaphysics: A Historical and Comparative Study*. Princeton, Princeton University Press, 1989.
Woolhouse, R. S., ed.: *Leibniz: Metaphysics and Philosophy of Science*. Oxford and New York, Oxford University Press, 1981.

Aristotle

SOURCES

Aristoteles' Philosophische Werke in der Philosophischen Bibliothek. 13 vols. Leipzig, Meiner, 1876–1922.
Hauptwerke. Ed. by W. Nestle. Leipzig, Meiner, 1934; 2nd ed., Stuttgart, Kröner, 1953.
Metaphysik. Ed. by A. Lasson. Jena, E. Diederichs, 1907.
Nikomachische Ethik. Ed. by A. Lasson. Jena, E. Diederichs, 1909.
The Basic Works of Aristotle. Ed. by Richard McKeon. New York, Random House, 1941.
The Complete Works of Aristotle: The Revised Oxford Translation. Ed. by Jonathan Barnes. Bollingen Series LXXI.2, Princeton, Princeton University Press, 1984.
Introduction to Aristotle. Ed. by Richard McKeon. 2nd, enlarged ed., Chicago, University of Chicago Press, 1973.
The Works of Aristotle. Ed. by W. D. Ross. 12 vols. London, Oxford University Press, 1952–62.

SECONDARY WORKS:

Ackrill, J. L.: *Aristotle the Philosopher*. Oxford, Oxford University Press, 1981.
Allen, Donald James: *The Philosophy of Aristotle*. Oxford, Clarendon Press, 1952.
Barnes, Jonathan: *Aristotle*. Oxford and New York, Oxford University Press, 1982.
Edel, A.: *Aristotle and His Philosophy*. Chapel Hill, University of North Carolina Press, 1982.
Grene, Marjorie: *A Portrait of Aristotle*. London, Faber & Faber, 1963.
Hardie, W. F.: *Aristotle's Ethical Theory*. 2nd ed., Oxford, Clarendon Press, 1980.
Jaeger, Werner: *Aristotle*. Oxford, Clarendon Press, 1934; repr., 1948.
————: *Aristotle: Fundamentals of the History of His Development*. New York, Oxford University Press, 1962.
————: *Paideia: The Ideals of Greek Culture*. Trans. by Gilbert Highet. 3 vols. New York, Oxford University Press, 1944.
Rose, Valentin: *Aristoteles Pseudepigraphus*. Leipzig, 1863. Trans. quoted from *The Complete Works of Aristotle*.
Veatch, H. B.: *Aristotle: A Contemporary Appreciation*. Bloomington, Indiana University Press, 1974.

Hegel

SOURCES

Georg Wilhelm Friedrich Hegels Werke, vollständige Ausgabe durch einen Verein von Freunden des Verewigten. Ed. by P. Marnheinecke *et al*. 19 vols. in 23 vols. Berlin, Duncker and Humblot, 1832–87.
Sämtliche Werke. Ed. by H. Glockner. 26 vols. Stuttgart, F. Fromann, 1927–40.
Sämtliche Werke: Neue Kritische Ausgabe. Ed. by J. Hoffmeister. 52 vols. Leipzig, Meiner, 1930–.
Encyclopädie der philosophischen Wissenschaften im Grundrisse. Ed. by G. Lasson. 3rd ed. Leipzig, F. Meiner, 1923.
Phänomenologie des Geistes. Ed. by J. Hoffmeister. In *Sämtliche Werke*. Ed. by G. Lasson. 6th ed., Philosophische Bibliothek, 1952.
Early Theological Writings. Trans. by T. M. Knox. Chicago, University of Chicago Press, 1948.

Encyclopedia of Philosophy. Trans. by G. Mueller. New York, Philosophical Library, 1959.

Hegel on the Arts. Ed. by H. Paolucci. New York, Ungar, 1979.

Hegel's Logic: Being Part One of the Encyclopaedia of the Philosophical Sciences *(1830)*. Trans. by William Wallace; with Foreword by J. N. Findlay. Oxford, Clarendon Press, 1975.

Introduction to Aesthetics. Trans. by T. M. Knox. Oxford, Clarendon Press, 1979.

Introduction to the Lectures on the History of Philosophy. Trans. by T. M. Knox and A. V. Miller. New York, Oxford University Press, 1985.

The Letters. Trans. by C. Butler and C. Seiler. Bloomington, Indiana University Press, 1984.

Phenomenology of Spirit. Trans. by A. V. Miller. Oxford, Clarendon Press, 1977.

The Philosophical Propaedeutic. Trans. by A. V. Miller. Oxford and New York, Blackwell, 1986.

The Philosophy of Hegel. Ed. by C. Friedrich. New York, Modern Library, 1954.

Philosophy of Right. Trans. by T. M. Knox. New York, Oxford University Press, 1973.

Political Writings. Trans. by T. M. Knox. Oxford, Clarendon Press, 1964.

Reason in History. Trans. by R. Hartman. New York, Liberal Arts Press, 1953.

SECONDARY WORKS:

Avineri, Shlomo: *Hegel's Theory of the Modern State*. Cambridge, Cambridge University Press, 1972.

Findlay, J. N.: *Hegel: A Re-Examination*. New York, Humanities Press, 1958; repr., 1976.

Harris, H. S.: *Hegel's Development: Toward the Sunlight, 1770–1801*. London, Oxford University Press, 1972.

Kaufmann, Walter: *Hegel: A Reinterpretation*. New York, Doubleday, 1965; repr., 1978.

Löwith, Karl: *From Hegel to Nietzsche*. New York, Holt, Rinehart and Winston, 1965; repr., 1984.

O'Brien, George: *Hegel on Reason and History: A Contemporary Interpretation*. Chicago, University of Chicago Press, 1975.

Rosen, Stanley: *G. W. F. Hegel: An Introduction to the Science of Wisdom*. New Haven, Yale University Press, 1974.

Taylor, Charles: *Hegel*. London, Cambridge University Press, 1975.

INDEX OF NAMES